Georgia Wills, Trusts, and Estate Administration

Georgia Wills, Trusts, and Estate Administration

SECOND EDITION

Antoinette France-Harris, J.D.

PROFESSOR OF LEGAL STUDIES
CLAYTON STATE UNIVERSITY

Teri D. Fields, J.D.

PARTNER
SOUTH ATLANTA INJURY LAWYERS, LLC

Sheryne Southard, J.D.

PROFESSOR OF LEGAL STUDIES
CLAYTON STATE UNIVERSITY

CAROLINA ACADEMIC PRESS
Durham, North Carolina

Library of Congress Cataloging-in-Publication Data
Names: France-Harris, Antoinette, author. | Fields, Teri D., author. | Southard, Sheryne, author.
Title: Georgia wills, trusts, and estate administration / Antoinette France-Harris, Teri D. Fields, Sheryne Southard.
Description: Second edition. | Durham, North Carolina : Carolina Academic Press, 2025. | Includes bibliographical references and index.
Identifiers: LCCN 2025021408 | ISBN 9781531029074 (paperback) | ISBN 9781531029081 (ebook)
Subjects: LCSH: Estate planning—Georgia. | Wills—Georgia. | Trusts and trustees—Georgia.
Classification: LCC KFG140 .F73 2025 | DDC 346.75805/2—dc23/eng/20250502
LC record available at https://lccn.loc.gov/2025021408

Carolina Academic Press
700 Kent Street
Durham, North Carolina 27701
(919) 489-7486
www.cap-press.com

Printed in the United States of America

Contents

Table of Exhibits

Preface

Since the first edition of *Georgia Wills, Trusts, and Estate Administration* was published, the legal landscape in this area has continued to evolve, and the use of artificial intelligence has become more prevalent. This second edition reflects these changes and builds upon the foundation established in the original text. We have meticulously updated the content to incorporate the latest developments in Georgia law and ethics, ensuring readers can access the most current forms and legal information available.

In addition to incorporating updates in case and statutory law, we have revised and expanded the practical tools included in the textbook. The most current forms and real-world case examples provide greater insight into how these laws are applied in practice. This edition also includes discussion prompts, reflective exercises, and digital resources to further enrich the learning experience.

As with the first edition, our goal remains to provide a clear and concise introduction to the substantive theory and practice of wills, trusts, estates, and administration in Georgia. While these topics can be intricate, this textbook continues to present them straightforwardly and practically, making it an essential resource for students, paralegals, and attorneys alike.

For educators, we provide excellent instructor materials including relevant PowerPoint presentations, test banks, and project ideas. These resources are designed to align with the changes in this edition and to facilitate continued dynamic and engaging classroom instruction.

We hope that *Georgia Wills, Trusts, and Estate Administration,* 2nd ed. serves as an invaluable resource for those entering the legal field and for those seeking to deepen their understanding of Georgia's laws in this area.

If you have questions about the teaching materials, please contact Beth Hall, at bhall@cap-press.com.

Antoinette France-Harris, J.D.

Teri D. Fields, J.D.

Sheryne Southard, J.D.

July 1, 2025

Acknowledgments

We would like to express our deepest gratitude to everyone who supported and guided us throughout the process of creating and revising this textbook. The contributions and encouragement of many individuals and institutions made this project possible.

First and foremost, we extend our heartfelt thanks to Clayton State University and South Atlanta Injury Lawyers for providing us with the resources and platform necessary to complete this work. Our colleagues' support has been invaluable.

Moreover, we are grateful to Olivia Smith and Nicola Robinson at the SR Law Group for the practical advice they have provided over the years and their generosity in allowing us to use some of their marketing materials as graphics throughout the book. We are certain these items will be particularly helpful for visual learners.

A special acknowledgment also goes to our students, whose curiosity and enthusiasm inspired much of the content in this textbook. Your questions and perspectives shaped our approach and made this endeavor truly rewarding.

We also wish to thank the team at Carolina Academic Press for their professionalism and dedication. Your meticulous attention to detail and commitment to excellence ensured that this work met the highest standards.

Finally, we are profoundly thankful to our families and friends for their patience, understanding, and encouragement. Your love and support kept us motivated during the countless hours of writing and revising.

Georgia Wills, Trusts, and Estate Administration, 2nd ed. is a testament to the collaborative spirit of everyone involved, and we hope it serves as a valuable resource for learners, educators, and those working in the legal field who experience it.

Georgia Wills, Trusts, and Estate Administration

Chapter 1

Purpose of and Need for Estate Planning

Learning Objectives

Upon completion of this chapter, you should be able to:

- Explain why some people never create a will or trust.
- Recognize the implications of dying without a will or trust.
- Analyze the purpose of and need for an estate plan.
- Discuss the importance of state statutes in wills, trusts, and probate law.
- Define basic terminology and concepts associated with wills, trusts, probate, and estate administration.

Why Some Fail to Plan

No one wants to think about death or dying. Nonetheless, these are realities that we all must face eventually. Caring.com, an organization that raises awareness of estate planning, conducted a 2024 survey on Americans and estate planning. As shown in Exhibit 1.1, it revealed that only 32% of Americans had a will, which means 68% of Americans die without leaving an outline of their final wishes for their loved ones. In most cases, we are growing increasingly unprepared for death and dying in the United States.

People tend to avoid planning for the inevitable for various reasons. Many recognize the importance but procrastinate for a time or indefinitely. They wish to put off the unpleasant thoughts of death and dying until another day, and may view discussing these topics as taboo. Others feel that they do not possess enough property to necessitate estate planning tools, such as a will or trust. They view **estate planning**, which involves preparing for the transfer of one's assets upon death (i.e., one's **estate**), as something for the rich and famous, not necessarily for "everyday" people with few possessions. Still others believe that since they are young, unmarried, or childless, they do not need to plan at all. They feel that somehow this discussion is premature, given the current

Exhibit 1.1 Percentage of Americans Who Have a Will

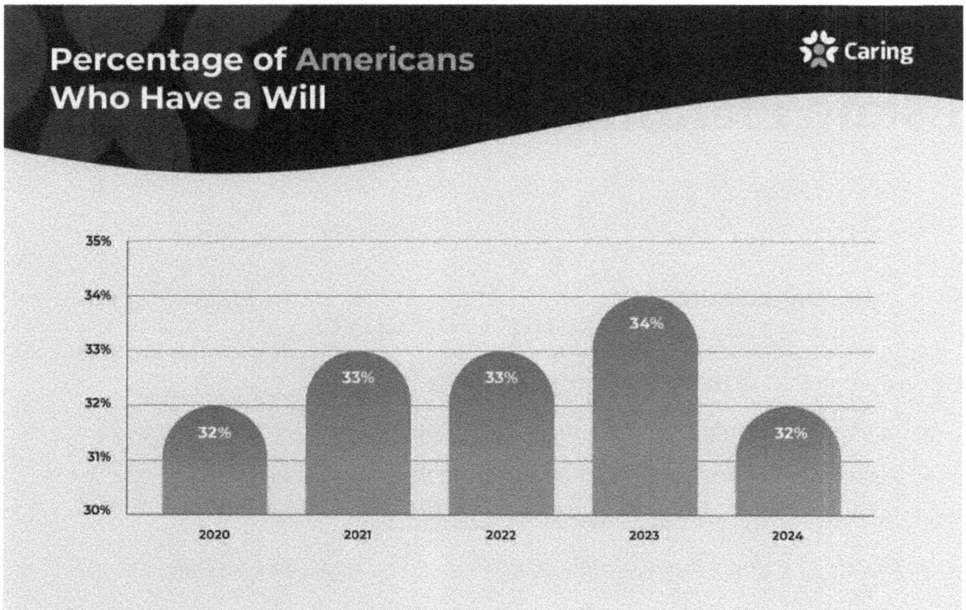

Source: https://www.caring.com/caregivers/estate-planning/wills-survey/

Exhibit 1.2 Reasons Why Americans Have Not Engaged in Estate Planning

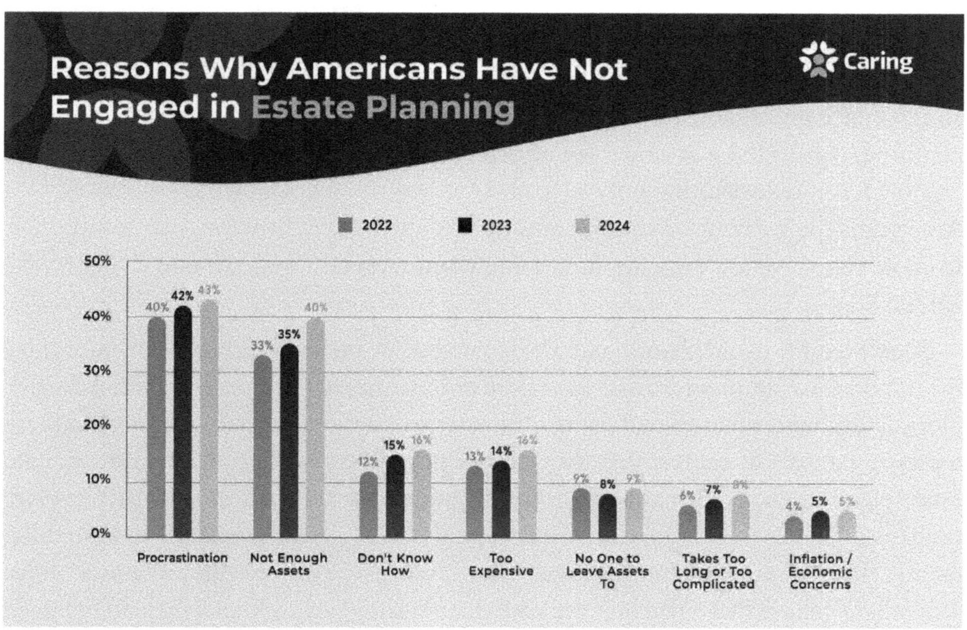

Source: https://www.caring.com/caregivers/estate-planning/wills-survey/

circumstances of their lives, and do not understand the personal relevance. Others may not comprehend or appreciate that in most circumstances, someone will be charged with administering their estate once they have passed away. In effect, putting a plan in place represents a gift to the person who will be so charged because it will make that process much easier. Some people are reluctant to plan because they envision that it will be too costly to have an attorney prepare the necessary documents. They may feel ill-equipped to draft these crucial documents for themselves and have been wisely cautioned against using forms sold on the Internet and at office supply stores. Furthermore, they may not consult an attorney to prepare the necessary documents because they have other more pressing financial concerns. Ironically, even celebrities, such as the singer Prince and billionaire Howard Hughes, who seemingly had extraordinary riches and were surrounded by a myriad of professional advisors, die without having created wills or trusts. Other reasons cited include having no one to leave assets to, the length and complexity of the process, and concerns about inflation or the economy. Exhibit 1.2 outlines the most common reasons and the percentages associated with each reason.

Consequences for Failing to Plan

Benjamin Franklin once stated, "If you fail to plan, you are planning to fail." The same can be said of estate planning. This failure to plan has profound legal and personal consequences for the **decedent**, who is a person who has died, and for the decedent's family and friends. Dying **intestate**, meaning without leaving a valid will, can potentially lead to unfortunate, unpredictable outcomes for the decedent and his or her loved ones. In the event of intestacy, the probate court in the decedent's **domicile**, the place of his or her principal and permanent residence, will have jurisdiction over the estate. Therefore, a court will have the power to decide how and to whom the decedent's assets are distributed. One exception to this rule occurs when the decedent dies with certain property in another state or country. Under those circumstances, the laws of the domicile may need to be considered in conjunction with the laws of the jurisdiction(s) where the property is located.

Property takes two forms: real and personal. We will discuss property and its importance to estate planning at greater length in Chapter 3. However, it is important to note here that **real property** includes land, buildings, items attached to land, and interests in land, such as water and mineral rights. **Personal property** consists of movable items, such as furniture, clothing, cash, and automobiles. Regarding real property owned by the decedent, the law of the state where the property is located will determine who receives it. Conversely, any personal property will be distributed according to the laws of the decedent's domicile. In either case, if the decedent has left no clear indication of his or her intent, the government determines the decedent's **heirs**, i.e., those who will inherit the property of the intestate decedent. **Assets** are defined as any property a decedent may own that has value. You will usually see the term juxtaposed with **liabilities**, which represent the financial obligations of the decedent.

Each state, including Georgia, has **intestate succession laws** (to be discussed in Chapter 4) which outline the order in which the decedent's relatives will inherit if the decedent has no will or trust. This means that the decedent forfeits the power to name his or her **beneficiaries**, that is, those who may inherit the decedent's property under a will or a trust. With intestacy, step-family, friends, alma maters, and charities will be foreclosed from receiving gifts from the decedent's estate. Additionally, those relatives whom the decedent may have otherwise wanted to **disinherit**, meaning preclude from receiving a gift, may inherit nonetheless.

Furthermore, suppose the decedent has minor or disabled children (or even pets). In that case, the decedent will not have an opportunity to nominate a **guardian**, someone to take care of their basic needs, or a **conservator**, someone to manage their inherited property. Instead, the court will select and appoint the individual(s) to assume these responsibilities. Again, the appointees may not be the person(s) that the decedent would have chosen. Consider a scenario where the decedent is estranged from her family and would have preferred to have a close friend serve as guardian and conservator for her minor child. Without a will expressing this intention, the court will not have a clear indication of this desire. Under those circumstances, the court is likely to appoint a family member of the decedent.

Finally, without a valid will, the decedent will not have a chance to nominate a **personal representative**, an individual, or an entity to carry out the final wishes usually expressed in a will and oversee the proper distribution of the decedent's property. If the decedent has a will, this individual will be called the **executor** (gender-neutral) or **executrix** (female). Without a will, the court will appoint someone of its or the potential heirs' choosing, who will be called the **administrator** (gender-neutral) or **administratrix** (female), to serve the same purposes. The problem is that the court may appoint a person or entity whom the decedent would not have chosen. Consider a scenario where the decedent's closest family member is not business-savvy and is a **spendthrift**, meaning that he or she spends money unwisely. It is unlikely that the decedent would have considered this individual to oversee his or her estate. Similarly, if the decedent was estranged from this family member, this individual would not have been a primary choice. However, if there is no will or trust to outline the decedent's wishes, and no one raises an objection, a court may appoint this individual as the administrator of the decedent's estate.

In light of all these possible consequences, it remains a daunting but necessary task for lawyers and paralegals to help clients understand the absolute urgency of estate planning and the documents related to the same. Legal advisors must convey that there is a measure of security and peace of mind that comes from preparing for the inevitable. Moreover, they need to explain that estate planning will make it much easier for the loved ones of the decedent. Leaving a clear outline in the form of an estate plan will make the process of settling the decedent's estate less time-consuming, costly, and stressful for those who are left behind. Everyone needs a plan.

One needs a thoughtful estate plan if one has a family. Consider a parent who has multiple children. Each child may have a different financial impact. Perhaps that parent has provided funding to start a business for one child or paid college tuition for that child during that parent's lifetime. If there is no estate plan, each child will receive equally upon the parent's death, which may not have been the parent's intention. The parent may have thought of the business funding or tuition payment as an advance on the inheritance that the child would receive upon the parent's death. In addition, consider a father who needs to ensure that there is no issue regarding the entitlement of any child/beneficiary of his whose paternity may be questioned. This may not be possible without a written expression of the father's intentions. Or, a situation may arise similar to that of the singer Prince who died without a will and the world thought he had no children. Suddenly, upon his death, hundreds of individuals claimed to be his long-lost relatives. As a result, it took six years to settle his estate. Also, consider the parents who have one disabled child who will never be able to care for himself and another child who has become a wealthy business owner; these children have different needs that must be addressed. Finally, think of a situation in which a man has married a woman who already has children. If he dies without leaving a will and has not formally adopted those children, they will not be entitled to take from his estate under Georgia law, even if he has loved and raised the children as his own for most of their lives. Given the complexity of family dynamics today, it is imperative to have a well-defined estate plan.

Moreover, it is important to have a careful estate plan even if one has no family. A person who has never married, has no children, has deceased parents, and no extended family still needs to have a plan. In this instance, without a will or trust, Georgia law dictates that one's property will go to the school board of one's domiciliary county. Most people would object to such a result and instead would prefer that their property go to benefit their close friends, church, a charity of their choosing, or their alma mater. Lastly, consider the person who has passed away with little to no assets and has never had any assets. Estate planning may be crucial for this individual, as legal claims could arise from the circumstances surrounding his or her death (e.g., medical malpractice). Any possible proceeds collected from such legal claims belong to the estate of the deceased and would be distributed according to the mandates of the existing estate plan, if any. Without a plan, those proceeds would end up in the hands of the government. Thoughtful estate planning is the only way to avoid such unfortunate results. Estate planning is crucial for everyone, with no exception.

Overview of the Law

This area of the law is primarily state-specific. Title 53 of the **Official Code of Georgia Annotated (O.C.G.A.)** contains statutes that govern wills, trusts, and the administration of estates in the State of Georgia. Under Georgia law, a person's estate consists of all the property, real or personal, that he or she owns at the time of death. Estate planning involves managing an individual's property using the laws of wills, trusts, tax, banking, insurance, and property to gain maximum financial benefit for the individual during life and upon death.

The **last will and testament**, also known as the **will**, is perhaps the most widely recognized and utilized estate planning document. O.C.G.A. § 53-1-2(17) defines a will as "the legal declaration of an individual's testamentary intention regarding that individual's property or other matters." Hence, the will may serve as an instrument by which an individual indicates how his or her property should be distributed upon death, who will oversee the distribution of the property, and to whom any minor or disabled children or pets should be entrusted. The person making the will, also known as the **testator** (gender-neutral) or **testatrix** (female), can express these intentions in various ways, which we will discuss later. Moreover, in Chapter 5, you will learn that the validity of a will depends on the observance of certain formal statutory requirements called **formalities.** The failure to have the will executed properly may make it null and void, having no legal effect. Therefore, it is important for an individual to consult with licensed professionals when he or she decides to create a will or other estate planning documents.

Another common, but more complex, estate planning tool is the **trust** (sometimes known as a revocable living trust or an inter vivos trust). It involves one person, the **trustee**, holding legal title to property for the benefit of another, the beneficiary. Some choose this instrument instead of a will because they have significant assets and want to avoid tax consequences. Others choose a trust to avoid the time and expense involved with settling an estate in probate court. Still others are attracted to the privacy that a trust affords because, unlike a will, it does not need to be filed with the probate court after an individual dies. We will discuss the many different types of trusts and their respective advantages more fully in Chapters 8 and 9.

In addition to a will or trust, estate planning attorneys in Georgia often recommend that their clients execute an **advance directive for health care** and a **financial power of attorney**. With an advance directive for health care (also known as a living will, health care power of attorney, or health care proxy in some states), the person creating the directive, referred to as the **declarant**, can designate someone to act on their behalf. This designated person is called the **agent**. The declarant grants his or her agent the power to make health care decisions on his or her behalf if the declarant is incapable of doing so. The declarant gives the agent the same access to the declarant's medical records as the declarant, including those protected by the **Health Insurance Portability and Accountability Act (HIPAA)**, a federal law that protects patients' health information. An advance directive also allows the declarant to specify his or her preferences for health care treatment in such circumstances. Moreover, one may use this document to express a desire to make an **anatomical gift**, that is, a gift of all or part of one's body. An advance directive may also provide the agent with clarity as to whether the declarant would like to be buried or cremated. Nonetheless, according to Caring.com, only one in three Americans has an advance directive.

A financial power of attorney allows the maker, also known as the **principal**, to name someone as his or her agent to make certain business and/or financial decisions on his or her behalf. Using this document, the principal may grant his or her agent authority to handle transactions involving the principal's property, business operations, insurance policies, estate, litigation, retirement plans, and taxes. Similar to a will, people often fail to prepare these important documents as well. We will discuss these ancillary estate planning documents in greater detail in Chapter 7.

Key Terms

administrator/administratrix
advance directive for health care
agent
anatomical gift
assets
beneficiaries
conservator
decedent
declarant
disinherit
domicile
estate
estate planning
executor/executrix
financial power of attorney
formalities
guardian
Health Insurance Portability and Accountability Act (HIPAA)
heirs
intestate
intestate succession laws
last will and testament
liabilities
Official Code of Georgia Annotated (O.C.G.A.)
personal property
personal representative
principal
real property
spendthrift
testator /testatrix
trust
trustee
will

Review Questions

1. What is estate planning?
2. What are some common reasons why people die without an estate plan?
3. Why is estate planning necessary?
4. Who needs to have an estate plan?
5. What law(s) govern(s) wills, trusts, probate, and administration of estates in the State of Georgia?
6. What is a domicile, and how is it relevant in this area of the law?

7. Name a few estate planning tools that an attorney may recommend to clients.
8. Why is it necessary to properly execute or sign estate planning documents?
9. What is an advance directive?
10. What is the financial power of attorney?

Practical Assignment

Conduct research on the Internet concerning a celebrity who died without leaving a will or a trust. Answer the following questions related to that celebrity:

1. Who is the individual that died, and why is he/she famous?
2. When was the celebrity born, and when and how did he/she die?
3. What are/were the legal and personal issues surrounding the celebrity's failure to plan?
   a. Who is/was involved?
   b. What or who caused the problem?
   c. What is/are the relationship(s) affected?

Chapter 2

The Estate Planning Team

Learning Objectives

Upon completion of this chapter, you should be able to:

- Identify the diverse members of the estate planning team.
- Discuss the respective roles of team members in creating the estate plan.

Various individuals work as a team and are critical to creating an effective and efficient estate plan. Each plays a role in meeting the diverse planning needs that clients express. In this chapter, we will explore the various actors of the estate planning team, depicted in Exhibit 2.1. We will also discuss their respective contributions to the estate planning process, including preparing the essential estate planning documents, which we will discuss in subsequent chapters.

Exhibit 2.1 Estate Planning Team

Estate Planning Attorney

As mentioned in Chapter 1, to develop an effective estate plan, it is advisable to consult an **estate planning attorney**, an individual authorized to practice law in the State of Georgia who specializes in the area of wills, trusts, and estate administration. While one can easily find do-it-yourself legal forms or services on the Internet and in office supply stores, using these measures is not recommended, as estate planning is not a "one-size-fits-all" proposition. On the contrary, estate planning involves complex tasks, including, but not limited to: assessing an individual's circumstances, needs, and desires; conducting legal and factual research; interpreting the law and its applicability to a specific client; advising the client related to his or her best interests; and, properly drafting and executing an effective will or trust and other estate planning documents.

Moreover, if a testator has a major life change, including relocating to another state, having a child, adopting a child, getting married, going through a divorce, or experiencing a substantial increase or decrease in their assets, then undoubtedly the client will need a new estate plan. In any event, it is recommended that clients review their estate planning documents regularly, perhaps every three to five years, to determine if it is time to amend these documents. Any revisions will require the same level of thoughtfulness and precision as was put into the original estate plan. Therefore, a licensed estate planning attorney should be consulted once again because he or she will have the requisite knowledge and training to competently address the individual's changing needs.

Paralegal/Legal Assistant

Paralegals, sometimes referred to as **legal assistants**, play an integral role in the estate planning process. They have specialized legal knowledge obtained either through education or on-the-job training. As in other areas of the law, paralegals will work alongside attorneys to accomplish the tasks requested by estate planning clients. Under the supervision of their attorneys, paralegals can perform a myriad of tasks on behalf of the client, including, but not limited to the following: interviewing clients; gathering facts and information; arranging appointments; conducting legal and factual research; drafting legal documents; filing and recording legal documents; corresponding with clients and third parties; organizing and maintaining files; and calendaring court dates.

Their assistance with obtaining client information is crucial as it will give the estate planning attorney a complete picture of the testator's financial situation and a comprehensive view of the assets and liabilities. In the initial meetings with a client, the legal team will gather personal information and financial data so that the attorney can properly advise the client and they can draft the necessary documents accordingly. Oftentimes, the attorney will create an **estate planning questionnaire**, a form that can be used to gather this vital information from each client. In the questionnaire, the legal team can also get the client to address who will inherit his or her property and make final choices related to health care and financial decisions and agents to act on his or her behalf. Paralegals can play a significant role in assisting the client in completing the firm's estate planning questionnaire. Exhibit 2.2 at the end of this chapter is an example of an estate planning questionnaire that may be used by the legal team.

While attorneys rely heavily on them for support, paralegals and legal assistants cannot offer **legal advice**, meaning they may not make a statement or conclusion that applies the law or legal principles to the facts of a specific person's legal problem. Furthermore, they cannot otherwise engage in the **unauthorized practice of law (UPL)**. What constitutes UPL varies from state to state, but according to O.C.G.A. § 15-19-50, the practice of law in Georgia includes the following:

> (1) Representing litigants in court and preparing pleadings and other papers incident to any action or special proceedings in any court or other judicial body; (2) Conveyancing; (3) The preparation of legal instruments of all kinds whereby a legal right is secured; (4) The rendering of opinions as to the validity or invalidity of titles to real or personal property; (5) The giving of any legal advice; and (6) Any action taken for others in any matter connected with the law.

It is unlawful for anyone who is not a duly licensed attorney to do these things per O.C.G.A. § 15-19-51(a). UPL is a criminal matter in the State of Georgia, and the penalty is outlined in O.C.G.A. § 15-19-56(a). It is a misdemeanor, which can result in a fine of up to $500, imprisonment for up to six months, or both.

Financial Advisors

In addition to legal assistance, and since estate planning involves the transfer of property, it is useful for the client to consult qualified financial professionals for advice. **Financial advisors**, such as accountants, bankers, financial planners, and investment managers, can assist a client in getting a realistic picture of his or her property, assets, and liabilities before the legal team drafts the necessary estate planning documents. In addition, financial advisors are important because they can provide invaluable advice on other estate planning tools, including informing the client on how to maximize savings and profits, invest in retirement plans, diversify an investment portfolio, name beneficiaries on investment accounts, and foresee and avoid possible tax and other financial consequences related to death and the transfer of property.

These advisors can also assist in **postmortem estate planning**, which is estate planning after someone dies that helps those receiving under a will minimize tax liability. For example, an advisor may recommend **renunciation** or **disclaimer**, whereby a gift under a will can be refused or rejected by the named beneficiary and passed by intestacy to other family members for tax-saving benefits. Other possibilities to avoid tax liability include (1) releasing the power of appointment and selecting optional provisions in life insurance policies; (2) selecting the tax year for income tax purposes and whether to file a joint return on the decedent's final return; (3) delaying the administration of the decedent's estate and distributing the estate over some time rather than all at one time; (4) choosing an alternative valuation date for the estate; and, (5) utilizing a qualified terminable interest property (QTIP) trust. We will discuss the QTIP trust and other tax-saving measures in later chapters.

Insurance Agent

Another component of a comprehensive estate plan is insurance. A licensed **insurance agent** will be in the best position to advise about possible expenses later in life and suggest the most appropriate insurance products to suit the estate planning objectives. Health insurance will be critical to address any medical concerns. If someone is unable to perform his or her job, **disability insurance** can be used to replace a portion of lost income. Disability insurance is available on both short-term and long-term bases, depending on the need. In addition, some individuals obtain **long-term care insurance** to pay for nursing homes or in-home care when they are older and unable to care for themselves. Oftentimes, these costly expenses are not covered by private insurance or government health benefits. Other individuals depend on **life insurance,** with policies payable on the death of the insured, to assist their loved ones in paying for the funeral and other final expenses. Moreover, life insurance can assist in meeting the income needs of the decedent's family and close friends who depended on him or her for financial support. There are many different options available for life insurance, and the insurance agent will assist in finding the best products for the client's specific needs and those of his or her loved ones. Finally, **pet insurance** is an insurance policy available for pet owners to protect against unexpected veterinary expenses.

Again, an estate planning attorney will want to determine what provisions their clients have made concerning insurance. As part of the estate planning process, the attorney may suggest that the client contact his or her insurance agent and obtain and provide exact details related to the nature of any policy, the listed beneficiaries, and the amount payable upon death.

Charities

As part of estate planning, some individuals may choose to make charitable donations **posthumously**, meaning after death. Charities that may be beneficiaries under a will or trust include, but are not limited to, churches, schools, or other not-for-profit organizations with which the donor may be affiliated. An estate planning client contemplating such a gift should meet with representatives from the charitable organization to determine its needs and the best way to coordinate a **testamentary** gift, meaning one that takes place under the donor's will. The estate planning attorney will want to include information related to this gift in the client's will or trust document to ensure that these wishes are honored posthumously.

Fiduciaries

One final component of the estate planning team is the testator's **fiduciaries**, those persons or organizations entrusted to act on his or her behalf to administer the will or trust and estate. The estate planning attorney will ask the client to carefully consider and select an executor and a trustee, whom the testator will nominate in his or her will. Either an individual (e.g., adult relative, friend, or attorney) or an entity (e.g., bank or trust company) may act as executor or trustee. The key is choosing a trustworthy fiduciary that is willing and able to serve, given the important role that the fiduciary plays. It is critical to understand that the fiduciary may face personal legal liability if this individual or entity does not perform tasks responsibly.

As stated earlier, the executor is the personal representative that the testator names in the will who has the task of distributing the decedent's property as directed, while the trustee has the role of conserving and managing estate assets for the beneficiary's sake. Usually, the will indicates when a testamentary trust is to be created and dictates how the trustee's duties should be performed. For example, a will may create a testamentary trust in case a beneficiary thereunder is a minor, disabled, or a spendthrift. Most estate planning attorneys will recommend that the testator name at least one successor executor and one successor trustee in case the person or entity named initially is unwilling or unable to act on the decedent's behalf.

Finally, testators who have minor or disabled children need to consider yet another fiduciary—someone to act as the guardian for these children and the conservator of their inherited property. Usually, if there is a **surviving parent**, meaning another parent who is still alive after the testator's death, this is not a concern as the survivor will generally act in this capacity. However, if the other parent is unfit or **predeceases**, that is, dies before the testator, or if the testator wants to nominate someone else to act in these capacities for another reason, the testator will need to nominate said individual(s) in the estate planning documents. In most cases, when it comes to matters involving guardianship and custody of a child, the courts, acting in the best interests of the child, will give preference to the child's biological parent. However, if the surviving parent is absent or it can be shown that this parent is unfit, unable, or unwilling to serve in this capacity, the court will likely honor the testator's nominee(s). Again, the estate planning attorney should advise the client to give careful consideration to the selection of a guardian and conservator, and possible successors. Moreover, it should be suggested that the client have a discussion with said individual(s) to confirm their willingness to take on this awesome responsibility. In addition, once the documents are fully executed, then the fiduciaries should be informed of the location of the originals for future reference.

Exhibit 2.2 Sample Estate Planning Questionnaire

BASIC ESTATE PLANNING QUESTIONNAIRE

Attach additional pages as necessary

I. Family Information

____

Your Name Date of Birth

____

Address

____

Phone Number and Email

____

Occupation Employer Name/Address

____

Spouse's Name Date of Birth

____

Address (if different from yours)

____

Phone number and Email

____

Occupation Employer Name/Address

____

Your Parents' Names Living?

____

Spouse's Parents' Names Living?

II. INFORMATION ON CHILDREN

___

Child's Name Date of Birth Age

___

Address

___

Email and Phone Number

___

Child's Name Date of Birth Age

___

Address

___

Email and Phone Number

___

Child's Name Date of Birth Age

___

Address

___

Email and Phone Number

If you have grandchildren, please list their information below:

___

Grandchild's Name Date of Birth Age

___

Name of grandchild's parent

___

(If Minor) Parent Address, Email and Phone Number (If not listed above)

____

Address, Email and Phone Number (if different from parent)

____

Grandchild's Name Date of Birth Age

____

Name of grandchild's parent

____

(If Minor) Parent Address, Email and Telephone Number (If not listed above)

____

Address, Email and Phone Number (if different from parent)

____

Grandchild's Name Date of Birth Age

____

Name of grandchild's parent

____

(If minor) Parent Address, Email and Phone Number (If not listed above)

____

Address, Email and Telephone Number (if different from parent)

III. DISPOSITION OF ASSETS

List any specific gifts of cash or specific items of property that you wish to make in your Will, either to individuals or to charity. For example, "$10,000 to my parents"/"$5,000 to Susan"/ "$2500 to the American Kidney Fund."

____

Beneficiary Cash/Property Amount

____

Beneficiary Cash/Property Amount

____

Beneficiary Cash/Property Amount

____

Beneficiary Cash/Property Amount

____

Beneficiary Cash/Property Amount

____

Beneficiary Cash/Property Amount

In general terms, please describe how you wish the balance of your estate to be distributed, i.e., to spouse and then to children/some portion to parents, the balance to spouse and then children, etc.

____

____

____

____

Beneficiaries of your estate if your line of descendants fails completely.

____

____

____

IV. DESIGNATION OF PERSONAL REPRESENTATIVES, TRUSTEES AND GUARDIANS

A "personal representative" gathers your assets immediately following your death, pays all your debts and taxes, and distributes the remaining assets to the beneficiaries under your Will. A "trustee" manages property held in trust and makes distributions to the beneficiaries. A "guardian" becomes the substitute parent for minor children (children under age 18). It may or may not be appropriate for the same person to act in all capacities.

If you can, please designate at least one successor in case the designated individuals are unable or unwilling to act.

A. PERSONAL REPRESENTATIVE

____

Name of Primary Personal Representative

____

Address

____

Email and phone number

____

Name of Secondary Personal Representative

____

Address

____

Email and phone number

B. TRUSTEE

____

Name of Primary Trustee (may be same as Executor)

____

____

Address, Email and phone number

____

Name of Secondary Trustee

____

____

Address, Email and phone number

C. GUARDIAN OF MINOR CHILDREN

____

Name of Primary Guardian

____

____

Address, Email and phone number

____

Name of Secondary Guardian

____

____

Address, Email and phone number

D. HEALTH CARE SURROGATE

In the event that you are determined to be incapacitated to provide informed consent for medical treatment and surgical and diagnostic procedures, whom do you wish to designate as your health care surrogate to make health care decisions for you?

____

Name

____

Address

____

Email and Phone number

____

Relationship

If your surrogate is unwilling or unable to perform his/her duties, whom do you wish to designate as your alternate surrogate?

____

Name

____

Address

____

Email and phone number

____

Relationship

Do you wish to be kept on artificial life support? Yes _____ No _____

Do you want food & water administered if you are in terminal condition?

Yes _____ No _____

Do you want any limitations on pain medication? Yes ____ No ____

If yes, describe:

Do you wish to donate organs? Yes _____ No _____

Will personal representative be able to authorize the disposal of body remains?

Yes ______ No ______

Will Personal Representative be able to authorize an autopsy? Yes _____ No ____

If there are any health care decisions you do not wish the Representative to make, please describe:

E. FINANCIAL POWER OF ATTORNEY

Name and relationship, if any, of person, if any, you wish to be appointed as your attorney-in-fact to handle on your behalf any of your personal or financial affairs, particularly if you lose the ability to manage your affairs.

____

Name

____

Address

____

Email and phone number

____

Relationship

Alternate, if your first choice is unable or unwilling to perform

____

Name

____

Address

____

Email and phone number

____

Relationship

V. MISCELLANEOUS INFORMATION

1. Are you the beneficiary or trustee of any trust? __________(y/n)

If yes, please supply a copy.

2. Is either individual in the couple likely to receive income or property from a parent or other relative? ________(y/n)

If yes, please specify the approximate value: _____________

3. Have you ever filed a gift tax return? ____________(y/n)

If yes, please supply a copy.

4. Have you ever created any trusts? ____________(y/n)

If yes, please supply a copy.

5. Has either individual in the couple ever executed an agreement relating to the nature of your property (i.e., a prenuptial agreement)? ____________(y/n)

If yes, please supply a copy.

6. Are both individuals in the couple citizens of the United States? _______(y/n)

7. Do you have a current will or living trust? ___________(y/n)

If yes, please supply a copy.

8. Do you have a safe deposit box? __________(y/n)

If yes, what is the location and who has access? ______________________________

9. Are all children listed in the questionnaire the natural or adopted children of both you and your spouse? ________ (y/n)

If not, please explain.

10. Do you have a presence on social media? ______ (y/n) If so, indicate the platform and your wishes for the accounts in the event of your death. That is, would you like the account immediately shut down? Do you have a list of passwords for each social media platform? If not, Please make a list of login and password information.

Reproduced with permission from South Atlanta Injury Attorneys

Key Terms

disability insurance
disclaimer
estate planning attorney
estate planning questionnaire
fiduciaries
financial advisors
insurance agent
legal advice
life insurance
long-term care insurance
paralegal/legal assistant
pet insurance
posthumously
postmortem estate planning
predecease
renunciation
surviving parent
testamentary
unauthorized practice of law (UPL)

Review Questions

1. Who are the members of an effective estate planning team?
2. What roles should an attorney play in the estate planning process?
3. What is an estate planning questionnaire, and how is it useful in estate planning?
4. What roles can a paralegal or legal assistant play in the estate planning process? What, if any, tasks are a paralegal prohibited from performing under Georgia law, without attorney supervision?
5. Why should an individual consult a financial advisor when planning his or her estate?
6. What different forms of insurance might someone contemplate as part of the estate planning process and for what purposes?
7. What does it mean to give to charities posthumously?
8. What is a fiduciary, and who may serve in this capacity?
9. Who ensures that the testator's property is distributed as outlined in the will?
10. Who is responsible for holding property on behalf of a beneficiary under a will if that beneficiary is unable to take possession upon the testator's death due to age or disability?

Practical Assignment

Conduct research on the Internet for a more complex estate planning questionnaire than the one contained in this chapter. Answer the following questions related to the questionnaire that you have located:

1. What are the similarities between the two questionnaires?
2. What are the general categories of questions in the more detailed questionnaire you found that were not included in the textbook example?
3. What other questions would you add and why?

Be sure to provide a link/citation for the questionnaire you have located.

Chapter 3

Property

Learning Objectives

Upon completion of this chapter, you should be able to:

- Distinguish among the forms of property ownership.
- Describe the "bundle of rights" concept of property.
- Identify and differentiate among types of property.
- Discuss the process for transferring property.

In this chapter, we will explore property ownership, the rights incidental to the same, and the various classifications or types of property. Property ownership is essential to estate planning. Uncovering the testator's assets will indicate whether he or she has anything to transfer upon death and the nature of such conveyance. In addition, it will give necessary insight to the estate planning team so that they can meet the client's needs given the unique circumstances. To effectively represent the client, the estate planning attorney, with the assistance of his or her paralegal or legal assistant, must gather complete information regarding the client's property. According to O.C.G.A. § 53-12-2(9), an estate planning client's property will encompass "any type of property, whether real or personal, tangible or intangible, legal or equitable," wherever such property is located. In the exercise of due diligence, the estate planning attorney will need to ask the client about such property and then research property records to confirm the client's property ownership and the type and quality of ownership.

As stated in Chapter 1, there are two forms that property will take: real and personal. Real property includes land, buildings, items so attached to the land that they become part of it (also known as **fixtures**), and interests in the land, such as water and mineral rights. Personal property consists of everything else or movable items such as furniture, clothing, cash, and automobiles.

O.C.G.A. § 53-12-2(9) also mentions tangible and intangible property. **Tangible property** is real or personal property that can be physically touched (e.g., house, car, and jewelry). On the other hand, **intangible property** is real or personal property that represents an ownership interest in something and has no physical substance (e.g., stocks, water and mineral rights, and bank accounts).

Exhibit 3.1 Items to Include in the Estate Plan

Furthermore, O.C.G.A. § 53-12-2(9) addresses legal and equitable property. **Legal property** refers to the fact that one has absolute ownership or title to the property, including the right to manage and control it. On the other hand, when one has **equitable property**, also known as **beneficial property**, then ownership is not absolute; instead, one may be entitled to use or enjoy the property legally owned by someone else. We will discuss these types of property more fully in Chapter 8 when we get to our discussion of trusts. You will learn that the trustee has legal title to the property, while the beneficiary has the equitable or beneficial title. In other words, the trustee holds and controls the property, not for his or her own benefit, but for the benefit of the beneficiary.

The Bundle of Rights

With absolute ownership, the highest and best form of ownership in real property, also known as **fee simple**, the title holder gains a **bundle of rights**. These include (1) the right to possess (i.e., occupy and access) the property; (2) the right to use and control the property; (3) the right to enjoy the property and exclude others; and, (4) the right to dispose of and encumber the property. From the estate planning perspective, our concern is this last ownership interest—the disposition of the property—upon a decedent's death. To **dispose** of property means to transfer possession or ownership. When referring to the gift of personal property in a will, the terms

bequest or **legacy** are used; when we are discussing a gift of real property in a will, it is called a **devise.**

According to O.C.G.A. § 44-6-20, a property owner has the power to transfer the property to a **devisee,** the person who will receive the decedent's property upon his or her death. Generally, it is in his or her will or trust that the decedent indicates the devisee(s). A testator can either transfer in fee simple or convey a **life estate.** A life estate represents a right to the property that is limited to a specific period (either the life estate owner's lifetime or a third party's lifetime) called the **measuring life.** The person obtaining this right is known as the **life tenant.** The life tenant must maintain the property. He or she may not commit **waste;** that is, the life tenant must not abuse or destroy the property, intentionally causing it to depreciate in value. If the life tenant commits waste or at the end of the measuring life, the property reverts to the person whom the testator named in the will as the owner of the remaining interest in the property. This person is known as the **remainderman.** For example, suppose Mary is married to Jim, and she is the sole owner of their home. When she dies, she would like Jim to continue to live in the home until he dies, but ultimately she would like to leave the home to her children (who are not Jim's), in equal shares. In this scenario, Mary could use her will to convey a life estate to Jim for his life, which is the measuring life, and name her children as the remaindermen. Jim would be the life tenant and during his lifetime, he would be obligated to upkeep the property and avoid its depreciation to the extent possible. When Jim dies, the property will then belong to Mary's children, who will own the property in fee simple, per Mary's wishes.

Finally, note that as indicated previously, if, at the time of death, the decedent has not named a devisee by will or trust, the property will be transferred under Georgia's laws of intestate succession. It is also important to recognize that, according to O.C.G.A. § 53-1-20(b), a devisee under a will or trust is not obligated to accept gifted property. On the contrary, he or she possesses the right to renounce the property, in whole or in part, meaning refuse or reject all or part of it. Renunciation may occur for various reasons, including the desire to avoid tax consequences, an inability to manage the financial burden associated with the assets, or a wish to maintain family harmony.

Classifications of Property

Several vs. Joint Property

As indicated earlier, when interviewing an estate planning client, it is important to ascertain how he or she owns the property. The attorney will want to know if: (1) the client owns the property in **severalty,** meaning he or she is the sole title holder; or (2) the client has **joint ownership,** meaning there are two or more concurrent owners of the property. Joint owners in Georgia will either hold the property as **tenants in common** (with their ownership right referred to as a **tenancy in common)** or as **joint tenants with the right of survivorship** (with their ownership right referred to as a **joint tenancy**). Per O.C.G.A. § 44-6-120, tenants in common possess an undivided interest in the property, meaning each owner can use and enjoy the entire property, but they each own only an agreed-upon percentage of the same. When a tenant in common dies, the decedent's share is distributed as indicated in that tenant's will or trust, or under the laws of intestate succession which we will discuss more fully in Chapter 4. According to O.C.G.A. § 44-6-190(a)(2), in Georgia, it is presumed that this is how joint owners hold the property unless the deed or another conveyance "instrument expressly refers to the takers as 'joint tenants,' 'joint tenants and not as tenants in common,' or 'joint tenants with survivorship' or as taking 'jointly with survivorship.'"

The other form of joint ownership, joint tenancy, is characterized by **four unities** (commonly referred to using the mnemonic "PITT"): (1) **unity of possession**—like tenants in common, joint tenants each have an undivided interest in the whole property; (2) **unity of interest**—the joint tenants must each own an equal percentage of the property; (3) **unity of time**—the joint tenants take ownership of the property at the same time and (4) **unity of title**—the joint tenants acquire ownership in the same instrument (e.g., deed or will). When a joint tenant dies, the decedent's share automatically becomes the property of the surviving joint tenant(s), if any, in equal shares. If there is no surviving joint tenant, then the decedent's share will be distributed as indicated in his or her will or trust, or following the laws of intestate succession.

Separate vs. Marital Property

For married estate planning clients in Georgia, there is an additional question related to property ownership: Is it **separate property** or **marital property**? Generally, separate property is real or personal property that the client owned before marriage or acquired during marriage by gift or inheritance, solely in his or her own name. On the contrary, marital property is acquired by either partner or jointly, or gifted to the couple during their marriage. Marital property is considered the property of both spouses in Georgia and must be dealt with accordingly for estate planning purposes.

As an illustration, consider the following couple, Sharon and Andrew:

- Before marriage, Sharon owned a car in her name and Andrew owned a motorcycle in his name.
- When they were married, they received a wedding gift of $25,000.
- During the marriage, they acquired a house and a truck in both their names.
- During the marriage, Andrew's mother died, and she left him the family business.

Exhibit 3.2 illustrates how the property would be classified. Generally, in Georgia, the car would be considered Sharon's separate property; the motorcycle and his family business would be considered Andrew's separate property; and the wedding gift, the house, and the truck would be considered marital property. Understanding these distinctions will be critical for an estate planning attorney as he or she is drafting wills or trusts for the couple.

Exhibit 3.2 Classification of the Couple's Separate and Marital Property

Probate vs. Nonprobate Property

A final important question for consideration in estate planning is whether the client's property will be deemed probate property or nonprobate property. **Probate property** is property that is owned solely by the decedent, or by the decedent as a tenant in common, at the time of his or her death. Property classified in this manner will be distributed as the decedent designated in his or her will, or by the laws of intestate succession if the decedent died intestate. The significance of property that falls under this category is that it will become a part of the decedent's estate and subject to the administration process and claims of creditors which you will learn more about in Chapter 12. Exhibit 3.3 illustrates the items that are considered probate property in Georgia.

Exhibit 3.3 Probate Property

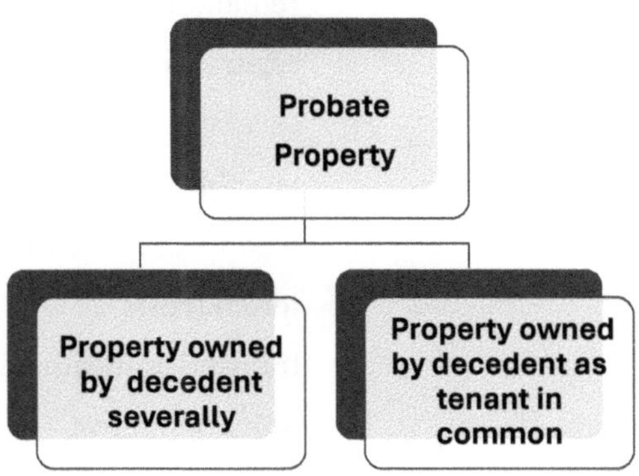

On the other hand, **nonprobate property** cannot be transferred by will or through the laws of intestate succession. Property classified in this manner will not be considered a part of the decedent's estate to be settled in probate court. Instead, it goes directly to the decedent's beneficiaries upon his or her death, free from administration costs and the claims of creditors. Nonprobate property includes: (1) jointly owned property, including (a) **transfer-on-death accounts**, which are accounts passing securities, such as stocks and bonds, directly to the named beneficiary upon the owner's death; (b) **pay-on-death accounts**, also known as **totten trusts**, which are bank accounts listing a beneficiary in the event the owner dies; and (c) joint tenancies with the right of survivorship; (2) property held in a living trust; (3) life insurance with a named beneficiary; (4) retirement and pension accounts with a named beneficiary; and (5) life estates. Exhibit 3.4 illustrates those items that are considered nonprobate property.

Exhibit 3.4 Nonprobate Property

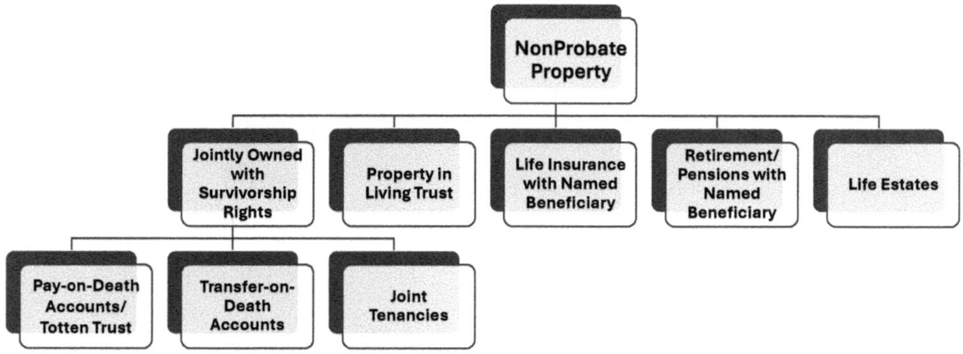

Key Terms

beneficial property
bequest
bundle of rights
devise
devisee
dispose
equitable property
fee simple
fixtures
four unities
intangible property
joint ownership
joint tenants with the right of survivorship/joint tenancy
legacy
legal property
life estate
life tenant
marital property
measuring life
nonprobate property
pay-on-death accounts
probate property
remainderman
separate property
severalty
tangible property
tenants in common/tenancy in common
totten trusts
transfer-on-death accounts
unity of interest
unity of possession
unity of time
unity of title
waste

Review Questions

1. What is the bundle of rights associated with property ownership in fee simple?
2. What is a life estate?
3. What are the devisee's options concerning property that he or she has inherited?
4. Describe what constitutes real property and provide some examples of the same.
5. Describe what constitutes personal property and provide some examples of the same.
6. What is the difference between tangible and intangible property?
7. What does it mean to have legal ownership as opposed to equitable or beneficial title?
8. What are the four unities, and how are they relevant to property ownership?
9. In Georgia, what is classified as separate property, and what is marital property?
10. In Georgia, what items are generally included as probate property, and what items are nonprobate property?

Practical Assignment

Today, most counties have property records available online but continue to maintain physical property record rooms. Either visit the website for the county in which you live or the records room and research a property (yours or someone else's). Then provide the following information related to your search in a detailed report:

1. Which of the two methods did you use to locate the property records?
2. What is the property that you attempted to research and your relation to the same?
3. What process did you use to locate the property records?
4. Describe the experience fully. What did you learn from it?

Chapter 4

Testate vs. Intestate Succession

Learning Objectives

Upon completion of this chapter, you should be able to:

- Differentiate between dying testate and intestate.
- Explain entitlement to a year's support.
- Summarize Georgia's laws related to intestate succession.
- Discuss the effect of intestacy upon the estate and the decedent's loved ones.

Testate Succession

As stated in Chapter 2, the goal of the estate planning team is to ensure that the client is prepared for the inevitable. In previous chapters, we have discussed all of the benefits for a client who dies **testate**, i.e., leaving a valid will. **Testate succession**, meaning the transfer of property according to a will, is far better for the decedent, his or her loved ones, and his or her estate for a myriad of reasons. The decedent will have outlined (1) who should receive his or her assets, (2) how they should be handled, (3) where minor or disabled children and pets should live and who should care for them and their inherited property, and (4) who should act as fiduciaries to oversee the testator's wishes as outlined in the will. Leaving a valid will can minimize court battles over who should receive the decedent's assets, and provide answers to issues like child custody and burial vs. cremation, which issues may threaten to divide a family during an extremely difficult time. Moreover, it will significantly reduce the time and expense that it takes to administer an estate. Therefore, a will is an essential tool to protect yourself, your loved ones, and your property.

Year's Support

It is important to note that in Georgia, as in many other states, there are some limitations related to the decedent's ability to disinherit certain family members totally. Under O.C.G.A. § 53-3-1(c), the decedent's surviving spouse (who has not remarried) and unmarried minor children (not stepchildren) are entitled to a **year's support**. They possess a fundamental right to inherit at least that portion of the decedent's estate, free from the claim of creditors, whether the decedent died intestate or testate. Therefore, even if a testator attempts to disinherit a spouse or minor children from whom he or she is estranged in his or her will, the disinherited family member may petition the probate court upon the decedent's death for a year's support. However, the petition must be filed within two years of the decedent's death. Upon filing, the court will determine the petitioner's entitlement to a year's support and the inheritance amount. Exhibit 4.3 at the end of this chapter includes a sample petition.

Intestate Succession Laws

Personal Property

According to O.C.G.A. § 53-2-1(c), if a decedent has died without leaving a valid will, then Georgia's rules of intestate succession are applicable to determine the heirs of the decedent's personal property. Exhibit 4.1, which follows, is a chart that summarizes Georgia's intestate succession laws.

Exhibit 4.2, which also follows, is a diagram demonstrating the intestate distribution of a decedent's assets. As you can see, the laws address just about every familial scenario. However, it is important to note in the unlikely event that the intestate decedent passes without leaving any relatives at all, then his or her property will **escheat**. In other words, per O.C.G.A. § 53-2-50, the property will go to the State of Georgia "upon a failure of heirs of a decedent to appear and make claim for or against property owned by the decedent at death for which no other disposition was provided either by will or otherwise." Needless to say, this is hardly the outcome that most people would want.

There are a few other interesting provisions of Georgia's intestacy laws. For example, according to O.C.G.A. § 53-2-3, children born out of wedlock may inherit from their mother, but can only inherit from their father after demonstrating some indicia of paternity. Also, according to O.C.G.A. § 53-2-5, children born from consensual artificial insemination during a marriage are entitled to a share of their parents' estates. Moreover, "half" relatives are treated as if they are "whole" for intestate inheritance purposes under O.C.G.A. § 53-2-1(b)(2). In other words, according to the Georgia laws of intestate succession, siblings who share only one parent may inherit from one another as if they share both parents.

Finally, the rules provide that those who are responsible for a decedent's death are barred from inheritance of his or her estate. According to Georgia's **slayer statute**,

Exhibit 4.1 Intestate Succession Laws

Applicable Code Section	If the decedent has:	The result is:
O.C.G.A. § 53-2-1(c)(1)	spouse and no children	spouse is the sole heir
O.C.G.A. § 53-2-1(c)(1)	spouse and children	spouse and children share equally, but spouse is entitled to at least ⅓ of estate
O.C.G.A. § 53-2-1(c)(3)	no spouse, but children	surviving children share equally, with any descendant of a deceased child taking his or her share, ***per stirpes****
O.C.G.A. § 53-2-1(c)(4)	no spouse and no children, but parents	surviving parents share equally
O.C.G.A. § 53-2-1(c)(5)	no spouse, no children, and no parents, but siblings	surviving siblings share equally, with any child of a deceased sibling taking his or her share, *per stirpes*
O.C.G.A. § 53-2-1(c)(6)	no spouse, no children, no parents, no siblings, but grandparents	surviving grandparents share equally
O.C.G.A. § 53-2-1(c)(7)	no spouse, no children, no parents, no siblings, no grandparents, but uncles and aunts	surviving uncle and aunts share equally, with any child of a deceased uncle or aunt taking his or her share, *per stirpes*
O.C.G.A. § 53-2-1(c)(8)	none of the above, but more remote relatives	the court will use a formula to calculate those in the nearest degree of kinship and they will share equally

***per stirpes** means distributing equal shares "by roots," that is, by family groups

O.C.G.A. § 53-1-5(a), "An individual who feloniously and intentionally kills or conspires to kill or procures the killing of another individual forfeits the right to take an interest from the decedent's estate ... and to serve as a personal representative or trustee of the decedent's estate or any trust created by the decedent."

While Georgia's intestacy laws attempt to distribute the decedent's property in a common-sense fashion, without a valid will, there is no way of confirming the decedent's true intentions.

Real Property

Similar issues arise concerning the distribution of an intestate decedent's real property. As indicated in Chapter 1, real property is governed by the laws of the county and state where the property is located. Therefore, in the event of a decedent's intestacy, the intestate succession laws of the property locale will govern. For decedents who own real property within Georgia, that property will pass according to the laws outlined

Exhibit 4.2 Diagram of the Intestate Distribution of a Decedent's Assets

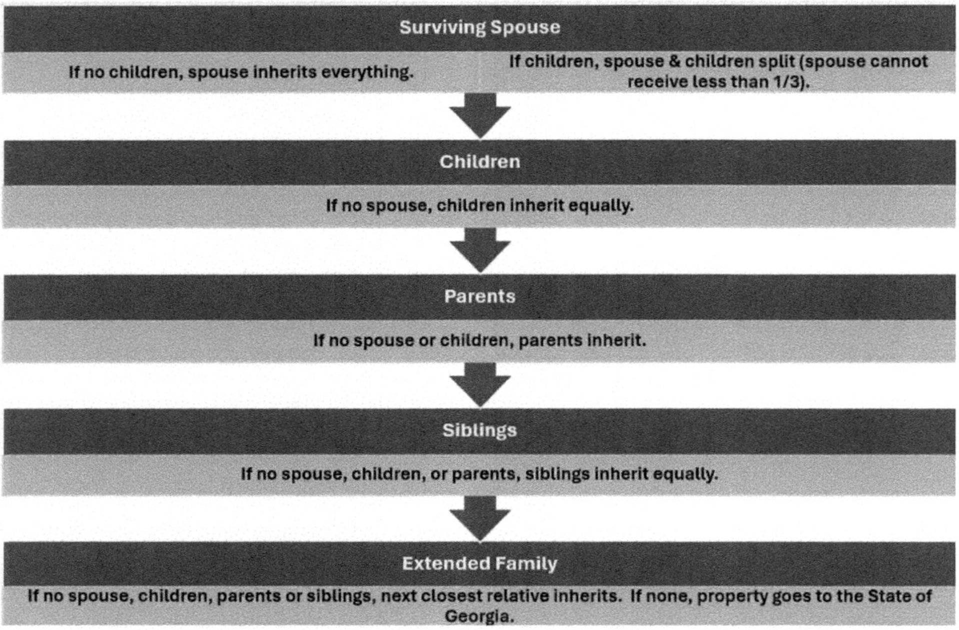

and summarized in Exhibit 4.1 from O.C.G.A. § 53-2-1(c). As is the case with personal property, if the decedent has no surviving relatives, then the real property will escheat.

In addition, some Georgia residents may own property outside of the state, so there is a possibility that another state's (or country's) laws of intestate succession may come into play when settling a decedent's estate. These foreign laws may conflict with the laws of the State of Georgia and the real property may be distributed in a manner not consistent with the Georgia laws of intestate succession. Moreover, potential heirs will likely need to consult with and hire additional local legal counsel for areas outside of Georgia to settle the estate in those jurisdictions. This parallel probate process is known as **ancillary administration** or **ancillary probate**. Needless to say, it will lead to added expense and time to settle the decedent's estate when there is an ancillary administration. This would further complicate the matter of handling the affairs of the decedent. Again, these added burdens on the decedent's loved ones can be avoided by careful estate planning before it is too late.

Exhibit 4.3 Petition for Year's Support

IN THE PROBATE COURT OF ____________________ COUNTY
STATE OF GEORGIA

IN RE:	)	
	)	
_______________________________,	)	**ESTATE NO.** __________
DECEASED	)	

PETITION FOR YEAR'S SUPPORT

The petition of ____
[Full name of petitioner] First Middle Last

whose physical address(es) is/are ____
Street City County State Zip Code

and mailing address(es) is/are ____
Street City County State Zip Code

shows the Court the following:

1.

The petitioner is:

_____ (a) the surviving spouse who has not married since the death of the decedent.

_____ (b) a guardian or other individual acting on behalf of minor child(ren), who have not turned 18 prior to the filing of this petition and have not married *[state specific relationship]*: ______________________________

____,
[Full name of decedent] First Middle Last

whose place of domicile was____,
Street City County State Zip Code

departed this life on ________________, 20 ______.

2.

[Initial one]

_____ (a) There is not a will. *[List in "Exhibit B" all of the decedent's heirs at law, with age or majority status, address and relationship to the decedent set opposite the name of each. For any minor, include the date of birth and the name and address of the parent or guardian.]*

_____ (b) There is a will, which has been offered for probate; however, a personal representative has not been appointed as of the date this petition was filed. *[List the personal representative to be appointed, all of the heirs at law of the decedent, with age or majority status, address and relationship to the decedent set opposite the name of each, the beneficiaries named in the will in "Exhibit B." For any minor, include the date of birth and the name and address of the parent or guardian.]*

_____ (c) There is a will, which will be offered for probate. *[List the personal representative to be appointed, all of the heirs at law of the decedent, with age or majority status, address and relationship to the decedent set opposite the name of each, the beneficiaries named in the will in "Exhibit B." For any minor, include the date of birth and the name and address of the parent or guardian.]*

_____ (d) There is a will, which will not be offered for probate but is hereby filed with this Court not for probate or is already on file with this Court. *[List the personal representative named in the will, all of the heirs at law of the decedent, with age or majority status, address and relationship to the decedent set opposite the name of each, the beneficiaries named in the will in "Exhibit B." For any minor, include the date of birth and the name and address of the parent or guardian.]*

_____ (e) There is a will, which has been probated. *[List the appointed personal representative. The names of the beneficiaries are not required to be listed in "Exhibit B" unless the appointed personal representative and the petitioner are the same person. For any minor, include the date of birth and the name and address of the parent or guardian.]* A copy of the final order and letters of appointment are attached as "Exhibit ____," in the event the letters were not issued by the probate court named in the style above.

_____ (f) There is an appointed administrator. *[List the appointed personal representative in "Exhibit B." The names of the heirs are not required to be listed in "Exhibit B" unless the personal representative and the petitioner are the same person. For any minor, include the date of birth and the name and address of the parent or guardian.]* A copy of the final order and letters of appointment are attached as "Exhibit ____," in the event the letters were not issued by the probate court named in the style above.

3.

Required for all estates in which the heirs must be listed in "Exhibit B." *[Provide sufficient factual information to enable the Court to conclude that all of the heirs of the decedent are included and that there are no heirs of the same or closer degree according to O.C.G.A. § 53-2-1. Provide the names of any deceased heirs and include the date of death for each (see instructions for further clarification). Also, state here all pertinent facts that may govern the method of giving notice to any party and that may determine whether or not a guardian ad litem should be appointed for any party. If any heirs listed in "Exhibit B" are cousins, grandchildren, nephews or nieces of the decedent, indicate the deceased ancestor through whom they are related to the decedent.]*

____

____

____

____

____

GPCSF 10 [2] Eff. July 2021

4.

Petitioner shows that the minor child(ren) of the decedent and/or the surviving spouse (is)(are) entitled, before the payment of debts of the decedent, to an allowance called "Year's Support," which petitioner hereby claims for the individual(s) named in paragraph 6 of this petition.

5.

The decedent's estate consists of real and/or personal property of the probable value of ____________________________________ dollars.

6.

A schedule of the property or a statement of the amount of money, or both, which the petitioner proposes to have set apart to the following individuals: ____

[List the full name(s) of the individual(s) whom the petitioner proposes the year's support be set apart to, usually the spouse and minor child(ren).] is attached hereto as "Exhibit A," and made a part hereof.

7.

In addition to all taxes and tax liens on real property accrued for years prior to the year of the decedent's death, petitioner elects to have property taxes on any real property set apart as year's support divested as follows:

[Only select one]

______ (a) Real property taxes accrued in the year of decedent's death;
______ (b) Real property taxes accrued in the year in which this petition is filed; or
______ (c) Real property taxes accrued in the year following the filing of this petition if this petition is filed in the year of the decedent's death.

8.

Additional data: *[Where full particulars are lacking, state here the reasons for any such omission.]*

____

____

____

____

____

____

____

____

____

WHEREFORE, petitioner prays:

1. That this petition be accepted and filed.
2. That notice issue and be published and served as required by law.
3. That any interested person who is a minor or an incapacitated adult have a guardian ad litem appointed for him or her.
4. That this Court grant such other and further relief as it deems proper under the circumstances.

This _____ day of __________________, 20 _____.

____
Signature of the Petitioner

____
Printed Name of the Petitioner

____

____
Mailing Address

____
Telephone Number

Signature of Attorney: ____

Printed Name of Attorney: ____

Address: ____

____

Telephone Number: __________________ State Bar #________________________

Source: https://www.gasupreme.us/probate-court-standard-forms/

Key Terms

ancillary administration
ancillary probate
escheat
per stirpes
slayer statute
testate
testate succession
year's support

Review Questions

1. What does it mean to die testate?
2. What is testate succession?
3. What is a year's support, and who is entitled to it under Georgia law?
4. Can you disinherit family under Georgia law? If so, are there any limitations?
5. What does it mean to die intestate, and where are Georgia's laws related to intestacy located?
6. What is the slayer statute?
7. What does *per stirpes* mean?
8. Tami, a Georgia resident with no property outside of Georgia, dies intestate, leaving a husband, parents, a grandmother, and no children. Who inherits her property and in what percentage(s)?
9. John, a Georgia resident with property in Georgia and New York, dies intestate, leaving a wife and three children. Who inherits his property and in what percentage(s)?
10. Alexis, a Georgia resident, passed away unexpectedly, without a will. She left behind her biological father, Bob; her biological mother, Jill; her sister, Britney; and her half-sister, Raven (they share the same mother, but not the same father). According to Georgia law, who inherits her property and in what percentage(s)?

Practical Assignment

After reading this chapter and reviewing Georgia's intestate succession laws, prepare a diagram indicating how your property would be distributed if you died without leaving a will.

Chapter 5

Wills—Validity, Modification, Revocation, and Contests

Learning Objectives

Upon completion of this chapter, you should be able to:

- Define basic terminology and concepts associated with wills.
- Outline Georgia's statutory requirements for a valid will.
- Describe formalities related to the execution of a will.
- Differentiate among types of wills.
- Explain procedures for will modification and revocation.
- List and define grounds for will contests.
- Identify the purpose and function of the self-proving affidavit.

Since we have established the importance of estate planning, in this chapter, we will shift to a discussion of the particulars of the last will and testament, one of the most widely used estate planning tools. As outlined below in Exhibit 5.1, choosing a will over a trust as the primary estate planning document has pros and cons. The estate planning team will advise the client about which instrument is better suited to address

Exhibit 5.1 Pros and Cons of a Will

PROS	CONS
SIMPLE TO CREATE & AMEND • Relatively easy to draft & change • Basic formality requirements NOMINATE GUARDIANS • Parents can designate guardians for minors FLEXIBLE • Freedom to distribute assets as desired and creatively	MUST BE PROBATED • Time consuming • Expense (varies by state) • Involves each state where property is located BECOMES PUBLIC RECORD SUBJECT TO CHALLENGES & DISPUTES LIMITED TO CERTAIN PROPERTY • Assets with beneficiaries are excluded (life insurance, retirement accounts)

the client's individual needs. We will discuss trusts more fully later, but, in this chapter, we will explore what is necessary to create a valid will in the State of Georgia. Then we will address reasons and procedures for (1) **modification**, which is amendment of the will, (2) **revocation**, meaning cancellation of the will, and (3) **will contests**, which are challenges to the validity of the will.

Validity

You may have noticed that in previous chapters, when we discussed testate succession, we spoke of the importance of everyone having a **valid**, meaning legally enforceable, will. That is because it is not enough to simply create a will. Instead, it is necessary to ensure that the will meets the statutory requirements, also known as formalities, within the domicile for validity and proper execution. Without taking these measures, the document may be invalid and have no legal effect. It will be as though the testator died intestate, and the laws of intestate succession will prevail over the testator's failed attempt to express his or her final wishes.

For example, many assumed that the singer, Aretha Franklin, died intestate in August 2018. However, in May 2019, three handwritten documents believed to be her wills were discovered in her home. Two, dated 2010, were found in a locked cabinet, and a third, dated 2014, was found under seat cushions in a sofa at her home. Despite Aretha Franklin's apparent attempts to express her final wishes, the discovery led to great confusion for her loved ones because the handwriting in the documents was messy, as shown in Exhibit 5.2, required verification, and the dispositive provisions were not well-drafted and, at times, contradictory. Some questioned whether the necessary formalities had been observed for the documents to be valid under Michigan law.

As O.C.G.A. § 53-4-3 indicates, in Georgia, "No particular form is necessary to constitute a will. To determine whether an instrument is a will, the test is the intention of the maker to be gathered from the whole instrument, read in light of the surrounding circumstances." In effect, no specific words or format are necessary for a valid will. Therefore, the will need not be typed, printed on fancy paper, or filled with legalese. A handwritten statement of the testator's wishes on a messy notepad, like Aretha Franklin's, or even on a crumbled napkin, will suffice as long as the necessary formalities related to execution are observed and the testator's intentions are clear. Note, however, that in Georgia, a **holographic will**, one that is handwritten but does not observe the formalities related to execution, is unacceptable.

Hence, even though the form is unimportant, each state, including Georgia, has set forth statutory requirements that must be met for a valid will to be created. The requirements are generally minimal to allow individuals to express themselves freely. First, as stated previously, the will must be written. Per O.C.G.A. § 53-4-20(a), **nuncupative wills**, also known as oral wills, which have been videotaped or tape-recorded, are no longer allowed in Georgia. Furthermore, to make a valid will, the testator must be at least 14 years old and have the capacity to understand the nature and importance

Exhibit 5.2 First Page of Aretha Franklin's 2014 Handwritten Will

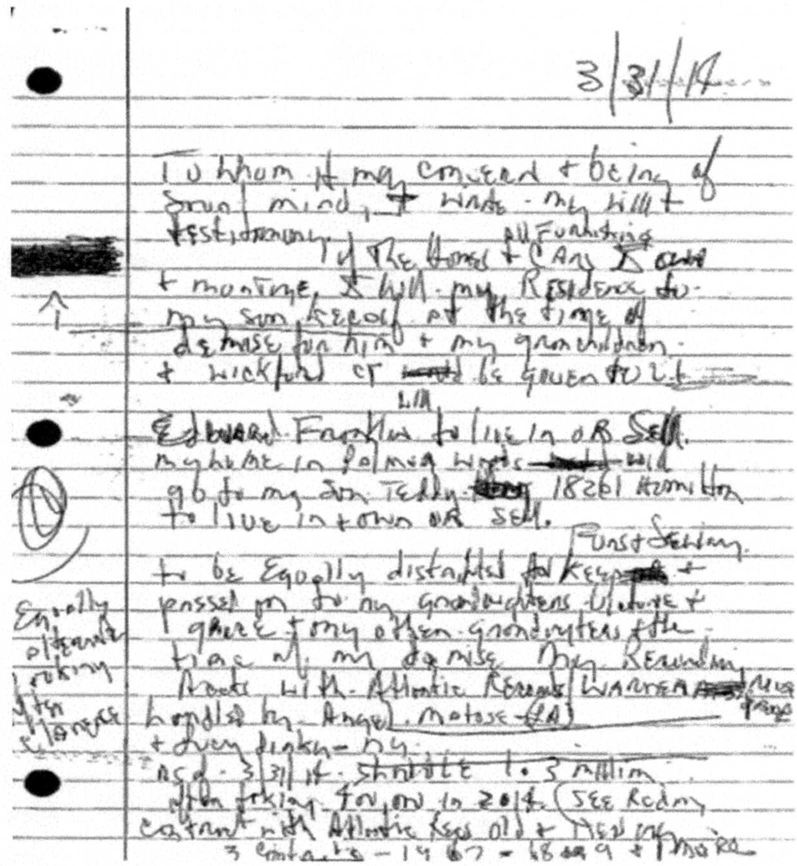
3/31/14

Source: Oakland County Probate Court

of transferring property. The testator must also know the contents of the will. Moreover, the testator must act at his or her own **volition** or free choice when making the will. The testator should not be under any form of duress, fraud, or undue influence that may be affecting his or her decision-making related to the disposition of property. Additionally, the will must be signed by the testator (or his or her appointed representative) and attested by two or more competent witnesses who are at least 14 years old. It is advisable to have two **disinterested witnesses**, meaning they are not beneficiaries under the will. Otherwise, while the will may be valid, the right of the interested witnesses to inherit thereunder will be forfeited. The testator and the subscribing witnesses may **execute**, that is, sign, the document, with either a signature or a mark, such as an "X." While the testator may direct someone to execute the will on his or her behalf, the witnesses may not.

Georgia's statutory requirements for a valid will and the corresponding Code sections are outlined in Exhibit 5.3, which follows.

Exhibit 5.3 Statutory Requirements for Will Validity

Code Section	Requirement
O.C.G.A. § 53-4-10(a)	age: testator must be 14 years or older to make a will
O.C.G.A. § 53-4-11(a)	capacity: testator must have a "decided and rational desire" as to the disposition of his or her property
O.C.G.A. § 53-4-12	freedom and volition: testator must be acting freely and voluntarily
O.C.G.A. § 53-4-20(a)	writing: will must be in writing
O.C.G.A. § 53-4-20(a)	signing: will must be signed by the testator (or someone else signing on behalf of the testator at his or her direction) with a mark (such as an "X") or a signature
O.C.G.A. § 53-4-20(b); O.C.G.A. § 53-4-22(a); O.C.G.A. § 53-4-2	witnesses: will must be attested and signed in testator's presence by two or more competent witnesses who are age 14 or older and not beneficiaries under the will
O.C.G.A. § 53-4-21	knowledge: testator must be aware of contents of the will

In addition to the will, O.C.G.A. § 53-4-5(a), allows the testator to draft a written statement or list called a **letter of instruction** to "dispose of items of tangible personal property, other than money, not otherwise specifically disposed of by the testator's will." The statement or list must be signed and dated by the testator; reasonably describe the items and beneficiaries; and reference the testator's will. This allows the testator to informally designate beneficiaries for property not specified in the will or acquired after the will is executed. The document can be revoked or modified, provided that it is signed and dated after the revision. While these letters are useful, they are not legally binding, since they are not executed with the same formalities as the will. Nonetheless, they provide added guidance on handling the testator's estate. For this reason, it is suggested that the testator execute at least three copies of any letter of instruction: (1) one for the executor; (2) one to be kept with the testator's other important documents; and (3) one to be kept with the will. Common matters addressed in the letters include, but are not limited to, the following:

- Location of important documents (insurance, will, bank statements, and so forth);
- List of financial, retirement, and investment accounts;
- Location of the safe or safe deposit box (combination and/or key location);
- Information related to assets and liabilities;
- Names and addresses of insurance agents, financial and legal advisors; and
- Details related to funeral/cremation arrangements.

Finally, related to the will, although it is not required, it is a common practice for attorneys to attach a **self-proving affidavit** to the will. It is a sworn statement signed by the testator and subscribing witnesses before a notary public. The value of this document is that a self-proved will may be admitted to **probate** without the testimony of

Exhibit 5.4 Self-Proving Affidavit

SELF PROVING AFFIDAVIT

STATE OF GEORGIA
COUNTY OF ____________________

Before me, the undersigned authority, on this day personally appeared the Testator, ___________________, and the witnesses, ______________________ and ___________________, whose names are subscribed to the annexed or foregoing instrument in their respective capacities, and all of said individuals being duly sworn, the Testator, declared to me and to the witnesses in my presence that said instrument is the Last Will and Testament of the Testator and that the Testator had willingly made and executed it as the Testator's free act and deed for the purposes expressed therein. The witnesses, each on oath, stated to me in the presence and hearing of the Testator that the Testator had declared to them that the instrument is the Testator's Last Will and Testament and that the Testator executed the instrument as such and wished each of them to sign it as a witness; and under oath each witness stated further that the witnesses had signed the same as witness in the presence of the Testator and at the Testator's request; that the Testator was fourteen (14) years of age or over and of sound mind; and that each of the witnesses was then at least fourteen (14) years of age.

_________________________________(SEAL)
______________________, Testator

____
_______________________, Witness

____
_______________________, Witness

Sworn to and subscribed before me by the Testator, ____________________ and the witnesses, ___________________ and _________________, this __________ day of ___________, 20__.

____
___________________, Notary Public

[NOTARY SEAL OR STAMP]

the witnesses under O.C.G.A. § 53-4-24(c). Exhibit 5.4 shows the form of affidavit suggested. Probate is the court-supervised process of administering the decedent's estate, which includes determining the validity of the will, settling estate debts, and distributing the decedent's property. This process will be discussed more fully in Chapter 12. However, it is important to note here that a will does not take effect until the death of the testator after the court admits the will to probate.

Pour Over Wills

Even if an attorney advises a client to utilize a trust, the attorney may still draft a basic will to accompany it, with the trust named as the primary beneficiary thereunder. This is called a **pour over will**. As you will learn in Chapter 8, with a trust, to enjoy all of its advantages, the client must transfer all property into the name of the trust during his or her lifetime. Needless to say, an issue with trusts is that inevitably, some client property is not properly transferred or titled. Hence, a simple pour over will is recommended to avoid this problem. When it accompanies the trust document, it demonstrates the testator's intention to "pour over" to the trust any property that has not been properly transferred to the trust during the decedent's lifetime. Appendix E of this textbook contains Michael Jackson's pour over will for your review of typical provisions. You will notice the catch-all pour over provision in Article III. The singer expressly states that he gives his entire estate to his Trustee(s) under the Michael Jackson Family Trust and all assets to be held, managed, and distributed as part of the Trust, in accordance with its terms.

Joint and Mutual Wills

In addition, under Georgia law, both **joint wills** and **mutual wills** (also known as **reciprocal wills**) are permissible. O.C.G.A. § 53-4-31(a) defines a joint will as "one will signed by two or more testators that deals with the distribution of the property of each testator. A joint will may be probated as each testator's will." While a joint will may seem like an easier, cheaper option for couples, it is ill-advised. Several circumstances may arise that could prove problematic: (1) the couple may separate or divorce; (2) one testator may possess the will, while the other has no access to it or no idea where it is located; and, (3) one testator may modify or destroy the will without the other's consent or knowledge.

For couples, it may be more prudent to execute mutual wills, which are also known as reciprocal wills. O.C.G.A. § 53-4-31(b) defines them as "separate wills of two or more testators that make reciprocal dispositions of each testator's property." For example, a husband's will may contain the following language: "I give my entire estate to my wife, and if she predeceases me, then I give said property to our children, in equal shares." His wife's mutual will would contain mirroring language such as: "I give my entire estate to my husband, and if he predeceases me, then I give said property to our children, in equal shares." To avoid some of the pitfalls of joint wills, in mutual wills,

Exhibit 5.5 Reasons for Modification or Revocation

When to Review an Estate Plan

- After a wedding or divorce
- After the birth or adoption of a child
- After relocating out of state
- After an increase or decrease in assets
- After the loss of a loved one
- After 3 or more years has passed since the estate plan was created

there is usually included a provision that no testator may change his or her will without the other's consent until after the death of the other.

Modification and Revocation

As indicated above, in Exhibit 5.5, one should periodically review the estate plan and make any necessary revisions based on a change in circumstances. Generally, wills are **ambulatory**, meaning that modification and revocation are possible. Per O.C.G.A. § 53-4-40, since a will does not take effect until the death of the testator, the testator has the power to modify or revoke his or her will at any time before death, as long as he or she remains competent. Unless the testator modifies or revokes the will, it remains valid. As stated in Chapter 2, major life changes, including moving out of state, giving birth, adopting, getting married or divorced, or receiving a significant increase or decrease in assets, or the passage of time since the original plan was created may prompt a testator to either modify or revoke his or her will. Just as there are formalities for properly executing a valid will, there are procedures for the effective modification and revocation of a will.

To modify, or amend, a will, a testator must either: (1) execute a **codicil**, a written supplement or addition to an existing will that changes it, or (2) create an entirely new will. According to O.C.G.A. § 53-4-20(c), "A codicil shall be executed by the testator and attested and subscribed by witnesses with the same formality as a will." Moreover, it is standard practice to include a self-proving affidavit with the codicil. If the testator chooses to create a new will, there is usually language included therein to the effect that the new will is replacing any prior wills and codicils. As a result of these formalities, a codicil is a binding document. A sample codicil is provided as Exhibit 5.6.

To revoke, or cancel, a will, a testator must either: (1) destroy it by some physical act, such as burning it, tearing it up, or crossing through it in its entirety; or (2) create an entirely new will. In other words, and according to O.C.G.A. § 53-4-42:

(a) A revocation may be express or implied.

(b) An **express revocation** occurs when the testator by writing or action expressly annuls a will. An express revocation takes effect instantly.

(c) An **implied revocation** results from the execution of a subsequent inconsistent will that does not by its terms expressly revoke the previous will. An

Exhibit 5.6 Sample Codicil

CODICIL

GEORGIA, ________________ [Name of County]

CODICIL TO LAST WILL AND TESTAMENT OF
____ [Name of Testator]

I, ________________________________ [name of testator], of
______________________________ [name of county], Georgia, do hereby make and declare this to be the first codicil to my Last Will and Testament dated
____ [date of last will and testament].
Item Number _______ [designation of item]

Different examples, i.e., modifications of simple will.

In the Fourth Item on page one of said Will I named as Trustee [name of trustee]. In the Eighth Item at subparagraph (b) I made reference to common trust funds administered by [name of trustee], and further in subparagraph (h) I made reference to any successor bank of said [name of trustee]. In the Fourteenth Item I named said [name of trustee] as successor Executor. I hereby delete from said Will every reference to [name of trustee], and revoke all appointments and authorizations conferred upon said [name of trustee], and do substitute in lieu thereof as Trustee under said Will and as successor Executor under said Will, [name of substitute]. I direct that as such Trustee and successor Executor [name of substitute] shall have all of the powers, duties and privileges as fully and amply as if it had been originally named in my said Will in lieu of [name of trustee]. Item [designation of item]

[Proceed to amend the will, giving original Item number and exact change to be made.] Item [designation of item]

Except as changed and amended hereby, I ratify, confirm, re-publish and re-declare my said Will of ______________________________ [date of will].

IN WITNESS WHEREOF, I have hereunto set my name and affixed my seal to this my CODICIL TO LAST WILL AND TESTAMENT dated
____ [date of last will and testament], this _____ day of ________________________________, 20____.

____
[Name of testator]

1

The above and foregoing instrument was on the day and year above set forth and in the presence of each of us, the undersigned witnesses, acknowledged by ______________________________ [name of testator] as his CODICIL TO LAST WILL AND TESTAMENT dated ______________________________, and said CODICIL was on said date and in our presence voluntarily signed and acknowledged by the said ______________________________[name of testator], who appeared at the time to be of sound and disposing mind and memory, and the undersigned in the presence of the said ______________________________ [name of testator] and at his request, and in the presence of each other, have hereunto subscribed our names and witnesses this _______ day of ______________________________, 20______.

WITNESSES:

____
[Name of witness 1]

____
____
____
[Address of witness 1]

____
[Name of witness 2]

____
____
____
[Address of witness 2]

2

Source: https://www.southernjudicialcircuit.com/selfhelp/miscforms/CodiciL.pdf

> implied revocation takes effect only when the subsequent inconsistent will becomes effective. If the subsequent inconsistent will fails to become effective from any cause, the implied revocation is not completed.

It is important to note that neither beneficiaries under a will nor family members have a right to know of its contents or any modifications or revocations related to the same. As indicated previously, creating a will is an expression of the testator's intent and his or her free will. Nonetheless, discussion of the will and its contents is prudent and advised to avoid surprise and possible will contests, which can be costly and waste estate assets.

Contests

While potential beneficiaries do not have the right to know about the contents of the testator's will or to get notice of any modification or revocation while the testator is alive, they may be able to contest the will once the testator has died and the will has been admitted to probate. A will contest is the name given to a lawsuit objecting to the validity of a will. To contest a will, the person doing so must have **standing**, meaning, a beneficial interest can be lost if the will is allowed. Those with standing could include close friends or family members of the testator who are not named as beneficiaries in the most recent iteration of the will. After the will is admitted to probate, these interested parties will get notice and the opportunity to challenge the will. The person contesting the will must file a **caveat**, which is a written document that states the reason he or she objects to the will. If the challenger prevails and the court confirms the will is invalid, the court will determine if there was an earlier valid will. If there is none, then Georgia's intestate succession laws come into play.

In addition, a disgruntled beneficiary may wish to contest a will because he or she is dissatisfied with the inheritance received. For this reason, many wills include a **no-contest clause,** also known as an **in terrorem clause**. This clause prevents a will challenger from being a beneficiary under the will. The language used in a no-contest clause may be similar to the following:

> Should any beneficiary contest or initiate proceedings to contest the validity of this will or to prevent any provision herein from being carried out in accordance with its terms, then all the benefits provided for such contesting beneficiary in this will are revoked and annulled.

It is important to note that will contests are difficult to win as courts are prone to honor the testator's desires as expressed in the will, without clear and convincing evidence (a very high standard) of other intentions. Following are the main grounds upon which a will may be contested in Georgia: (1) capacity; (2) undue influence; (3) fraud; (4) forgery; and (5) improper execution.

Capacity

First, someone might question whether the decedent had the required testamentary capacity at the time he or she made the will. O.C.G.A. § 53-4-11(a) provides, "Testamentary capacity exists when the testator has a decided and rational desire as to the disposition of property." A simple test for the interviewing attorney of a testator's capacity is to ask him or her the day of the week and the purpose for the meeting. If the client lacks the capacity or even a basic understanding of the purpose or necessity of the meeting, the attorney should consider discontinuing the representation of the client. As stated earlier in this chapter, the standard is pretty low regarding capacity. To prevail in a will challenge, substantial evidence will need to be submitted to the court to establish that the testator was not of sound mind at the time that he or she made the will.

Undue Influence

A second closely related ground upon which someone can challenge a will is by alleging that the testator was subject to undue influence at the time that he or she made or executed the will. As you may recall, one of the statutory requirements for will validity is that the testator acts freely and voluntarily in making his or her will. In asserting undue influence, the challenger is stating that freedom of volition was absent and he or she must present evidence related to the same. The probate court will consider four factors to determine whether the testator was unduly influenced: (1) whether the testator was in a weak mental state; (2) the background and relationship of the accused undue influencer relative to the testator; (3) the interactions between the testator and the accused undue influencer; and, (4) whether the provisions of the will are reasonable.

Melican v. Parker, 657 S.E.2d 234 (Ga. 2008) is an illustrative case that involved a will contest on the bases of incapacity and undue influence. The testator, Harvey Strother, had an extramarital affair during the last decade of his life and executed three codicils to his will during that time to make provisions for his mistress, Anne Melican, and her son. Melican petitioned the court to probate the codicils along with the will; however, the executor and testamentary trustee, Sydney Parker, contested. The Georgia Supreme Court ruled against Melican. It was persuaded by evidence that the "[t]estator was 79 years old when he died and, because of his extraordinary alcohol dependency, was suffering from numerous severe physical maladies and was, near the time of execution of the second and third codicils, in an incapacitated state, vulnerable, and easily manipulated." *Id.* at 238. Moreover, the Court found it convincing that the testator required constant in-home care and he was completely dependent on Melican for the same. In fact, when two of the three codicils were executed, she drove him to the attorney's office, who also served as her attorney, with Melican and her son sitting on each side of the testator during one signing ceremony. *Id.* at 238–39.

Fraud

Thirdly, someone may challenge a will in Georgia by alleging that a fraud or deception was perpetrated upon the testator and that the testator relied on the fraudulent act(s) when he or she made or executed the will. This contest ground is extremely fact-specific, and the burden of proof will be on the challenger to demonstrate the existence of fraud based on the circumstances. For example, it could be claimed that the testator's signature was obtained through some nefarious conduct that took place surrounding the will creation or execution, such as a "bait-and-switch" where the testator was unaware that it was a will execution and thought he or she was signing something else. Another example is that a testator may have been led to believe that a potential beneficiary has died when he or she is very much alive. Under the belief that the person is dead, the testator may leave assets to another.

Forgery

A fourth potential ground to contest a will is based on forgery. Again, this is a fact-specific ground; the challenger must illustrate to the court that the signature on the will is not actually the signature of the testator. The challenger is likely to allege that someone signed on the testator's behalf for his or her own benefit and without the testator's knowledge or direction. It may be necessary for the challenger to consult and hire a handwriting expert who would testify in court to support this claim. In *Harvey v. Sullivan*, 529 S.E.2d 889 (Ga. 2000), the Georgia Supreme Court rejected forgery claims in a will contest due to a lack of sufficient evidence. William Sullivan, a nephew of the testator, Francis Sullivan, admitted her will to probate, and another nephew (Harvey) challenged the will, suggesting that it was a forgery. Harvey alleged that when he first examined the will, there was no signature on the first page, but that when he later looked at it, there was a signature. However, since he could not provide sufficient evidence to support his contention, Harvey's claim was denied. *Id.* at 891.

Improper Execution

The fifth and final common ground for will contests in Georgia is when someone alleges that there was a problem in the execution of the will. To prevail on this ground, it must be shown that the formalities related to execution were not followed. For example, a will challenger might allege that: (1) the testator was not at least 14 years old; (2) the testator did not sign a written will; or (3) there were not two competent, disinterested witnesses over the age of 14 who were present when testator signed and who signed to attest to the same.

All these grounds for will contests offer a reminder of the importance of the self-proving affidavit discussed earlier. If you will recall, the affidavit is a sworn statement by the testator and witnesses that the testator: (1) appeared to have capacity, (2) acted freely, without the presence of undue influence or fraud, and (3) signed the will or had a designated representative sign, and asked them to attest and sign as witnesses.

So, needless to say, there is a high burden of proof on the challenger to show otherwise when the affidavit is annexed to the will.

Key Terms

ambulatory	mutual will
caveat	no-contest clause
codicil	nuncupative will
disinterested witnesses	pour over will
execute	probate
express revocation	reciprocal will
holographic will	revocation
implied revocation	self-proving affidavit
in terrorem clause	standing
joint will	valid
letter of instruction	volition
modification	will contests

Review Questions

1. What does it mean to say that wills are ambulatory?
2. What are the methods by which a will can be revoked?
3. What is the difference between express and implied revocation? Give concrete examples.
4. How can a testator modify a will?
5. What is a codicil, and how must it be executed?
6. What are the requirements for a valid will in Georgia?
7. What is a self-proving affidavit, and why is it important?
8. Define joint wills and mutual wills. Which are more advisable?
9. What is a will contest, and when is it possible?
10. List and describe the grounds upon which one can contest a will in Georgia.

Practical Assignment

Survey 10 family members or close friends who are over the age of 14. Ask the following questions and then summarize your results in a chart:

1. How old are you?

2. Do you have a will or a trust?
3. If not, why not?
4. If so, did you consult an attorney to draft it?
5. If so, how old is it?

After preparing the chart, explain what you found interesting about the results.

Chapter 6

Wills—Preparation and Drafting Considerations

Learning Objectives

Upon completion of this chapter, you should be able to:

- Gather pertinent facts and documents for will preparation.
- Identify the components of a basic will and their purposes.
- Assist in conducting research and drafting wills.

Because careful and deliberate estate planning is a must, it is best to consult an attorney to draft the necessary documents instead of attempting to prepare them on your own. Some of the reasons for doing so are outlined in Exhibit 6.1.

In this chapter, we describe some of the steps that are helpful to the drafting process.

Information Gathering

In Chapter 2, we discussed the importance of the client questionnaire as an essential tool to collect information for drafting the necessary estate planning documents, including the will. A good estate planning questionnaire will enable the attorney and his or her paralegal to gather facts concerning the client's domicile, property, assets, liabilities, beneficiaries, dispositive intentions, and so forth. Additionally, it will alert the estate planning team to any issues that require attention before the completion of an effective estate plan. For example, the questionnaire may reveal title issues for certain estate assets.

Although the questionnaire covers a wide range of subject matters, the attorney or paralegal may still need to follow up with client interviews for additional information. In fact, the legal team should ask the client to present government identification and appear in person early in the process for an interview, if possible, so that the legal team may verify his or her identity and confirm capacity. Furthermore, the client may need to produce copies of deeds, mortgages, insurance policies, bank statements, and other vital financial documents. If the client cannot locate these important records,

Exhibit 6.1 Why a Lawyer to Draft Your Will?

Reproduced with permission from SR Law Group, Douglasville, GA

then the paralegal may need to conduct research and investigate to obtain them on the client's behalf.

In their interactions, the legal team must manifest excellent interpersonal skills and treat their estate planning clients with a considerable amount of sensitivity, given the nature of this area of the law. As we stated in Chapter 1, many people are often uncomfortable talking about issues related to death and dying. Similarly, some clients may not have discussed their final wishes with family or friends who are reluctant to even think such unpleasant thoughts. Moreover, for other clients, familial relations and friendships may be complicated, strained, or non-existent. For these individuals, it may be difficult to decide upon beneficiaries or those who can be entrusted with carrying out their final wishes. Still other clients may be hesitant to share their sensitive financials and other personal information with the legal team for fear of fraud or identity theft.

As a result of the foregoing, the attorney and paralegal may need to reassure the estate planning client that they are determined to work in his or her best interests. In Chapter 14, we will discuss the various ethical rules that govern the conduct of attorneys and their paralegals. Informing the client of the special attorney-client relationship and the related ethical protections may put the client at greater ease and make disclosure flow more freely. In the end, patience and good listening skills will be critical to make the information-gathering process the most productive.

Drafting Considerations

By now, it should be apparent that the estate planning paralegal has many important roles to play. While the paralegal is not allowed to give the client legal advice and must act under the supervision of his or her attorney, the paralegal may interview clients, gather facts and information, complete the estate planning questionnaire, conduct legal research, and assist the attorney by drafting crucial estate planning documents.

Oftentimes, to draft legal documents, including the will, the legal team utilizes forms as a starting point. However, as we discussed earlier, generic forms will not suffice. Estate planning forms can come from various sources: some are created by the courts (many examples of which you will find in this textbook); others may have been developed by attorneys in previous cases; and still others may come from formbooks or electronic sources. Whatever their origin, when drafting estate planning documents, the paralegal and attorney must carefully tailor any form documents to address the client's specific situation and intentions. It is essential for the legal team to employ good listening skills and be mindful of the client's needs and desires to produce a well-drafted will. Each estate planning client presents a unique set of circumstances that must be addressed in the drafting process. It is paramount that the provisions of the will are relevant to the client and further his or her intentions.

Will Structure

A will is just like many other types of writing: it has a beginning, a middle, and an end. It contains sections, which are sometimes referred to as articles or **clauses**, that outline the testator's final wishes, which have been articulated to the attorney and his or her paralegal. Per our discussion in Chapter 5, there is no single particular format that a will must take. Furthermore, as indicated earlier in this chapter, no two wills look alike. Some may be short and simple, while others may be longer and more complex. According to O.C.G.A. § 53-4-55, when drafting, the construction of the will is unimportant, but capturing the testator's intentions is key. This Code provision reinforces the idea that a will must be specifically tailored to address the unique needs of each testator. However, wills do possess certain common features that we will discuss next.

Introductory Paragraphs

Take a look at the sample will included at the end of this chapter as Exhibit 6.3. It, like most wills, begins with the **exordium clause**, also known as the **publication clause**. The goals of this opening section of the will are to: (1) identify the testator, listing his or her full legal name and any other names by which he or she may hold title to property; (2) indicate the testator's domicile to establish the probate court which has jurisdiction over the testator's estate; (3) publish or declare that the document is, in fact, the testator's last will and testament; and (4) revoke any wills and codicils that the testator may have executed previously.

You will notice that following the publication clause, in Article I of Exhibit 6.3, information is provided regarding the testator's family. This introductory clause is often included because family members may later be named as beneficiaries in the will, and it helps to identify these persons and their relationship to the testator. Moreover, in the event the testator chooses to disinherit a family member in the will, listing that family member in this introductory paragraph manifests the testator's intentionality regarding such disinheritance. Sometimes, the city and state where the family members are located are also included to make it easier to track them down. Finally, in Article I of the sample will, the **guardianship clause**, the testator who has minor children at the time of his or her death nominates a guardian for the person and a conservator for the property of those children. The same individual may be named to serve as both guardian and conservator. Similar language may be used in that article to nominate a guardian and conservator for any disabled members of the testator's family.

Other introductory provisions in the sample will that are common to many wills concern (1) burial or cremation arrangements (Article II) and (2) instructions related to final debts (Article III). Regarding preferences for burial or cremation arrangements, these should be expressed in the advance directive for health care (which we will discuss more fully in Chapter 7) in addition to the will. This is because burial or cremation arrangements will need to be attended to immediately upon the decedent's death, and the will may not be found right away. On the other hand, the advance directive is often on file with the decedent's healthcare provider or agent and can usually be accessed more readily. Finally, the provision giving directions about the payment of debts is frequently included in wills. Usually, it instructs the executor to pay the testator's final expenses out of the estate, including burial or cremation costs, taxes, administration expenses, and so forth, as we see in Article III of the sample will. However, if the testator chooses to have such expenses paid by the executor, it is advisable to include additional language related to a specific source to ensure that funds are available to cover those costs. For example, the testator may indicate that her Bank of America savings account funds be used for final expenses. This provision is wise because, as noted earlier, not all property of a decedent is part of the probate estate; certain items such as life insurance, pension plans, and accounts with named beneficiaries or joint owners will not be part of the estate, and as a result, are not subject to the claims of creditors. Instead, they will go directly to the beneficiaries. O.C.G.A. § 53-4-63, which is included in Appendix A, provides direction to the executor concerning in what order the debts of the decedent should be paid from the estate funds. We will also discuss this matter in Chapter 12, related to estate administration.

Body of Will

The main part, or body, of the will may consist of a wide variety of other provisions, depending on the needs and desires of the testator. In this section of the text, we will explain some common clauses included in the body of the sample will provided in Exhibit 6.3.

Dispositive Provisions

First, in the most substantive portion, or body, of the will, you can usually find **dispositive provisions,** clauses by which the testator designates the beneficiaries of his or her real and personal property. In this section, where the testator disposes of or gifts his or her property to designated beneficiaries, different language is used to convey the same. Words like "give," "bequest," "bequeath," and "devise" are often used interchangeably to indicate the desired disposition of the testator's property.

According to O.C.G.A. § 53-4-59, "Testamentary gifts may be specific, demonstrative, general, or residuary," or a combination of these. A **specific bequest** refers to the gift of a particular object from the testator to a beneficiary. For example, a testator may choose to give her boat to her son and her house to her daughter; these are both specific bequests. More concretely, the gift of a particular item of personal property in the will (the boat, in this example) is referred to as a **specific legacy**; and the gift of a particular parcel of real property in the will (the house, in this example) is commonly known as a **specific devise.** Note that a **demonstrative gift** refers to the testator's gift of property (usually money) that must be taken from a specific source. For example, a testator may choose to leave $25,000 from Truist bank account # 12345 to his mother; this would constitute a demonstrative gift.

Usually, after naming the beneficiaries of specific gifts under the will, the testator makes a **general bequest**. A general bequest is a gift from the testator that does not specify the precise property that the beneficiary will receive. For instance, a husband may choose to leave for his wife "all items of personal property" that he owns at the time of his death. So, rather than listing each item individually, a general gift has been made. Another example of a general bequest occurs in the **residuary clause** of a will. This clause amounts to a catch-all provision, by which the testator disposes of all other property that has not been gifted in previous will provisions. In Paragraph 4.2 of the sample will provided in Exhibit 6.3, the residuary clause employs typical language:

> I give all the rest, residue, and remainder of my property and estate, both real and personal, of whatever kind and wherever located, including any inheritance I may be entitled to as well as any lapsed or void legacy or devise under this will, that I own or am in any manner entitled at the time of my death to
>
> ______________.

A residuary clause is a necessary component of any well-drafted will because, without it, any property that is left over, without a named beneficiary, would be distributed according to the laws of intestate succession and not necessarily as the testator intended.

In a pour over will, which we discussed in Chapter 5, this residuary clause is used to ensure that property that was not properly transferred to the trust before the testator's death ends up there posthumously. Language such as the following is used to accomplish this task:

> I give all the rest, residue, and remainder of my property and estate, both real and personal, of whatever kind and wherever located, including any inheri-

> tance I may be entitled to as well as any lapsed or void legacy or devise under this will, that I own or am in any manner entitled at the time of my death ("residuary estate") to the trustee under the following trust to be held and disposed of in accordance with the terms, covenants and conditions of such trust: ______________________ Living Trust dated ______________.

Finally, the last of the dispositive provisions that you will notice in Exhibit 6.3 relates to distributions to minor beneficiaries. It is important to note that minors can inherit property under Georgia law. However, per O.C.G.A. § 44-5-81, a minor beneficiary under a will cannot accept the gifted property in his or her own name. Instead, a parent, guardian, or other responsible adult must act as conservator of the minor's inherited property. The conservator must manage the property wisely for the minor beneficiary, at least until the minor reaches the age of majority, which is 18 in Georgia. Smaller gifts to minors during a donor's lifetime are frequently made by creating custodial accounts with banks and other financial institutions under The Georgia Transfer to Minors Act, O.C.G.A. § 44-5-110 *et seq.* When the minor reaches the age of majority, he or she is usually entitled to receive the gift directly. Posthumous gifts to minors that are more substantive can be made either by creating a living trust, which you will learn more about in Chapter 8, or by creating a testamentary trust, as outlined in Article V of the sample will. Note that a testator can provide another appropriate age for the minor to receive the property. Many choose the age of 21 or 25 as the time for disbursement, or a particular occurrence (e.g., after the beneficiary has completed college), rather than the age of 18. Oftentimes, this is done to ensure that the beneficiary can manage the property responsibly on his or her own. Note also that while the minor cannot receive the entrusted property outright, the trustee of either a living trust or a testamentary trust has the discretion to use trust income for the health, education, maintenance, and support of the minor beneficiary at any time. Similar language can be used to create a testamentary trust for disabled beneficiaries. For example, a testator might provide that the disabled beneficiary's inherited property be held in trust by the trustee until the beneficiary's disability ends or the trust funds are exhausted.

Other Provisions

The remaining provisions in the body of a will may vary. One common provision is a clause naming the testator's executor(s) and trustee(s) and listing their respective responsibilities. Articles VI and VII of Exhibit 6.3 provide examples of such clauses. While our sample will references the sections of the O.C.G.A. that outline the various powers of fiduciaries, some testators choose to spell out these powers explicitly in their wills and indicate any limitations thereto. Moreover, in these provisions, a testator may indicate that the named fiduciaries, who should be trusted individuals or entities, will not need to post a bond, file reports, or be audited as they carry out their functions on behalf of the testator. These measures are usually part of the fiduciary's responsibilities to ensure his or her proper management of the testator's estate, free of fraud, embezzlement, and other wrongdoing. However, a testator may choose to waive these requirements in his or her will. It is prudent for the testator to nominate at least one **successor**

trustee and one **successor executor**. A successor fiduciary may be necessary in case the testator's primary choice is unwilling or unable to act or does not qualify to serve.

Article VIII of Exhibit 6.3 manifests another common feature of wills: the **survivorship clause**. It indicates that the beneficiary cannot inherit under the will unless he or she outlives the testator for a certain amount of time (usually at least 30 days). The survivorship clause exists to fulfill the testator's intention for a specifically designated beneficiary to receive the property. If the named beneficiary predeceases the testator or does not survive for the specified period after the testator's death, then the named alternate beneficiary inherits the property. If there is no named alternate, then the property becomes a part of the testator's residuary estate and is dispersed accordingly.

We discussed Georgia's provision for a year's support in Chapter 4, and Article IX of the sample will in Exhibit 6.3 addresses the same. As stated previously, the decedent's surviving spouse who has not remarried and his or her unmarried minor children are entitled to at least a year's support, regardless of the contents of a will. However, in Article IX and similar provisions, a testator may indicate that he or she has named those individuals as beneficiaries under the will and that the testamentary gifts are meant to take the place of Georgia's requirement for a year's support.

Finally, in Article X of the sample will is a section referred to as the **disinheritance clause**, **in terrorem clause**, or **no-contest clause**. The purpose of this provision is to make clear the testator's desire that certain individuals be disinherited and indicate that it was not an oversight nor a mistake. Moreover, this section of the will is often used to delineate disinheritance as the penalty for those who complain about the contents of the will and seek to contest it.

Closing Paragraphs

Testimonium Clause

The **testimonium clause**, a short paragraph that marks the end of the body of the will, includes the date of execution and comes just before the testator's signature line. In the sample will, the following language is used: "**IN WITNESS WHEREOF**, I have set my hand and seal this _______ day of _________, 20__."

Attestation Clause

Finally, the **attestation clause** follows the testator's signature and appears before the self-proving affidavit (the value of which we discussed in Chapter 5). In this section, before the witnesses sign and include their addresses, they acknowledge that the formalities for will validity required under Georgia law have been observed. The attestation clause in Exhibit 6.3 is typical:

> The foregoing instrument was signed, sealed, published, and declared by _______________, the above-named Testator to be such Testator's Last Will and Testament in our presence, all being present at the same time, and we, at

such Testator's request and in such Testator's presence and in the presence of each other, have subscribed our names as witnesses on the date above written.

Generally, the testator executes only one copy of the will at the signing ceremony to avoid confusion and since only the original will can be admitted to probate. Lawyers should advise their clients to store the original will and other important documents in a fireproof, waterproof safe, or lock box at home. If the client chooses to utilize a bank safe deposit box, the client should complete paperwork with the bank to allow someone else access to it in the event of the client's death. Otherwise, a court order will be necessary to gain access to the safe deposit box, which will cost additional time and money. In addition, the client should be cautioned about altering the will in any way to avoid possible contests.

In conclusion, there are many considerations for the client and legal team as they work together to draft the client's will. Some of them are summarized below.

Exhibit 6.2 Do's and Don'ts of Will Drafting

Reproduced with permission from SR Law Group, Douglasville, GA

Exhibit 6.3 Sample Basic Will

LAST WILL AND TESTAMENT OF

____

[name of testator]

exordium/publication clause

I, ____________________, a resident of ______________ County, within the State of Georgia, make, publish and declare this to be my Last Will and Testament, revoking all wills and codicils previously made by me.

ARTICLE I: FAMILY

1.1 At the time of the making of this will, I am ________________ [marital status and if married, state to whom].

1.2 I have ___________ [number of] children. The name and dates of birth of my children are: ___________________________. All references in this will to my "child" or "children" are to these named children as well as any child subsequently born to or adopted by me.

guardianship clause

1.3 If at the time of my death a guardian is needed to care for my then minor children, I appoint ____________________________, currently of __________, Georgia, as guardian(s) for the person and conservator(s) for the property to serve the best interests of such children. In the event ____________________________ is(are) unwilling or unable to serve as guardian(s) and conservator(s), I appoint ________________________________, currently of ___________, Georgia, as guardian(s) and conservator(s) to serve the best interests of such children.

ARTICLE II: BURIAL/CREMATION

2.1 I desire to be buried and request that my Executor make arrangements for funeral services to be conducted at _______________________________ and for my remains be buried at _______________________________

[Or]

2.1 I desire to be cremated and ask that my Executor do the following with my ashes: ___________________________________

2.2 All costs and expenses associated with these requests shall be paid from my estate.

Initials: _______

ARTICLE III: DEBTS

I direct that all of my due and payable debts, including funeral (or cremation), memorial and burial expenses, the expenses of the administration of my estate, all estate, inheritance and similar taxes payable with respect to property included in my probate estate, including any interest or penalties thereon, shall be paid out of my estate in accordance with the laws of the State of Georgia, without apportionment or right of reimbursement from any beneficiary under my will.

body of will

ARTICLE IV: BEQUESTS

dispositive provisions

4.1 I give, bequeath, and devise the following specific property: ________________ to ________________________________. If ____________

specific bequest

does not survive me, then I give such property to ________________________________.

[And/or]

general bequest and residuary clause

4.2 I give all the rest, residue and remainder of my property and estate, both real and personal, of whatever kind and wherever located, including any inheritance I may be entitled to as well as any lapsed or void legacy or devise under this will, that I own or am in any manner entitled at the time of my death ("residuary estate") to ____________________.

4.3 If ________________________ does not survive me, then I give my residuary estate to ________________________________.

testamentary trust

ARTICLE V: DISTRIBUTION TO MINOR BENEFICIARIES

If any beneficiary shall be under the age of ____________________ at the time of my death (each of such being hereinafter referred to as a "Beneficiary"), the share of such Beneficiary shall not be paid or distributed to such Beneficiary directly. Instead, such Beneficiary's share shall be held by my Trustee **IN TRUST**, pursuant to the following provisions:

(a) My Trustee shall hold, manage, invest, and reinvest each share set aside for each Beneficiary in a separate trust for the benefit of such Beneficiary and shall pay so much or all of the net income from each such trust to or for the benefit of the Beneficiary thereof, for the health, education, maintenance and support of the Beneficiary, to such extent and at such time or times and in such manner as may be determined in the absolute discretion of my Trustee. Any net income not so paid shall be accumulated and added to the principal at least annually and thereafter shall be held, administered and disposed of as part thereof.

(b) In addition, my Trustee may pay to or for the benefit of each Beneficiary, for the health, education, maintenance and support of each Beneficiary, from the principal of each Beneficiary's trust, such amounts, including the whole thereof, as determined by my Trustee in her absolute discretion. The determination of my Trustee as to the amount and the advisability of any discretionary payment shall be final and conclusive on all persons, whether or not then in being, having or claiming any interest in such trust.

(c) When any Beneficiary shall attain the age of ________ years, the trust for such Beneficiary shall terminate and any remaining principal and income shall be paid and distributed to such Beneficiary, discharged of trust. If such Beneficiary dies before said age, such principal and income shall be paid and distributed to any then living issue of such Beneficiary, in equal shares per stirpes. If there are no then living issue, the same shall be paid or distributed to the beneficiaries of my residuary estate then in being as provided in this will, or if there are none, to those who would take from me as if I were then to die without a will, unmarried and the absolute owner of the same, and a resident of the State of Georgia.

ARTICLE VI: EXECUTOR AND TRUSTEE

6.1 I appoint ________________________ to serve as the Executor of this will, and if my Executor is unwilling or unable to serve, I appoint ________________________ to serve as the Successor Executor of this will.

6.2 I appoint ________________________ to serve as Trustee of any trust created under this will, and if my Trustee is unwilling or unable to serve, I appoint ________________ to serve as the Successor Trustee of any trust created under this will.

6.3 Any Executor or Trustee serving under this will shall be a Fiduciary granted all of the powers conferred by *O.C.G.A. §§53-12-261* and *263*, as amended.

ARTICLE VII: BONDS/AUDITS NOT REQUIRED

7.1 The term "Fiduciary" shall mean any Executor, Trustee or successor qualifying and serving under this will.

7.2 No Fiduciary shall be required to file or furnish any bond, surety or other security in any jurisdiction, nor shall any Fiduciary hereunder be required to file any inventory or other reports with any court.

7.3 No Fiduciary shall be required to inquire into or audit the acts or doings of any predecessor Fiduciary or to make claim against any such predecessor or their estate.

ARTICLE VIII: SURVIVORSHIP

survivorship clause

I direct that, for purposes of this will, a beneficiary shall be deemed to predecease me unless such beneficiary survives me by more than thirty (30) days.

-3- Initials: ______

ARTICLE IX: YEAR'S SUPPORT

The provisions made in this Will for my ________________________________ are in lieu of Year's Support; provided, however, if my spouse is the sole beneficiary of this will, this provision shall be null and void.

disinheritance/in terrorem/ no-contest clause

ARTICLE X: DISINHERITANCE

I have intentionally omitted to provide for and specifically direct that under no circumstances shall any property, part, share or interest of my estate vest in, or be taken by ________________________. I generally and specifically disinherit each and every person identified within this Article, regardless of whether they claiming to be or are ay be lawfully determined to be my heirs at law, notwithstanding anything to the contrary in this will.

testimonium clause

IN WITNESS WHEREOF, I have set my hand and seal this ______ day of ________, 20__.

________________________________(SEAL)
__________________, Testator

ATTESTATION CLAUSE

The foregoing instrument was signed, sealed, published and declared by ______________________, the above-named Testator to be such Testator's Last Will and Testament in our presence, all being present at the same time, and we, at such Testator's request and in such Testator's presence and in the presence of each other, have subscribed our names as witnesses on the date above written.

Addresses:

________________________________	________________________________
____________________, *Witness*	________________________________
________________________________	________________________________
____________________, *Witness*	________________________________

Initials: ______

SELF-PROVING AFFIDAVIT

STATE OF GEORGIA
COUNTY OF ______________________

Before me, the undersigned authority, on this day personally appeared the Testator, ___________________, and the witnesses, ______________________ and ___________________, whose names are subscribed to the annexed or foregoing instrument in their respective capacities, and all of said individuals being duly sworn, the Testator, declared to me and to the witnesses in my presence that said instrument is the Last Will and Testament of the Testator and that the Testator had willingly made and executed it as the Testator's free act and deed for the purposes expressed therein. The witnesses, each on oath, stated to me in the presence and hearing of the Testator that the Testator had declared to them that the instrument is the Testator's Last Will and Testament and that the Testator executed the instrument as such and wished each of them to sign it as a witness; and under oath each witness stated further that the witnesses had signed the same as witness in the presence of the Testator and at the Testator's request; that the Testator was fourteen (14) years of age or over and of sound mind; and that each of the witnesses was then at least fourteen (14) years of age.

_________________________________(SEAL)
______________________, Testator

____
______________________, Witness

____
______________________, Witness

Sworn to and subscribed before me by the Testator, ____________________ and the witnesses, ____________________ and _________________, this __________ day of ___________, 20__.

____
__________________________, Notary Public

[NOTARY SEAL OR STAMP]

Initials: _______

Key Terms

attestation clause
clause
demonstrative gift
disinheritance clause
dispositive provisions
exordium clause
general bequest
guardianship clause
in terrorem clause
no-contest clause
publication clause
residuary clause
specific bequest
specific devise
specific legacy
successor executor
successor trustee
survivorship clause
testimonium clause

Review Questions

1. What type of information must the legal team gather to draft a client's will?
2. What skills are necessary for the legal team to serve an estate planning client effectively?
3. What are potential sources for forms that can be used to draft a client's will?
4. What is an exordium clause, and for what purpose is it included?
5. Under Georgia law, what forms can a testamentary gift take?
6. Can a minor in Georgia inherit property? If so, are there any limitations on the minor receiving the property directly? Be specific.
7. What is a residuary clause, and why is it important to include?
8. Why is it advisable for a testator to name at least one successor executor and trustee?
9. Where does the testimonium clause appear in the will?
10. What is the purpose of the attestation clause?

Practical Assignment

In Exhibit 6.3, you were presented with a simple basic will. Find a more complex will on the Internet and in a brief report, compare the two documents. First, describe the similarities between the simple will and the document you found. Do they contain similar clauses? If so, which ones? Second, indicate the differences that you notice. Are there additional provisions in the more complex form? If so, what are they, and what do you suppose is the purpose for each? Be sure to provide a citation or link to the will you have found on the Internet.

Chapter 7

Advance Directive, Power of Attorney, and Anatomical Gifts

Learning Objectives

Upon completion of this chapter, you should be able to:

- Compare and contrast the purposes and functions of advance directives and financial powers of attorney.
- Produce drafts of advance directives and financial powers of attorney.
- Explain the importance and methods of making anatomical gifts.

As indicated in Chapter 1, a comprehensive estate plan in Georgia includes at least a will or trust, an advance directive for health care, and a financial power of attorney. We discussed wills in Chapters 5 and 6. In this chapter, we will describe the ancillary documents and anatomical gifts before we discuss trusts in Chapter 8.

Advance Directive for Health Care

Before July 1, 2007, Georgians utilized two documents—the living will and the durable power of attorney for health care—to accomplish all that the advance directive for health care does today. Oftentimes, those unfamiliar with the law confuse the will with the living will. Some may even mistakenly use the terms interchangeably. As you learned in previous chapters, the will (also known as the last will and testament) is an estate planning tool used to dispose of one's property after death. On the other hand, a living will (also known as an advance directive for health care in some jurisdictions, including Georgia) is an estate planning tool used to nominate a health care agent to act on one's behalf and to outline other medical treatment choices. Additionally, as stated in Chapter 1, this document gives the agent access to the declarant's medical records, including those protected by the Health Insurance Portability and Accountability Act (HIPAA). Nonetheless, as an added measure, some estate planning attorneys also have their clients execute a separate document, a **HIPAA Authorization and Waiver,** which provides written authorization for certain uses and disclosures of protected health information.

Exhibit 7.1 Health Care Directive Definition

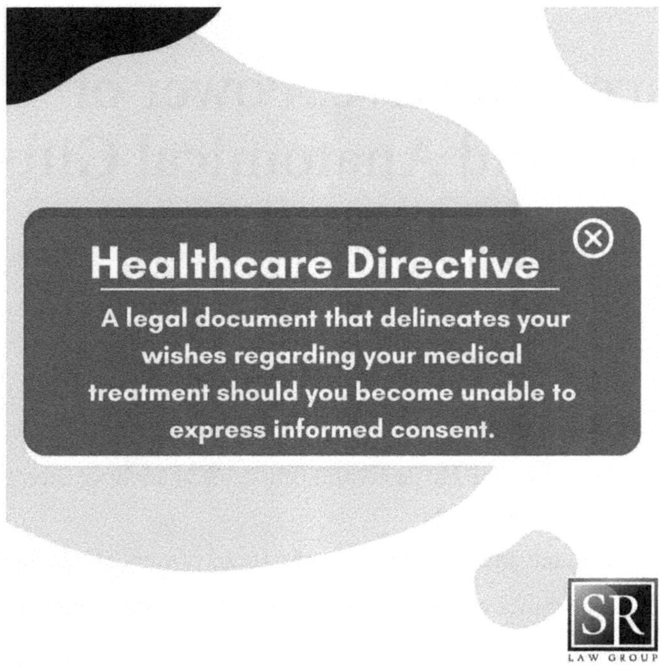

Reproduced with permission from SR Law Group, Douglasville, GA

O.C.G.A. § 31-32-5(a) states that an **emancipated minor** (i.e., one who is no longer under the care, custody, or control of parents) or anyone over the age of 18 who has a sound mind may execute an advance directive for health care. As stated earlier, the individual who makes an advance directive is referred to in the Code as a declarant. Regarding required formalities, O.C.G.A. § 31-32-5(a)(3) indicates that the document "shall be in writing, signed by the declarant or by some other person in the declarant's presence and at the declarant's express direction, and witnessed...." In addition, O.C.G.A. § 31-32-5(c)(1) explains that the two witnesses must be at least 18 years old and of sound mind and need not be together or present when the declarant signs the document. While this document does not require notarization, it may be notarized for an added measure of authenticity.

The **statutory form** of advance directive for health care that was adopted in 2007 is located in O.C.G.A. § 31-32-4. Exhibit 7.3 at the end of this section of the chapter includes the form and its amendments that became effective July 1, 2022. This form was adopted by the Georgia General Assembly to serve as a model for public use. However, it is optional, and other forms are also acceptable. You will notice that the form document consists of four parts, which we will now describe.

Part I

Part I allows the declarant to choose a health care agent who will make health care decisions for the declarant if the declarant cannot do so. Previously in Georgia, this was the essential function of the durable power of attorney for health care. In Section 1, the declarant nominates the agent and provides the agent's contact information so that he or she may be reached in the event of a medical emergency. Additionally, the declarant can name a backup agent or two in Section 2 in case the first choice cannot be reached after a good faith effort, or if the declarant's first choice is otherwise unavailable, unable, or unwilling to act. Even though this section is optional, it is a common practice for the legal team to have their client name at least one alternate agent. Sections 3 and 4 outline the various duties and responsibilities of the health care agent. These are also articulated in O.C.G.A. § 31-32-7. Finally, in Section 5, the declarant expresses his or her wishes related to autopsy, anatomical gifts (which we will explore further later in this chapter), and final disposition of the body (i.e., burial or cremation).

Part II

In Part II, the declarant indicates his or her treatment preferences when he or she has a terminal condition or is in a state of permanent unconsciousness (Section 6). Previously, this was the main purpose of the living will. Note, however, that Part II only takes effect when the declarant is unable to communicate his or her medical choices directly for himself or herself.

In Section 7, the declarant states what should be done under such circumstances as it relates to hydration, nutrition, and the use of medications, machines, and other medical procedures. Exhibit 7.2, which follows, explains more fully the three choices for treatment preferences that are available to the declarant in Section 7.

If the declarant has other specific treatment preferences to express, this can be done in Section 8. For a female declarant, Section 9 explains that generally, Part II will not be effective if she is pregnant unless: (1) the fetus is not viable (able to survive outside of the womb) and (2) she indicates by initialing that she wants Part II to be carried out under such circumstances.

A recent unpublished Georgia case highlights the importance of having an advance directive that clearly outlines one's medical treatment preferences. In 2018, Vinit Shinde, a 45-year-old software consultant from Atlanta, suffered a brain aneurysm that left him unresponsive and unable to communicate. As a result of his severe neurological injury, Vinit was placed on life support, and for years, his family members sought treatment and held out hope for his recovery. Since he was divorced and had no children, his brother, Rajesh Shinde, was named his guardian and conservator during Vinit's incapacity. Then, in 2020, since Vinit was still showing no signs of improvement, Rajesh decided he would move his brother to hospice and take him off of life support, claiming that his brother would not want to continue to be kept alive by machines. However, Vinit's ex-wife, Mala Pillutla, who was a frequent visitor during his incapacity, objected

Exhibit 7.2 Treatment Preferences

PREFERENCE	DESCRIPTION
A—Extend Life as Long as Possible	Extend the declarant's life as long as possible through medications, machines, or other medical procedures that could keep the declarant alive. If the declarant is unable to take nutrition or fluids by mouth, then nutrition or fluids will be administered by a tube or other medical means.
B—Natural Death	The declarant's death occurs naturally. Medications, machines, or other medical procedures that could keep the declarant alive but cannot cure the declarant will not be used. The declarant will not receive nutrition or fluids by tube or other medical means, except as needed to provide pain medication.
C—No Extension of Life Except the Aid Selected by the Declarant	The declarant will not receive medications, machines, or other medical procedures that in reasonable medical judgment could keep the declarant alive but could not cure him or her, except the specific aid selected by the declarant: ❑ Feeding tube ❑ Tube for fluids ❑ Ventilator ❑ CPR

to the cessation of life-sustaining treatment. She asserted that Vinit would want to be kept alive by any means necessary. Hence, in 2021, she filed a petition with the Fulton County Probate Court to enjoin Rajesh from removing life support and replace him as Vinit's guardian. The Court ruled in Mala's favor, and Vinit remained on life support. Rajesh filed an appeal, and the Georgia Court of Appeals affirmed the lower court's decision in 2023. The Georgia Supreme Court denied Rajesh's petition for certiorari in 2024. Needless to say, this court battle that lasted for years compounded the emotional and financial burden on the family. However, without his advance directive for healthcare, it is still unclear what Vinit Shinde would have wanted under these circumstances.

Part III

Related to guardianship, Part III, Section 10 of the document gives the declarant the option to appoint someone to act as his or her guardian if a court determines one is necessary to manage the declarant's personal support, safety, or welfare. The declarant can choose to have his or her agent act in this capacity or the declarant may choose someone else. Again, the advance directive is valuable because it puts important decisions in the hands of the declarant rather than having a court determine what is best. We will discuss adult guardianship more fully in Chapter 10.

Exhibit 7.3 Advance Directive Form

Georgia Advance Directive for Health Care

By: ______________________________ Date of Birth: ______________
(Print Name) *(Month/Day/Year)*

This advance directive for health care has four parts:

PART ONE—Health Care Agent. *This part allows you to choose someone to make health care decisions for you when you cannot (or do not want to) make health care decisions for yourself. The person you choose is called a health care agent. You may also have your health care agent make decisions for you after your death with respect to an autopsy, organ donation, body donation, and final disposition of your body. You should talk to your health care agent about this important role.*

PART TWO—Treatment Preferences. *This part allows you to state your treatment preferences if you have a terminal condition or if you are in a state of permanent unconsciousness. PART TWO will become effective only if you are unable to communicate your treatment preferences. Reasonable and appropriate efforts will be made to communicate with you about your treatment preferences before PART TWO becomes effective. You should talk to your family and others close to you about your treatment preferences.*

PART THREE—Guardianship. *This part allows you to nominate a person to be your guardian should one ever be needed.*

PART FOUR—Effectiveness and Signatures. *This part requires your signature and the signatures of two witnesses. You must complete PART FOUR if you have filled out any other part of this form.*

You may fill out any or all of the first three parts listed above. You must fill out PART FOUR of this form in order for this form to be effective.

You should give a copy of this completed form to people who might need it, such as your health care agent, your family, and your physician. Keep a copy of this completed form at home in a place where it can easily be found if it is needed. Review this completed form periodically to make sure it still reflects your preferences. If your preferences change, complete a new advance directive for health care.

Using this form of advance directive for health care is completely optional. Other forms of advance directives for health care may be used in Georgia.

You may revoke this completed form at any time. This completed form will replace any advance directive for health care, durable power of attorney for health care, health care proxy, or living will that you have completed before completing this form.

PART ONE—Health Care Agent

PART ONE will be effective even if PART TWO is not completed. A physician or health care provider who is directly involved in your health care may not serve as your health care agent. If you are married, a future divorce or annulment of your marriage will revoke the selection of your current spouse as your health care agent. If you are not married, a future marriage will revoke the selection of your health care agent unless the person you selected as your health care agent is your new spouse.

1. Health Care Agent

I select the following person as my health care agent to make health care decisions for me:

Name: ______________________________

Address: ______________________________

Telephone Numbers: ______________________________
(Home, Work, and Mobile)

2. Back-Up Health Care Agent

This section is optional. PART ONE will be effective even if this section is left blank.

If my health care agent cannot be contacted in a reasonable time period and cannot be located with reasonable efforts or for any reason my health care agent is unavailable or unable or unwilling to act as my health care agent, then I select the following, each to act successively in the order named, as my back-up health care agent(s):

Name: ______________________________

Address: ______________________________

Telephone Numbers: ______________________________
(Home, Work, and Mobile)

Name: ______________________________

Address: ______________________________

Telephone Numbers: ______________________________
(Home, Work, and Mobile)

3. General Powers of Health Care Agent

My health care agent will make health care decisions for me when I am unable to communicate my health care decisions or I choose to have my health care agent communicate my health care decisions.

My health care agent will have the same authority to make any health care decision that I could make. My health care agent's authority includes, for example, the power to:

- **Admit me to or discharge me from any hospital, skilled nursing facility, hospice, or other health care facility or service;**
- **Request, consent to, withhold, or withdraw any type of health care; and**
- **Contract for any health care facility or service for me, and to obligate me to pay for these services (and my health care agent will not be financially liable for any services or care contracted for me or on my behalf).**

My health care agent will be my personal representative for all purposes of federal or state law related to privacy of medical records (including the Health Insurance Portability and Accountability Act of 1996) and will have the same access to my medical records that I have and can disclose the contents of my medical records to others for my ongoing health care.

My health care agent may accompany me in an ambulance or air ambulance if in the opinion of the ambulance personnel protocol permits a passenger, and my health care agent may visit or consult with me in person while I am in a hospital, skilled nursing facility, hospice, or other health care facility or service if its protocol permits visitation.

My health care agent may present a copy of this advance directive for health care in lieu of the original and the copy will have the same meaning and effect as the original.

I understand that under Georgia law:

- **My health care agent may refuse to act as my health care agent;**
- **A court can take away the powers of my health care agent if it finds that my health care agent is not acting properly;**
- **My health care agent does not have the power to make health care decisions for me regarding sterilization, involuntary hospitalization, or involuntary treatment for mental or emotional illness, developmental disability, or addictive disease; and**
- **My health care agent does not have the power to make health care decisions that are otherwise covered under a psychiatric advance directive that I have executed pursuant to Chapter 11 of Title 37 of the Official Code of Georgia Annotated, including decisions related to treatment or hospitalization for mental or emotional illness, developmental disability, or addictive disease.**

4. Guidance for Health Care Agent

When making health care decisions for me, my health care agent should think about what action would be consistent with past conversations we have had, my treatment preferences as expressed in PART TWO (if I have filled out PART TWO), my religious and other beliefs and values, and how I have handled medical and other important issues in the past. If what I would decide is still unclear, then my health care agent should make decisions for me that my health care agent believes are in my best interest, considering the benefits, burdens, and risks of my current circumstances and treatment options.

5. Powers of Health Care Agent After Death

(A) AUTOPSY

My health care agent will have the power to authorize an autopsy of my body unless I have limited my health care agent's power by initialing below.

_________ *(Initials)* **My health care agent will not have the power to authorize an autopsy of my body (unless an autopsy is required by law).**

(B) ORGAN DONATION AND DONATION OF BODY

My health care agent will have the power to make a disposition of any part or all of my body for medical purposes pursuant to the Georgia Anatomical Gift Act, unless I have limited my health care agent's power by initialing below.

Initial each statement that you want to apply.

_________ *(Initials)* **My health care agent will not have the power to make a disposition of my body for use in a medical study program.**

_________ *(Initials)* **My health care agent will not have the power to donate any of my organs.**

(C) FINAL DISPOSITION OF BODY

My health care agent will have the power to make decisions about the final disposition of my body unless I have initialed below.

_________ *(Initials)* **I want the following person to make decisions about the final disposition of my body:**

Name: ______________________________

Address: ______________________________

Telephone Numbers: ______________________________
(Home, Work, and Mobile)

I wish for my body to be:

_________ *(Initials)* **Buried**

OR

_________ *(Initials)* **Cremated**

PART TWO—Treatment Preferences

PART TWO will be effective only if you are unable to communicate your treatment preferences after reasonable and appropriate efforts have been made to communicate with you about your treatment preferences. PART TWO will be effective even if PART ONE is not completed. If you have not selected a health care agent in PART ONE, or if your health care agent is not available, then PART TWO will provide your physician and other health care providers with your treatment preferences. If you have selected a health care agent in PART ONE, then your health care agent will have the authority to make all health care decisions for you regarding matters covered by PART TWO. Your health care agent will be guided by your treatment preferences and other factors described in Section (4) of PART ONE.

6. Conditions

PART TWO will be effective if I am in any of the following conditions:

Initial each condition in which you want PART TWO to be effective.

________ *(Initials)* **A terminal condition, which means I have an incurable or irreversible condition that will result in my death in a relatively short period of time.**

________ *(Initials)* **A state of permanent unconsciousness, which means I am in an incurable or irreversible condition in which I am not aware of myself or my environment and I show no behavioral response to my environment.**

My condition will be determined in writing after personal examination by my attending physician and a second physician in accordance with currently accepted medical standards.

7. Treatment Preferences

State your treatment preference by initialing (A), (B), or (C). If you choose (C), state your additional treatment preferences by initialing one or more of the statements following (C). You may provide additional instructions about your treatment preferences in the next section. You will be provided with comfort care, including pain relief, but you may also want to state your specific preferences regarding pain relief in the next section.

If I am in any condition that I initialed in Section (6) above and I can no longer communicate my treatment preferences after reasonable and appropriate efforts have been made to communicate with me about my treatment preferences, then:

(A) ________ *(Initials)* **Try to extend my life for as long as possible, using all medications, machines, or other medical procedures that in reasonable medical judgment could keep me alive. If I am unable to take nutrition or fluids by mouth, then I want to receive nutrition or fluids by tube or other medical means.**

OR

(B) ________ *(Initials)* **Allow my natural death to occur. I do not want any medications, machines, or other medical procedures that in reasonable medical judgment could keep me alive but cannot cure me. I do not want to receive nutrition or fluids by tube or other medical means except as needed to provide pain medication.**

OR

(C) ________ *(Initials)* **I do not want any medications, machines, or other medical procedures that in reasonable medical judgment could keep me alive but cannot cure me, except as follows:**

Initial each statement that you want to apply to option (C).

________ *(Initials)* **If I am unable to take nutrition by mouth, I want to receive nutrition by tube or other medical means.**

________ *(Initials)* **If I am unable to take fluids by mouth, I want to receive fluids by tube or other medical means.**

________ *(Initials)* **If I need assistance to breathe, I want to have a ventilator used.**

________ *(Initials)* **If my heart or pulse has stopped, I want to have cardiopulmonary resuscitation (CPR) used.**

8. Additional Statements

This section is optional. PART TWO will be effective even if this section is left blank. This section allows you to state additional treatment preferences, to provide additional guidance to your health care agent (if you have selected a health care agent in PART ONE), or to provide information about your personal and religious values about your medical treatment. For example, you may want to state your treatment preferences regarding medications to fight infection, surgery, amputation, blood transfusion, or kidney dialysis. Understanding that you cannot foresee everything that could happen to you after you can no longer communicate your treatment preferences, you may want to provide guidance to your health care agent (if you have selected a health care agent in PART ONE) about following your treatment preferences. You may want to state your specific preferences regarding pain relief.

____

____

____

9. In Case of Pregnancy

PART TWO will be effective even if this section is left blank.

I understand that under Georgia law, PART TWO generally will have no force and effect if I am pregnant unless the fetus is not viable and I indicate by initialing below that I want PART TWO to be carried out.

________ *(Initials)* **I want PART TWO to be carried out if my fetus is not viable.**

PART THREE—Guardianship

10. Guardianship

PART THREE is optional. This advance directive for health care will be effective even if PART THREE is left blank. If you wish to nominate a person to be your guardian in the event a court decides that a guardian should be appointed, complete PART THREE. A court will appoint a guardian for you if the court finds that you are not able to make significant responsible decisions for yourself regarding your personal support, safety, or welfare. A court will appoint the person nominated by you if the court finds that the appointment will serve your best interest and welfare. If you have selected a health care agent in PART ONE, you may (but are not required to) nominate the same person to be your guardian. If your health care agent and guardian are not the same person, your health care agent will have priority over your guardian in making your health care decisions, unless a court determines otherwise.

State your preference by initialing (A) or (B). Choose (A) only if you have also completed PART ONE.

(A) ________ *(Initials)* **I nominate the person serving as my health care agent under PART ONE to serve as my guardian.**

OR

(B) ________ *(Initials)* **I nominate the following person to serve as my guardian:**

Name: ________________________________

Address: ________________________________

Telephone Numbers: ________________________________
(Home, Work, and Mobile)

PART FOUR—Effectiveness and Signatures

This advance directive for health care will become effective only if I am unable or choose not to make or communicate my own health care decisions.

This form revokes any advance directive for health care, durable power of attorney for health care, health care proxy, or living will that I have completed before this date.

Unless I have initialed below and have provided alternative future dates or events, this advance directive for health care will become effective at the time I sign it and will remain effective until my death (and after my death to the extent authorized in Section (5) of PART ONE).

________ *(Initials)* **This advance directive for health care will become effective on or upon ____________________ and will terminate on or upon ____________________.**

You must sign and date or acknowledge signing and dating this form in the presence of two witnesses. Both witnesses must be of sound mind and must be at least 18 years of age, but the witnesses do not have to be together or present with you when you sign this form.

A witness:

- *Cannot be a person who was selected to be your health care agent or back-up health care agent in PART ONE;*

- *Cannot be a person who will knowingly inherit anything from you or otherwise knowingly gain a financial benefit from your death; or*
- *Cannot be a person who is directly involved in your health care.*

Only one of the witnesses may be an employee, agent, or medical staff member of the hospital, skilled nursing facility, hospice, or other health care facility in which you are receiving health care (but this witness cannot be directly involved in your health care).

By signing below, I state that I am emotionally and mentally capable of making this advance directive for health care and that I understand its purpose and effect.

______________________________ ______________
(Signature of Declarant) *(Date)*

The declarant signed this form in my presence or acknowledged signing this form to me. Based upon my personal observation, the declarant appeared to be emotionally and mentally capable of making this advance directive for health care and signed this form willingly and voluntarily.

______________________________ ______________
(Signature of First Witness) *(Date)*

Print Name: ______________________________

Address: ______________________________

______________________________ ______________
(Signature of Second Witness) *(Date)*

Print Name: ______________________________

Address: ______________________________

This form does not need to be notarized.

Source: O.C.G.A. § 31-32-4

Part IV

The final section of the advance directive for health care addresses its effective date and includes the signature block. As indicated earlier, the directive is only effective upon signature and when the declarant cannot articulate his or her own medical decisions. The document remains effective until the declarant's death unless he or she indicates alternate dates of effectiveness and termination in this section of the advance directive.

Before the declarant's signature, the document indicates other criteria for witnesses. It states that a witness:

> Cannot be a person who was selected to be your health care agent or back-up health care agent in PART ONE;
>
> Cannot be a person who will knowingly inherit anything from you or otherwise knowingly gain a financial benefit from your death; or
>
> Cannot be a person who is directly involved in your health care.
>
> Only one of the witnesses may be an employee, agent, or medical staff member of the hospital, skilled nursing facility, hospice, or other health care facility in which you are receiving health care (but this witness cannot be directly involved in your health care).

The witnesses sign below the declarant, indicating that the declarant appeared to have capacity and signed willingly and voluntarily, similar to the attestations we see in a will.

It is advisable to have the declarant and witnesses execute at least three originals of the advance directive for health care at the signing ceremony: (1) one to be given to the agent to use in the event of a medical emergency; (2) one for the declarant to keep with his or her other important personal documents, including the will or trust; and, (3) one to be kept with the declarant's primary health care provider.

Financial Power of Attorney

While the advance directive allows for the nomination of an agent to handle health care decisions on behalf of a declarant, the financial power of attorney provides for the nomination of an agent to complete financial and business transactions on behalf of the principal. As stated earlier, the individual who creates a financial power of attorney is referred to in the Code as a principal. Like the advance directive, Georgia has an optional statutory form for the financial power of attorney. It is located in O.C.G.A. § 10-6B-70 and is included as Exhibit 7.5 at the end of this section of the chapter.

This form has been effective since July 1, 2018, and it forces third parties, like banks and other financial institutions, to accept and abide by the terms of the financial power of attorney if certain conditions are met. Before that date, many financial institutions refused to accept the document and allow the agent to act on behalf of the principal because they feared liability. However, the Georgia General Assembly approved this

Exhibit 7.4 The Powerful Power of Attorney

Reproduced with permission from SR Law Group, Douglasville, GA

form, which explicitly offers greater protection to third parties and imposes liability and punishment directly on those agents who abuse the powers conferred on them. For example, right before the signature lines of the document, the form indicates: "Any person, including my agent, may rely upon the validity of this power of attorney or a copy of it...." Moreover, at the end of the document in the Important Information for Agent section, it states: "If you violate O.C.G.A. Chapter 6B of Title 10 or act outside the authority granted, you may be liable for any damages caused by your violation."

Regarding required formalities, according to O.C.G.A. § 10-6B-5, to properly execute a financial power of attorney: (1) it must be signed by the principal or by another individual in the principal's presence at the principal's express direction; (2) it must be signed by one or more competent (being of sound mind and at least 14 years of age) witnesses who attest to the principal's actions in the presence of the principal and each other; and, (3) all signatures and attestations must be done in the presence of a notary public who must notarize the document. The power of attorney is effective immediately upon signing unless otherwise stated in the Special Instructions, and it is **durable**, meaning that the document remains effective if the principal becomes incapacitated and unable to handle matters on his or her own.

You will notice in Exhibit 7.5, that, as with the advance directive, the first section of the financial power of attorney is reserved for the principal's designation of an agent.

Exhibit 7.5 Financial Power of Attorney Form

State of Georgia }

County of________________}

STATUTORY FORM POWER OF ATTORNEY
IMPORTANT INFORMATION

This power of attorney authorizes another person (your agent) to make decisions concerning your property for you (the principal). Your agent will be able to make decisions and act with respect to your property (including your money) whether or not you are able to act for yourself. The meaning of authority over subjects listed on this form is explained in O.C.G.A. Chapter 6B of Title 10.

This power of attorney does not authorize the agent to make health care decisions for you.

You should select someone you trust to serve as your agent. Unless you specify otherwise in the Special Instructions, generally the agent's authority will continue until you die or revoke the power of attorney or the agent resigns or is unable to act for you.

Your agent is not entitled to any compensation unless you state otherwise in the Special Instructions. Your agent shall be entitled to reimbursement of reasonable expenses incurred in performing the acts required by you in your power of attorney.

This form provides for designation of one agent. If you wish to name more than one agent, you may name a successor agent or name a coagent in the Special Instructions. Coagents will not be required to act together unless you include that requirement in the Special Instructions.

If your agent is unable or unwilling to act for you, your power of attorney will end unless you have named a successor agent. You may also name a second successor agent.

This power of attorney shall be durable unless you state otherwise in the Special Instructions.

This power of attorney becomes effective immediately unless you state otherwise in the Special Instructions.

If you have questions about the power of attorney or the authority you are granting to your agent, you should seek legal advice before signing this form.

DESIGNATION OF AGENT

I __________________________ (Name of principal) name the following person as my agent:

Name of agent: ____________________________

Agent's address: ____________________________

Agent's telephone number: ____________________________

Agent's e-mail address: ____________________________

DESIGNATION OF SUCCESSOR AGENT(S)
(OPTIONAL)

If my agent is unable or unwilling to act for me, I name as my successor agent:

Name of successor agent: ____________________________

Successor agent's address: ____________________________

Successor agent's telephone number: ____________________________

Successor agent's e-mail address: ____________________________

If my successor agent is unable or unwilling to act for me, I name as my second successor agent:

Name of second successor agent: ____________________________

Second successor agent's address: ____________________________

Second successor agent's telephone number: ____________________________

Second successor agent's e-mail address: ____________________________

GRANT OF GENERAL AUTHORITY

I grant my agent and any successor agent general authority to act for me with respect to the following subjects as defined in O.C.G.A. Chapter 6B of Title 10:

(**INITIAL** each subject you want to include in the agent's general authority. If you wish to grant general authority over all of the subjects you may initial "all preceding subjects" instead of initialing each subject.)

_____ Real property

_____ Tangible personal property

_____ Stocks and bonds

_____ Commodities and options

_____ Banks and other financial institutions

_____ Operation of entity or business

_____ Insurance and annuities

_____ Estates, trusts, and other beneficial interests

_____ Claims and litigation

_____ Personal and family maintenance

_____ Benefits from governmental programs or civil or military service

_____ Retirement plans

_____ Taxes

_____ All preceding subjects

GRANT OF SPECIFIC AUTHORITY (OPTIONAL)

My agent SHALL NOT do any of the following specific acts for me UNLESS I have INITIALED the specific authority listed below:

(CAUTION: Granting any of the following will give your agent the authority to take actions that could significantly reduce your property or change how your property is distributed at your death. INITIAL ONLY the specific authority you WANT to give your agent. You should give your agent specific instructions in the Special Instructions when you authorize your agent to make gifts.)

_____ Create, fund, amend, revoke, or terminate an inter vivos trust

_____ Make a gift, subject to the limitations of O.C.G.A. § 10-6B-56 and any Special Instructions in this power of attorney

_____ Create or change rights of survivorship

_____ Create or change a beneficiary designation

_____ Authorize another person to exercise the authority granted under this power of attorney

_____ Waive the principal's right to be a beneficiary of a joint and survivor annuity, including a survivor benefit under a retirement plan

_____ Exercise authority over the content of electronic communications sent or received by the principal

_____ Exercise fiduciary powers that the principal has authority to delegate and that are expressly and clearly identified (including the persons for which the principal acts as a fiduciary) in the Special Instructions

_____ Renounce an interest in property, including a power of appointment

LIMITATION ON AGENT'S AUTHORITY

An agent that is not my ancestor, spouse, or descendant SHALL NOT use my property to benefit the agent or a person to whom the agent owes an obligation of support unless I have included that authority in the Special Instructions.

SPECIAL INSTRUCTIONS (OPTIONAL)

You may give special instructions on the following lines (you may add lines or place your special instructions in a separate document and attach it to the power of attorney):

____

____

____

EFFECTIVE DATE

This power of attorney is effective immediately unless I have stated otherwise in the Special Instructions.

NOMINATION OF CONSERVATOR (OPTIONAL)

If it becomes necessary for a court to appoint a conservator of my estate, I nominate the following person(s) for appointment:

Name of nominee for conservator of my estate: ________________________

Nominee's address: ________________________

Nominee's telephone number: ________________________

Nominee's e-mail address: ________________________

RELIANCE ON THIS POWER OF ATTORNEY

Any person, including my agent, may rely upon the validity of this power of attorney or a copy of it unless that person has actual knowledge it has terminated or is invalid.

SIGNATURE AND ACKNOWLEDGMENT

Your signature __________________________ Date __________________________

Your name printed __________________________

Your address __________________________

Your telephone number __________________________

Your e-mail address __________________________

This document was signed in my presence on __________________________, (Date) by

__________________________ (Name of principal)

Witness Signature __________________________

Witness's name printed __________________________

Witness's address __________________________

Witness's telephone number __________________________

Witness's e-mail address __________________________

State of Georgia }

County of ________________ }

This document was signed in my presence on __________________________ (Date) by

__________________________ (Name of principal).

(Seal)

Signature of notary __________________________

My commission expires __________________________

This document prepared by __________________________

IMPORTANT INFORMATION FOR AGENT

Agent's Duties

When you accept the authority granted under this power of attorney, a special legal relationship is created between you and the principal. This relationship imposes upon you legal duties that continue until you resign or the power of attorney is terminated or revoked. You must:

(1) Do what you know the principal reasonably expects you to do with the principal's property or, if you do not know the principal's expectations, act in the principal's best interest;

(2) Act in good faith;

(3) Do nothing beyond the authority granted in this power of attorney; and

(4) Disclose your identity as an agent whenever you act for the

principal by writing or printing the name of the principal and signing your own name as "agent" in the following manner:
__________________________ by __________________________ as Agent.

(Principal's name) (Your Name)

Unless the Special Instructions in this power of attorney state otherwise, you must also:

(1) Act loyally for the principal's benefit;

(2) Avoid conflicts that would impair your ability to act in the principal's best interest;

(3) Act with care, competence, and diligence;

(4) Keep a record of all receipts, disbursements, and transactions made on behalf of the principal;

(5) Cooperate with any person that has authority to make health care decisions for the principal to do what you know the principal reasonably expects or, if you do not know the principal's expectations, to act in the principal's best interest; and

(6) Attempt to preserve the principal's estate plan if you know the plan and preserving the plan is consistent with the principal's best interest.

Termination of Agent's Authority

You must stop acting on behalf of the principal if you learn of any event that terminates this power of attorney or your authority under this power of attorney. Events that terminate a power of attorney or your authority to act under a power of attorney include:

(1) Death of the principal;

(2) The principal's revocation of your authority or the power of attorney;

(3) The occurrence of a termination event stated in the power of attorney;

(4) The purpose of the power of attorney is fully accomplished; or

(5) If you are married to the principal, a legal action is filed with a court to end your marriage, or for your legal separation, unless the Special Instructions in this power of attorney state that such an action will not terminate your authority.

Liability of Agent

The meaning of the authority granted to you is defined in O.C.G.A. Chapter 6B of Title 10. If you violate O.C.G.A. Chapter 6B of Title 10 or act outside the authority granted, you may be liable for any damages caused by your violation.

If there is anything about this document or your duties that you do not understand, you should seek legal advice.

Source: O.C.G.A. § 10-6B-70

In the next paragraph, the principal is asked to nominate one or more successor(s) if the first choice is unable or unwilling to act. Again, this is an optional provision, but it is always a good idea for legal advisors to recommend that clients name at least one successor agent.

In the section entitled "Grant of General Authority," the principal initials to indicate the specific types of matters for which he or she is authorizing the agent to act. If the principal wants to give the agent broad discretion to handle any type of financial decision, then the principal grants general authority by initialing the last blank in this section. If the principal desires to somehow limit the authority of his or her agent, he or she may also do so in the remaining sections before the Effective Date. Finally, there is an optional provision that allows the principal to appoint a conservator of his or her estate, which is followed by the signature lines. The agent may serve as the conservator, or someone else may be named. We will discuss adult conservatorship more fully in Chapter 10.

It is advisable to have the principal and witnesses execute at least three originals of the financial power of attorney at the signing ceremony: (1) one to be given to the agent to use in the event of an emergency; (2) one for the principal to keep with his or her other important personal documents, including the will or trust; and, (3) one to be produced upon request from a financial institution.

Anatomical Gifts

O.C.G.A. § 44-5-141(3) defines an anatomical gift as "a donation of all or part of a human body to take effect after the donor's death for the purpose of transplantation, therapy, research, or education." As this definition indicates, there is tremendous value attached to an anatomical gift. There are various reasons why individuals may donate parts of their anatomy while they are living or when they are deceased. Most donors are motivated by the simple desire to help others in need. Moreover, the research that is conducted with such gifts leads to many life-saving medical discoveries for years to come.

According to the U.S. Department of Health & Human Services (HHS), currently, one organ donor can save up to eight lives and enhance over 75. However, the demand for donations is overwhelming. As Exhibit 7.6 indicates below, in June 2024, almost 114,000 individuals were awaiting an organ transplant in the United States, with most looking for a replacement kidney.

Additionally, Exhibit 7.7, which follows, illustrates the total number of donors in the United States in 2023. There were only 16,336 living donors and 9,462 deceased donors. This data follows a historical trend in which the supply of donated organs has simply not been enough to keep up with the demand.

In fact, according to the HHS, in 2024, 17 people died each day waiting for an organ transplant, and every eight minutes, someone was added to the transplant waiting list. Given these grim statistics and the growing therapeutic, research, and educational

Exhibit 7.6 National Organ Donation Statistics

U.S. Department of Health & Human Services HRSA

OPTN

ORGAN PROCUREMENT AND TRANSPLANTATION NETWORK

National data

Overall by Organ

Current U.S. Waiting List

Based on OPTN data as of June 20, 2024

	Registrations
All Organs	113,923
Kidney	96,475
Liver	9,711
Pancreas	848
Kidney / Pancreas	2,250
Heart	3,440
Lung	945
Heart / Lung	41
Intestine	197
Abdominal Wall	2
VCA - head and neck	3
VCA - upper limb	3
VCA - uterus	8

Source: https://optn.transplant.hrsa.gov/data/view-data-reports/national-data/#

Exhibit 7.7 Living and Deceased Donors

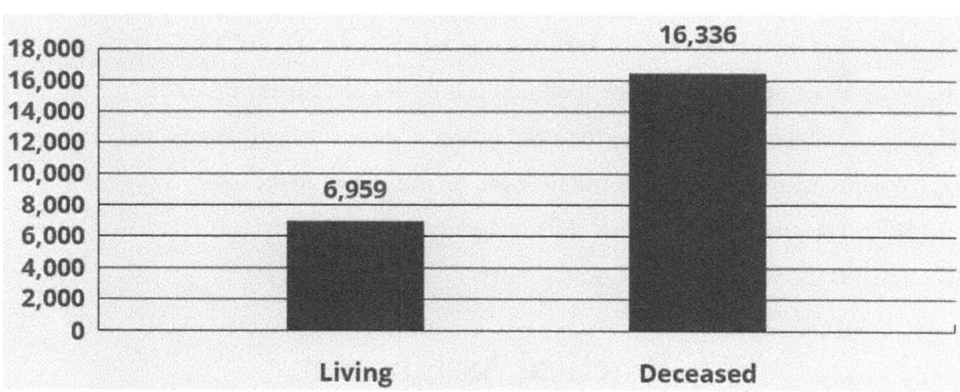

Source: https://www.organdonor.gov/learn/organ-donation-statistics#numbers

needs for organs, anatomical gifts are extremely important. They can help bridge the gap between supply and demand.

As stated earlier, Georgians can use the advance directive for healthcare to let their loved ones know of their intentions to make anatomical gifts upon their death. More specifically, related to organ and tissue donation and donating one's body for medical research, the following is included in Section 5(B) of the document, "My health care agent will have the power to make a disposition of any part or all of my body for medical purposes according to the Georgia Anatomical Gift Act, unless I have limited my health care agent's power by initialing below."

Furthermore, O.C.G.A. § 44-5-143 indicates other methods by which Georgians may make an anatomical gift. For instance, a donor may choose to do so by "authorizing a statement or symbol indicating that the donor has made an anatomical gift to be imprinted on the donor's driver's license or identification card." Another alternative is to include provisions in one's will indicating these wishes. Finally, a donation is possible "during a terminal illness or injury of the donor, by any form of communication addressed to at least two adults, at least one of whom is a disinterested witness." However it is done, the decision to make an anatomical gift has far-reaching consequences.

Key Terms

durable

emancipated minor

HIPAA Authorization and Waiver

statutory form

Review Questions

1. What is an advance directive, and what is its purpose?
2. What is a statutory form, and why is it useful?
3. In other jurisdictions, what names may be given to an advance directive?
4. What are the requirements for a valid advance directive?
5. What is a financial power of attorney, and what is its purpose?
6. Why was a new statutory form of financial power of attorney needed?
7. What is the relevance of the financial power of attorney being durable?
8. What is an anatomical gift, and how can an individual make one?
9. What law governs anatomical gifts in Georgia?
10. What is the value of an anatomical gift?

Practical Assignment

There is much debate surrounding the topics of organ and tissue donation. Conduct some research on the Internet to determine the arguments for and against anatomical giving. Create and submit a diagram or chart that illustrates both sides of this debate. Be sure to provide citations for the source(s) of your information.

Chapter 8

Trusts

Learning Objectives

Upon completion of this chapter, you should be able to:

- Define basic terminology and concepts associated with trusts.
- Explain trust creation and termination.
- Expound upon the respective roles of the trustee, settlor, and beneficiary.
- Discuss classifications of trusts.
- Distinguish between testamentary trusts and living trusts.
- Assist with drafting a trust.

In Chapter 1, we discussed that a valid will or trust is recommended as a crucial part of a well-crafted estate plan. In this chapter and the next, we will move on to a discussion of the trust. You will learn that a client may have various reasons to prefer a trust over a will as his or her primary estate planning tool. Some of those considerations are outlined in Exhibit 8.1.

Trust Characteristics

As stated previously, a trust is an arrangement by which property is transferred from one person to another for the benefit of yet another. To know how a trust works, it is essential to know that the right to property may be split into two interests: legal and equitable (or beneficial). The legal right is the right to manage and invest the property (e.g., investing money in the stock market, moving it from one account to another, or moving it from one bank to another). The equitable right is the right to enjoy the property (e.g., spending money on vacation, education, food, housing, or clothing).

There are three main participants in a trust. First, the person who creates the trust is known as the **settlor, trustor, creator, donor**, or **grantor**. Usually, a trust is created using one of two primary trust instruments: the **trust agreement** or the **declaration of trust**. A trust agreement is a written contract between the settlor and another actor, the trustee, to create and direct the operations of the trust. In a trust agreement, the trustee

Exhibit 8.1 Will or Trust?

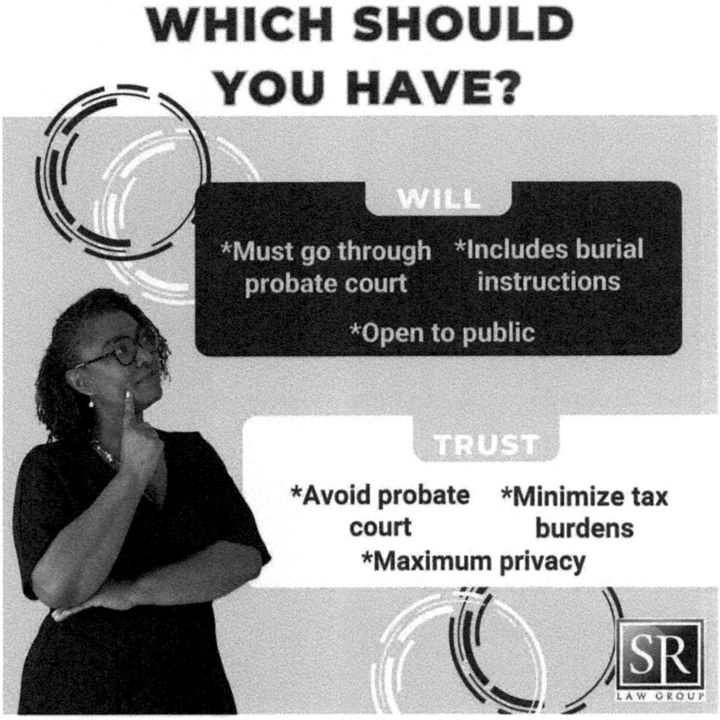

Reproduced with permission from SR Law Group, Douglasville, GA

and the settlor do not share the same interests, so the settlor can never be the sole trustee. On the other hand, a declaration of trust is a written document creating a trust in which the settlor is the sole trustee. Trusts are confidential documents, a fact that may be of importance to certain individuals who want to protect their privacy in estate planning. Unlike a will, a trust document is not required to be filed with the probate court upon the death of a creator. Therefore, oftentimes, the exact contents of a trust instrument cannot be easily verified. Michael Jackson's trust is an example of this. In addition to his pour over will, which we mentioned in Chapter 5, the singer executed a declaration of trust and in doing so, he created the Michael Jackson Family Trust. Many have speculated about its contents, but a verified copy of the trust has not been made public. However, according to court documents related to his estate, it is clear that Michael Jackson was the sole trustee of the revocable trust, and the beneficiaries under the Michael Jackson Family Trust were his children, his mother, and certain charities.

The patent requirement of a settlor that bears emphasis here is that he or she must fund the trust. The assets placed into the trust are what enable the trust to fulfill its purpose. Transferring ownership of the designated assets, such as cash, property, or investments, from the settlor into the trust's name is funding the trust. Funding the trust allows the trustee to manage and distribute these assets according to the trust's terms. An unfunded trust serves no purpose. Without funding, a trust is essentially an empty shell with no resources to carry out the settlor's intentions, such as providing for beneficiaries, paying debts, or facilitating proper care for dependents or pets. Furthermore, properly funding a trust ensures that those assets avoid probate, leading to a smoother, more private transfer of property upon the settlor's death. Avoidance of probate is one of the main reasons some prefer a trust over a will, particularly in states where the probate process can be long and arduous.

As noted above, the second actor in a trust is the trustee. A trustee may be a person, corporation, or other legal entity that holds and manages the legal interest in the trust property. Generally, a trust will not fail for lack of a trustee since the court may appoint one, if necessary. However, as stated above, a valid trust requires property. Many who choose a trust over a will do so because they possess a substantial amount of property, and upon their death, they wish to avoid related tax and other financial consequences for their beneficiaries. We will discuss tax considerations more fully in Chapter 13. Here, it is important to note that **trust property** is also referred to by various names, including **trust corpus, trust fund, trust principal**, and **trust res**. In handling trust property, the trustee acts in a fiduciary capacity and must perform all duties with honesty, loyalty, prudence, and good faith as outlined in the trust instrument. Moreover, trustees have numerous duties and powers which are spelled out in O.C.G.A. §§ 53-12-240 and 53-12-261, respectively. These provisions are included in Appendix A for your review. One of the most important trustee duties is to make regular reports to beneficiaries. According to O.C.G.A. § 53-12-243, these reports must include an accounting of the current assets as well as assets coming into and out of the trust. The reports must be made at least annually. If the trustee fails to properly manage trust assets, the trustee may be sued in a personal capacity and, thus, may be liable to satisfy any judgment from assets that the trustee owns personally. For example, in 2022, the sister of deceased rapper Tupac Shakur sued the trustee for the rapper's estate, alleging numerous misdeeds, including the trustee's embezzlement of over $5.5 million. He was ordered to provide a full accounting and was personally liable for any mishandled funds.

The third participant in a trust is the beneficiary, that is, a person or entity owning the equitable interest in the trust assets with the right to enjoy and benefit from the property. During trust administration, the beneficiary usually has the right to object to actions taken or proposed to be taken by the trustee. According to O.C.G.A. § 53-12-221, the beneficiary also can have the trustee(s) removed. Even when no specific beneficiary is named, the trust is still valid as long as it serves a specific purpose.

A trust is a legal entity that can sue and be sued. O.C.G.A. § 53-12-4 indicates the governing law in disputes related to a trust as follows:

(a) As to real property, the validity of a trust shall be determined by the law of the situs of the real property.

(b) As to all other property, the validity of a trust shall be determined by:

(1) The law of the jurisdiction designated in the trust instrument unless the effect of the designation is contrary to the public policy of the jurisdiction having the most significant relationship to the matter at issue; or

(2) In the absence of an effective designation in the trust instrument, the law of the jurisdiction having the most significant relationship to the matter at issue.

Trust Creation

We discussed earlier that trusts may be created with a formal written instrument, namely a trust agreement or a declaration of trust; however, they can also be created informally. For example, suppose Mary is going out of town for work and asks Sue, a pet sitter, to care for her pets. Sue accepts payment for the pet-sitting services and extra money that Mary gives her to use as needed for pet food and any other expenses or emergencies. In the foregoing example, there is no writing, and the word "trust" was never likely uttered. Nonetheless, this is a trust arrangement. Keep this scenario in mind throughout the rest of the chapter as we contemplate the basic ways of classifying trusts.

General Classifications of Trusts

Express Trusts v. Implied Trusts

Express trusts are those which have been created by the grantor intentionally, usually by a written trust instrument (e.g., a trust agreement or declaration of trust) signed by the grantor or the grantor's agent. Under O.C.G.A. § 53-12-21(a), as with a will, no formal words are necessary to create an express trust.

Instead, O.C.G.A. § 53-12-20(b) sets forth the elements for a valid express trust:

An express trust shall have, ascertainable with reasonable certainty:

(1) An intention by a settlor to create such trust;

(2) Trust property;

(3) Except for charitable trusts or a trust for care of an animal, a beneficiary who is reasonably ascertainable at the time of the creation of such trust or reasonably ascertainable within the period of the rule against perpetuities;

(4) A trustee; and

(5) Trustee duties specified in writing or provided by law.

On the other hand, per O.C.G.A. § 53-12-133, **implied trusts** arise based on the nature of the transactions, facts and circumstances, and the conduct of the parties. This was the case with our pet-sitting example above—an implied trust was formed. Mary, the pet owner, was the settlor; Sue, the pet sitter, was the trustee; and the pets were the beneficiaries. In other words, with an implied trust, if a dispute arises, a court might find a trust exists even though there is no formal, written trust instrument if there is an intention on the part of the property owner that the property is used for a particular purpose or goes to a particular person.

A **constructive trust** is another example of an implied trust; it is established by operation of law for equitable (or fairness) purposes. According to O.C.G.A. § 53-12-132(a), "[a] constructive trust is implied whenever the circumstances are such that the person holding legal title to property, either from fraud or otherwise, cannot enjoy the beneficial interest in the property without violating some established principle of equity." For instance, Bernie Madoff was a hedge fund manager in New York whose clients turned over their money to him so that he could invest it on their behalf and for their economic benefit. Instead, Madoff used the funds for other purposes, including to cover his own personal expenses and to hide his mismanagement of other clients' funds. Once the theft and fraud were uncovered, the court deemed that a trust arrangement was implied. It found that Madoff was holding the clients' funds in trust; therefore, he was liable for breach of trust.

Had the incident occurred in Georgia, investors would have been able to bring an action for breach of trust and misapplication of funds under O.C.G.A. § 53-12-301(a):

(1) To recover damages;

(2) To compel the trustee to perform the trustee's duties;

(3) To require an accounting;

(4) To enjoin the trustee from committing a breach of trust;

(5) To compel the trustee to redress a breach of trust by payment of money or otherwise;

(6) To appoint a temporary trustee to take possession of the trust property and administer the trust or to suspend a trustee with or without the appointment of a temporary trustee;

(7) To remove the trustee; and

(8) To reduce or deny compensation of the trustee.

Living Trusts vs. Testamentary Trusts

Another way of classifying trusts is according to when the trust becomes effective. If the trust is effective while the grantor is alive, it is considered an **inter vivos trust**, also known as a **living trust**. Pursuant to O.C.G.A. § 53-12-23, "A person has capacity to create an inter vivos trust to the extent that such person has legal capacity to transfer title to property inter vivos." On the other hand, a **testamentary trust** is a trust created by a testator in his or her will and takes effect after the grantor has passed away. Moreover, according to O.C.G.A. § 53-12-23, "A person has capacity to create a testamentary trust to the extent that such person has legal capacity to devise or bequeath property by will." You saw an example of a testamentary trust in Article V of the basic will provided in Exhibit 6.3. Because it is part of a will, more formalities are required to create a valid testamentary trust. Furthermore, once the testator dies, a testamentary trust cannot be amended or revoked. Also, unlike a living trust, a testamentary trust does not become effective until the testator's death and the will is probated. Because testamentary trusts are part of the will and must be probated, the terms of the trust eventually become public. In contrast, the terms of a living trust tend to remain private since it does not need to be filed with the probate court.

Revocable Trusts vs. Irrevocable Trusts

According to O.C.G.A. § 53-12-40, a **revocable trust** is a trust created during the lifetime of the grantor, and this type of trust explicitly states that it can be modified or, as the name suggests, revoked entirely. Language such as the following must be included in the trust to indicate these possibilities: "The Trustor hereby expressly reserves the right during his lifetime, at any time or from time to time, to amend this agreement in writing, in whole or in part, and to add to or withdraw all or part of the principal of this trust." Aside from the ability to amend the document, with a revocable trust, the grantor possesses the ability to add or remove property from the trust. Any property properly transferred to a revocable trust during the grantor's lifetime will avoid probate. A sample revocable trust is included at the end of this chapter as Exhibit 8.2. You will notice that Item Two, Paragraph A, addresses the revocability of the trust. Moreover, Item Two, Paragraph B indicates that additional property may be added to the trust after its creation.

While a revocable trust may be advantageous to avoid probate, it has its disadvantages. Trust property may be subject to the claims of the decedent's creditors and estate and gift taxes. An **estate tax** represents tax liability based on the value of the decedent's estate that exceeds the limits set by the taxing authority. A **gift tax** represnts a tax liability based on a gift that has a value that exceeds the annual or lifetime limits set forth by the taxing authority. These tax consequences result from the fact that when one creates a revocable living trust and transfers property to it, one retains all **incidents of ownership** to that property. In effect, the grantor of a revocable trust can still control the trust property, sell it, give it away, and determine how it is managed or invested.

In contrast, an **irrevocable trust** is a trust that generally cannot be revoked after its creation. It represents a total transfer of property since, upon transfer, the grantor forfeits any right to the property, including the right to dictate or modify its use. In other words, there are no incidents of ownership that remain for the grantor. In addition to the usual clauses one may find in a trust instrument, a clause related to irrevocability must be included to create an irrevocable trust. Typical language related to irrevocability is similar to the following:

> This trust shall be irrevocable, and the Grantor expressly waives all rights and powers to alter, amend, revoke, or terminate the trust, or any of its terms, in whole or in part. By this instrument, the Grantor relinquishes absolutely and forever all his possession or enjoyment of, or right to the income from, the trust property, and all his right and power, whether alone or in conjunction with others, to designate the persons who shall possess or enjoy the trust property or the income.

Despite its lack of flexibility, a person may choose an irrevocable trust for various reasons. For some, transferring property to an irrevocable trust may allow them to qualify for Medicaid or other benefits. Moreover, irrevocable trusts are useful tools to protect property from creditor claims. Finally, perhaps the most popular reason to establish an irrevocable living trust is the avoidance of federal estate taxes. We will discuss estate taxes more fully in Chapter 13. And, in the next chapter, we will discuss more specialized trusts, those created for a specific purpose, but for now, we will end with a discussion of trust modification and termination.

Trust Modification and Termination

By now, it may have occurred to you that trusts are like people: they are born (created), they live (exist and may be modified), and they also die (terminate). O.C.G.A. § 53-12-61 outlines how various types of trusts may be modified or terminated in diverse ways. It states in relevant part:

(a) The trust instrument may confer upon a trustee or other person a power to modify, consolidate, divide, or terminate the trust without court approval.

(b) During the settlor's lifetime, the court shall approve a petition to modify or terminate a noncharitable irrevocable trust, even if the modification or termination is inconsistent with a material purpose of the trust, if the settlor and all the beneficiaries consent to such modification or termination and the trustee has received notice of the proposed modification or termination.

(c) Following the settlor's death the court shall approve a petition to:

(1) Modify a noncharitable irrevocable trust if all the beneficiaries consent, the trustee has received notice of the proposed modification, and the court concludes that modification is not inconsistent with any material purpose of such trust; and

(2) Terminate a noncharitable irrevocable trust if all the beneficiaries consent, the trustee has received notice of the proposed termination, and the court concludes that continuance of such trust is not necessary to achieve any material purpose of such trust.

(d) The court may, upon petition:

(1) Modify the trust if, owing to circumstances not anticipated by the settlor, modification would further the purposes of such trust;

(2) Modify the administrative provisions of a trust if continuation of such trust under its existing provisions would impair such trust's administration;

(3) Modify the trust by the appointment of an additional trustee or special fiduciary if such appointment is necessary or helpful to the administration of such trust;

(4) Modify the trust to achieve the settlor's tax objectives, with such modification to have either prospective or retroactive effect;

(5) Order the division of a single trust into two or more trusts or the consolidation of two or more trusts, whether created by the same or different trust instruments or by the same or different persons, into a single trust if the division or consolidation would be helpful to the administration of such trust or trusts; or

(6) Terminate a trust and order distribution of the trust property if the:

(A) Costs of administration are such that the continuance of such trust, the establishment of such trust if it is to be established, or the distribution from a probate estate would defeat or substantially

(B) Purpose of such trust has been fulfilled or become illegal or impossible to fulfill; or

(C) Continuance of such trust would impair the accomplishment of the purposes of such trust.

To summarize, according to O.C.G.A. § 53-12-61(a), no court approval is necessary to modify or terminate a trust if the trust instrument indicates the same. However, court permission for modification or termination is necessary and must be granted under the conditions outlined in O.C.G.A. §§ 53-12-61(b) and (c). Stated another way, if the grantor and all beneficiaries, or just the beneficiaries after the grantor's death, unanimously agree to terminate or modify the terms of a noncharitable irrevocable trust, the court will approve such petition for modification or termination.

Moreover, the court may approve the modification or termination of a trust under the circumstances listed in O.C.G.A. § 53-12-61(d)(1) when there is a situation that the settlor could not have foreseen. For example, in circumstances where the settlor establishes an irrevocable trust to benefit a charity and the charity is no longer operational, the **cy pres doctrine** will allow the substitution of a similar charitable cause. Cy pres simply means "as near as possible," and the doctrine allows for modification of the trust when the settlor's original intent is frustrated. For instance, if one were to establish an irrevocable trust to benefit breast cancer research and then breast cancer is cured, the cy pres doctrine can then be used to substitute ovarian cancer research for breast cancer research. O.C.G.A. § 53-12-61(d)(1) can also be used in a situation where a trust purpose has been frustrated by technology, an act of god, or an act of government. Suppose, for example, an irrevocable trust is established to develop electric cars, but then the government passes a law banning the development of electric cars. Or, if an irrevocable trust is established to fund oil exploration in an area where it later becomes unsafe to do so. In those instances, the statute can be invoked to modify the terms of the trust so that the trust can endure.

Finally, we must note the significant changes to Georgia trust laws, which took effect on July 1, 2018, following a national trend. Most importantly, these changes allowed more flexibility to modify irrevocable trusts. For example, those laws provided for methods of modifying a trust agreement or even terminating it by: (1) the terms of the agreement itself; (2) judicial modification; (3) private agreements; (4) decanting, which is transferring the assets of one trust into another trust, and (5) terminating small trusts. These provisions are located in O.C.G.A. § 53-12-61 and O.C.G.A. § 53-12-62 and are fully outlined in Appendix A.

Exhibit 8.2 Sample Revocable Trust

______________________________ REVOCABLE LIVING TRUST
[insert chosen name of trust]

I, ______________________________[insert name of person creating the trust], as Grantor, hereby transfer and deliver the sum of Ten and No Dollars ($10.00), and the property described on Schedule "A", attached hereto and made a part hereof, to ______________________[insert name of Trustee], as Trustee (hereinafter "Trustee"), in trust, to be held as the "________________ REVOCABLE TRUST" and to be administered and distributed upon the following terms:

ITEM ONE - FAMILY STATUS

A. As of the execution of this trust agreement, I am _________________ [insert marital status (e.g, married to ______, or single)], and I have _______ natural born or adopted child(ren): [insert name(s)].

B. Whenever in this trust the term "descendants" (or any similar term denoting class for purposes of inheritance) is used, such term shall be deemed to include those naturally born as well as any legally adopted by me.

ITEM TWO - FACTS AND DECLARATIONS

A. Revocability. I reserve the right to alter, amend, modify, or revoke this trust in whole or in part at any time and from time to time by an instrument in writing signed by me and delivered to the Trustee, provided that no such change shall increase the duties or liabilities or decrease the compensation of the Trustee without the Trustee's consent. If this trust is revoked in its entirety, the Trustee shall deliver all the trust assets to me as soon thereafter as may be reasonably possible.

B. Additional Property. I, as well as others, shall have the right at any time to add to this trust by depositing, assigning, transferring or conveying additional money or property with the Trustee hereunder, provided that such property is acceptable to the Trustee. All such money or property shall be held and distributed by the Trustee in all respects as if it had been a part of the property originally deposited hereunder.

C. Transfer of Trust to Another Jurisdiction. Should any successor Trustee appointed under this trust as provided in this agreement be a person or entity domiciled outside the State of Georgia, such Trustee shall be authorized to remove the trust assets to the domicile of such Trustee, and then and thereafter the administration of such trust shall be governed by the laws of the state in which such Trustee is domiciled, but the construction of such trust and the rights of the beneficiaries thereof shall continue to be governed by the laws of the State of Georgia.

D. Applicable Law. This agreement shall be construed and the validity of any trust under

 Initials ______

this agreement shall be determined in accordance with the laws of the State of Georgia.

E. Titles and Headings. Titles and headings contained in this agreement shall not be deemed to govern, limit, modify or in any manner affect the scope, meaning or intent of the provisions in this agreement.

F. Gender and Number. As used in this agreement, the masculine, feminine or neuter gender, and the singular or plural number, include the others whenever the context so indicates.

G. Definition of Term "Trustee." Any reference in this agreement to "Trustee" shall include all Trustees at any time acting under this agreement, including any successor Trustees.

H. Definition of Term "Code." Unless otherwise specified in this agreement, any reference to the "Code" refers to the Internal Revenue Code of 1986, as amended, and shall be deemed to refer to the corresponding provisions of any subsequent tax laws.

ITEM THREE - ADMINISTRATION OF TRUST DURING GRANTOR'S LIFETIME

A. Capacity. While I am physically and mentally able to properly manage my affairs, the Trustee shall pay all net income from this trust to me and shall encroach on the principal hereof in such amounts as I may request.

B. Incapacity. At any time while I am physically or mentally unable properly to manage my affairs, as determined in accordance with Item Four hereof, the Trustee shall be authorized to use such part of the net income and principal of this trust as the Trustee may deem necessary, in the Trustee's sole discretion, to provide for my proper support, comfort, health, welfare, and maintenance (which shall be liberal) and to provide for any medical expenses or other expenses that I may incur, accumulating any income not used currently as principal. To these ends, the Trustee shall be authorized to pay any such expenses of mine directly or to pay over any money to me without the intervention of a guardian; or the Trustee, in his or her sole discretion, may make any such payment for my benefit to my attorney-in-fact or to any duly appointed guardian of my person or conservator of my property. All such payments made to or for me or to any such attorney-in-fact, guardian, or conservator shall be final and conclusive in favor of the Trustee on any accounting. While I am so physically or mentally unable to manage my affairs as determined under Item Four, any purchaser, seller, transfer agent, or other person dealing with the Trustee may act on the sole signature and direction of the Trustee and may conclusively presume that the Trustee has my direction for or consent to a purchase or sale or that my direction or consent is not then necessary. The accomplishment of the purposes set forth herein (primarily my proper support and maintenance) rather than the preservation of the trust assets until my death, shall govern the decisions of the Trustee.

ITEM FOUR-DETERMINATION OF GRANTOR'S CAPACITY

A. Composition of Committee. In the event a determination is necessary regarding the Grantor's capacity, there shall be a committee consisting of at least three (3) attending physicians.

B. Documentation. All decisions of the committee shall be by majority rule, and shall be documented by a signed, written and dated instrument.

C. Determinations. The members of the committee, by a signed, written and dated instrument delivered to the Trustee, shall determine solely for purposes of this trust that the said Grantor is physically or mentally incapable of managing his or her affairs (although he or she may not be legally incompetent), or may by like instrument delivered to the Trustee, determine that the said Grantor's condition has improved, and he or she is no longer unable properly to manage his or her own affairs. The Trustee shall be authorized to rely conclusively on any such determination by the committee, until a properly signed written determination to the contrary is received by the Trustee.

D. HIPAA Authority. Solely for the purpose of determining whether said Grantor is physically or mentally incapable of managing his or her own affairs (although he or she may not be legally incompetent), I authorize any health care provider to disclose (in verbal, written or electronic form, via hand delivery, mail, fax, electronic transmission or in any other way) to any or all of the committee members named in paragraph A. of this Item, any relevant individually identifiable health information, including any protected health information, sufficient to make such determination. This consent is valid until revoked by me in writing, making specific reference to this HIPAA authorization, which written revocation shall constitute an "expiration event" for purposes of the Health Insurance Portability and Accountability Act of 1996 ("HIPAA").

ITEM FIVE - ADMINISTRATION OF TRUST UPON DEATH OF GRANTOR(S)

A. Tangible Personal Property.

(i) Upon the death of the Grantor, I direct my Trustee to distribute my tangible personal property to my spouse.

(ii) If my spouse does not survive me, then I direct my Trustee to distribute such personal property to my children, in shares as nearly equal as practicable, if they survive me, and if not, to their then living lineal descendants, per stirpes.

(iii) If my children do not survive me and do not leave any living lineal descendants then I direct my Trustee to distribute such property in accordance with the order of intestate succession in the State of Georgia.

(iv) Notwithstanding the provisions of the foregoing sub-paragraphs, I may deliver to the Trustee a separate signed, written instrument containing instructions for the distribution of tangible personal property. If I do deliver such an instrument to the Trustee, then the Trustee is directed to distribute any tangible personal property listed in such instrument in accordance with the tenus of such instrument.

B. Real Property.

(i) Upon the death of the Grantor, I direct my Trustee to convey my principal residence, and any other real property owned by me, wherever located, to my spouse.

(ii) If my spouse does not survive me, then the Trustee shall convey such real property to my children, in shares as nearly equal as practicable, if they survive me, and if not, to their then living lineal descendants, per stirpes.

(iii) If my children do not survive me and do not leave any living lineal descendants then I direct my Trustee to sell all of said real property and add the net proceeds of such sale to the Residue (as hereinafter defined).

C. Residue.

After paying any debts, claims, taxes and expenses authorized under paragraph A. of Item Seven, and after making all of the conveyances and distributions provided for in paragraphs A. and B. of this Item, I direct my Trustee to distribute all remaining trust property of every kind and description then held by my Trustee, including, without limitation, any lapsed or void legacy or devise (collectively, the "Residue"), as follows:

(i) Upon the death of the Grantor, thus terminating this trust, all of the Residue shall be distributed to my spouse.

(ii) If my spouse does not survive me, then the Trustee shall distribute the Residue to my children, in shares as nearly equal as possible, if they survive me, and if not, to their then living lineal descendants, per stirpes.

(iii) If my children do not survive me and do not leave any living lineal descendants then I direct my Trustee to distribute such property in accordance with the order of intestate succession in the State of Georgia.

ITEM SIX - DISTRIBUTIONS TO MINORS

A. Distributions to Guardian or Custodian. Whenever my Trustee is directed or authorized to deliver any money or property to any person who is a minor, or, in my Trustee's absolute and uncontrolled discretion, is otherwise determined to be under a disability, or to use the same for the benefit of any such beneficiary, my Trustee need not, in my Trustee's sole discretion, require the appointment of a guardian, but shall be authorized to deliver the same to the person having custody of such beneficiary; to deliver the same to a legal guardian for such beneficiary if one has been appointed, to deliver the same to a custodianship for the benefit of such beneficiary created under or governed by the Georgia Transfers to Minors Act or the similar act of any other state, or to use the same for the benefit of such beneficiary. My Trustee shall have no duty to see to the proper application of such assets by any such recipient.

Initials ______

B. Distributions Held in Trust. In addition to the options described in paragraph A. of this Item, whenever my Trustee is directed to distribute any money or property to a person who has not attained age twenty-one (21), my Trustee, shall continue to hold the share of such beneficiary in trust for such beneficiary until he or she attains age twenty-one (21) and in the meantime shall use such part of the income or principal (or both) of the share of such beneficiary as my Trustee may, in his or her sole discretion, deem necessary or appropriate to provide for the proper support, maintenance, medical care and education of such beneficiary.

ITEM SEVEN - DEBTS AND DIVERSIFICATION

A. Debts, Claims, Taxes. Upon my death, my Trustee is authorized to pay all debts, claims and expenses properly chargeable to me or my estate. Upon my death, my Trustee shall pay all estate taxes, together with any interest and penalties thereon, other than any taxes imposed by section 2032A, section 2056A, section 2507 or Chapter 13 of the Code imposed at the time of my death and that may by reason of my death be attributable to my probate estate or to my interest in any trust created under this agreement.

B. Payments. My Trustee, in my Trustee's sole discretion, may make any payment described in paragraph A. of this Item directly to the creditor or taxing agency involved, or may pay all or any portion thereof to my personal representatives. My Trustee shall have no duty to verify any information furnished by my personal representatives and such personal representatives' information shall be conclusive and binding upon all persons interested in any trust under this instrument. All payments made by my Trustee under paragraph A. of this Item shall be conclusive and binding upon all persons interested in any trust under this agreement.

C. Diversification. I have confidence in the investments that will be found in this trust at the time of my death, and no change need be made by my Trustee in these investments solely for the purpose of creating a diversity of investments, but my Trustee shall be authorized to sell or otherwise dispose of any such investments, if and to the extent the Trustee deem such sale or disposition to be in the best interest of this trust, without being constrained to do so.

ITEM EIGHT – TRUSTEE PROVISIONS

A. Succession. I, ____________________ [insert Grantor's name], have appointed myself as the initial Trustee hereunder. Should I die, resign, be deemed incapable of managing my own affairs in accordance with Item Four hereof, or for any reason fail or cease to act as Trustee hereunder, then I appoint _______________ [insert successor's name] as successor Trustee. Should _______________ [insert name of first successor] die or for any reason fail or cease to act as successor Trustee hereunder, then I appoint ___________________ [insert second successor's name], as successor Trustee hereunder.

B. Accountability of Successor. No successor Trustee shall be required to inquire into or audit the acts or doings of any predecessor Trustee or to make any claim against such predecessor Trustee or such predecessor's estate.

C. Powers Granted to Successor. Any successor Trustee shall have and may exercise

 Initials ______

any or all of the powers herein conferred on the original Trustee of this trust, as fully and to the same extent as if such successor had originally been named to serve in such capacity.

D. Resignation and Appointment of Success or Trustee. Any Trustee hereunder may at any time and for any reason resign as Trustee of any trust created hereunder by a signed and dated document delivered to the successor Trustee and to the sui juris persons who are then income beneficiaries of the subject trust, if any. If there is no successor Trustee then willing and able to act, the sui juris persons who are then income beneficiaries of such trust shall be entitled to designate in writing a successor Trustee, forwarding such designation to the incumbent Trustee. If there are no sui juris income beneficiaries of such trust, or if no written designation of a successor is made by any such sui juris income beneficiaries within sixty (60) days from the delivery of notice of resignation, the resigning Trustee may file notice with any court having jurisdiction of this trust, whereupon the resignation of such Trustee shall be complete. Then and thereafter the resigning Trustee shall be relieved of all further duties, liabilities, and responsibilities. Any court having jurisdiction of this trust shall be authorized to appoint successors.

ITEM NINE - GENERAL ADMINISTRATIVE PROVISIONS

A. No Bond or Returns Required. All Trustees hereunder are relieved from any obligation to file or make any bond, inventory, appraisement, return or report to any court, but shall render semiannually a statement to all income beneficiaries and beneficiaries with vested remainder interests showing the condition of the trust and the receipts and disbursements during the preceding six (6) months.

B. Independent Application. The Trustee provisions of this agreement shall apply to each trust created hereunder, independent of the application of such provisions to any other trust under this agreement.

C. Rule Against Perpetuities. Anything in this agreement to the contrary notwithstanding, all property of every trust created hereunder shall vest in and be distributed to the persons then entitled to the income from such property at the expiration of twenty-one (21) years after the death of the last surviving beneficiary of this trust who was in life on the date this agreement is executed, unless sooner vested as herein provided. The purpose of this provision is to prevent any possible violation of the rule against perpetuities, and this provision should be so construed.

D. Statutory Powers Granted to Trustee. In the management, care and disposition of each trust established hereunder, my Trustee (and my Trustee's successors in office) shall have the power to do all things and to execute such instruments as may be deemed necessary or proper, including, without limitation, the powers set forth in Official Code of Georgia Annotated Section 53-12-232, as amended to the date of execution of this agreement, which powers are incorporated by reference herein. All such powers may be exercised without order of or report to any court.

E. Additional Powers Granted to Trustee. In addition to, and not in limitation of, the powers granted in paragraph D. of this Item, my Trustee (and my Trustee's successors in office)

Initials ______

shall have the following powers, privileges and exemptions, all of which may be exercised without order of or report to any court:

(1) Sell, exchange, partition or otherwise dispose of the property of any trust created hereunder, at public or private sale, for cash or upon terms, with or without advertisement;

(2) Improve or repair or lease (as lessor or lessee) any real estate and to grant or receive options to purchase property; and a lease or option may be made for a term that may extend beyond the term of any trust created hereunder;

(3) Insure the property of any trust created hereunder against damage or loss and my Trustee against liability with respect to beneficiaries and other persons;

(4) Retain any property which my Trustee may receive or acquire, including any stock and securities of any corporate fiduciary serving hereunder; to invest in stocks, bonds, loans, securities, mutual funds, money market funds, or any other property, real or personal, or in any collective or common trust fund (including those of any corporate fiduciary serving hereunder or any of its subsidiaries or affiliates); to buy securities from or sell securities to any corporate fiduciary serving hereunder as principal or as agent, and to pay reasonable compensation therefor, all without regard to any statute or rule of law now or hereafter in force limiting the class of investments for fiduciaries; to hold securities or other property in the name of a nominee, without disclosure of the fiduciary relationship, or unregistered so that ownership may pass by delivery, and transfer possession of such property to a nominee; and to do all of same without obligation to diversify investments or liability for failure to diversify investments;

(5) Borrow money for any purpose that my Trustee may deem proper, including the power to borrow from any corporate fiduciary serving hereunder, upon reasonable terms, and to secure such indebtedness by trust or loan deed, or otherwise;

(6) Employ real estate brokers, attorneys, accountants or other expert assistants, including any who may be subsidiaries or affiliates of any corporate fiduciary serving hereunder, and to pay reasonable compensation from fiduciary funds for their services;

(7) Compromise, adjust, arbitrate, bring or defend actions on, abandon or otherwise deal with and settle any and all claims for or against any trust created hereunder in the Trustee's sole discretion; and to make, rescind or modify any contract affecting any trust created hereunder, all in such manner and upon such terms as the Trustee deems best;

(8) Make division or distribution in kind or in money, or partly in kind and partly in money; and any asset distributed in kind need not be distributed pro rata or in fractional shares among beneficiaries;

(9) Vote any stock by itself or by proxy; to enter into any plan or agreement for the sale, merger, consolidation, liquidation, recapitalization or other disposition of any

Initials ______

trust property or of any corporation issuing securities held as part of any trust created hereunder, and to accept in such transaction any cash, securities or property that the Trustee deem proper;

(10) Exercise any and all options, whether such be options to purchase stock (qualified, non-qualified, restricted or other), or whether such shall be options to purchase other types or kinds of property;

(11) Make, fail to make, or terminate any election permitted under the Code, without liability for any reasonable exercise of discretion. Adjustments may, but need not, be made because of any such election but no adjustments may be made which would adversely affect any deductible bequest;

(12) Determine the allocation of dividends, distributions, profits resulting from the maturity or sale of any asset, and any other receipts and the allocation of payments and expenses as between income and principal; provide (or not provide) reserves from income otherwise distributable for depreciation, obsolescence, or other prospective loss, reduction in value, or casualty; amortize (or not amortize) premiums, and accumulate (or not accumulate) discounts, at which securities or other assets were acquired; provided that all such determinations, allocations and other actions are reasonable;

(13) Initiate, terminate, continue or participate in any business or other enterprise, effect incorporation, dissolution, or other change in the form of any business or other enterprise, and act without limitation as director, officer, limited partner or general partner in any business or other enterprise, at the risk of the trust and without any personal liability on the part of the Trustee for any resulting losses;

(14) When property is to be held as part of a separate trust, share or part under this agreement, my Trustee shall not be required to segregate physically or divide any such property except as segregation or division may be required by the terms of or termination of the trust, but my Trustee shall keep separate accounts for the different undivided interests; and

(15) Do all things which may be necessary or proper to protect and preserve the trust estate or any part thereof, and my Trustee hereunder shall be liable only for the use of ordinary care in its execution of this trust.

Initials ______

IN WITNESS WHEREOF, I have hereunto set my hand and affixed my seal, this ______ day of ______________, 20___.

Signed, sealed and delivered
in the presence of:

GRANTOR:

____
Unofficial Witness

____
[insert Grantor's printed name]

____

Notary Public

My Commission Expires: ________

The Trustee hereby acknowledges receipt of the property described in Schedule "A" attached hereto, and made a part hereof, accept every trust created by this agreement and agrees to execute the same in accordance therewith, this _______ day of _______________, 20___.

Signed, sealed and delivered
in the presence of:

TRUSTEE:

____
Unofficial Witness

____
[insert Trustee's printed name]

____

Notary Public

My Commission Expires: ________

Initials _____

SCHEDULE A

[describe trust property here]

Initials: _____

Key Terms

constructive trust
creator
cy pres doctrine
declaration of trust
donor
estate tax
express trust
gift tax
grantor
implied trust
incidents of ownership
inter vivos trust
irrevocable trust
living trust
revocable trust
settlor
testamentary trust
trust agreement
trust corpus
trust fund
trust principal
trust property
trust res
trustor

Review Questions

1. What is a trust?
2. What are the basic elements of a valid trust?
3. Who are the different parties involved in the creation of a trust, and what are their respective roles?
4. Distinguish between a trust agreement and a declaration of trust.
5. Will a trust fail (be deemed invalid) for lack of a trustee? Why or why not?
6. What is the difference between express and implied trusts?
7. What is the difference between inter vivos and testamentary trusts?
8. What is the difference between revocable and irrevocable trusts?
9. How is a testamentary trust created? When does it become effective?
10. Can an irrevocable trust be modified or terminated? If so, how?

Practical Assignment

You can preview an irrevocable trust agreement form for free at https://www.ilrg.com/forms (do not pay to download it). Review the form, and in a Word document, indicate in your own words the purpose for each clause therein. Be sure to provide a direct citation to the webpage where the form you found is located.

Chapter 9

Specialized Trusts

Learning Objectives

Upon completion of this chapter, you should be able to:

- Name and describe various specialized trusts.
- Explain the purpose of each type of specialized trust.

Classifying Trusts by Purpose

In this chapter, we will discuss another, more specific method by which trusts may be classified—by their unique purposes. As indicated previously, most trusts are established primarily to take advantage of gift, income, or estate tax benefits. However, to take advantage of those benefits, trust instruments must contain certain language as outlined in the applicable provisions of the **Internal Revenue Code (I.R.C.)** The I.R.C. contains federal tax laws, including those related to gift, income, and estate taxes, which we discuss in this chapter and others. Sections of the I.R.C. to which we refer are included in Appendix B for your review.

The legal team must have insight into the purpose of a trust to ensure that the necessary language is included in the trust instrument. Oftentimes, in crafting the trust document, the name of the trust will be reflective of its unique purpose. So, a lawyer drafting a trust agreement in our pet-sitting example might name it "The Mary/Sue Pet-Sitting Trust." A descriptive title for a trust helps convey its purpose and characteristics.

Typically, a trust is created with a particular purpose in mind, and that purpose will dictate the terms of the trust arrangement or instrument. To illustrate this point, let us return to our pet-sitting example first discussed in Chapter 8. Based on the circumstances and the conduct of the parties, we were able to ascertain that it amounted to an implied, inter vivos, revocable trust that was created by the pet owner for the benefit of her pets. Moreover, the trust was likely funded by the pet owner/grantor giving the pet sitter/trustee compensation and a small amount of additional money to care for the pets/beneficiaries for a short duration while the pet owner was away.

Common Specialized Trusts

The remainder of this chapter will be devoted to describing some of the more common special purpose trusts. In each case, we have included the elements that are particular to the trust's purpose. Exhibit 9.1, which follows, summarizes the various trusts described herein. Although this list is not all-inclusive, it should provide a good basis for understanding some of the trusts that you will likely encounter as you work in this area of law.

Exhibit 9.1 Trusts Categorized by Purpose

Specialized Trust	Description
A/B trust	trust for married couples that divides into two upon the death of the first spouse
bypass trust	See credit shelter trust
charitable trust	benefits a particular charity or the public in general
credit shelter trust	designed to hold as much of the grantor's property as is sheltered from or bypasses federal estate tax by virtue of the unified credit; also referred to as bypass trust
Crummey trust	life insurance trust (named after its founder) transfers to which qualify for the annual gift tax exclusion
dynasty trust	See generation-skipping trust
generation-skipping trust	designed to allow a gift to skip a generation; lasts beyond the time permitted by the rule against perpetuities; also known as dynasty trust
irrevocable life insurance trust (ILIT)	designed to hold life insurance on the life of the grantor or another person in order to exclude the life insurance proceeds payable on the death of the grantor from federal estate taxation
life insurance trust	See irrevocable life insurance trust (ILIT)
marital trust	designed to hold the remainder of the decedent's property and is sheltered from the federal estate tax by virtue of the unlimited marital deduction
pet trust	permits pet owners to provide instructions and set aside funds and other resources to care for their pets in the event of the owner's death or incapacitation
qualified terminable interest property (QTIP) trust	marital trust that holds property for a surviving spouse who will not incur tax liability due to the unlimited marital deduction
special needs trust	enables the grantor to provide for the continuing care of a disabled spouse, child, relative or friend for those supplemental needs in excess of those provided for by public benefit programs
spendthrift trust	includes certain language giving the trustee discretion to avoid making distributions to irresponsible beneficiaries or their creditors
supplemental needs trust	See special needs trust
totten trust	created during the lifetime of the grantor by depositing money into an account at a financial institution in his or her name as the trustee for another and is not completed until the grantor's death

A/B Trust

An **A/B trust** is a trust for married couples that is divided in two upon the death of the first spouse. It can be created either as a living trust or a testamentary trust and is designed to reduce or eliminate the couple's tax liability. The first component of an A/B trust is the **credit shelter trust**, also known as a **bypass trust**. Its name is derived from the fact that the grantor's property is held by the trustee; and as a result, it is sheltered from or bypasses federal taxes up to the amount of the **unified credit**, as outlined in I.R.C. § 2010. In other words, by virtue of the unified credit, a person may transfer a certain amount of property without being liable to pay estate, gift, or generation-skipping transfer taxes, which we will discuss shortly.

The second component of an A/B trust is the **marital trust**. After the first spouse dies, the remainder of the decedent's property (above the amount of the unified credit) is transferred into the marital trust. It is then sheltered from tax liability by virtue of the **unlimited marital deduction** provided for in I.R.C. § 2523. This deduction allows one spouse to transfer property without restriction to the other spouse at any time. The surviving spouse will have access to income from the marital trust. Once the surviving spouse dies, the remaining assets go to his or her designated beneficiaries. Use of an A/B trust is prudent for a couple whose wealth exceeds the **exclusion amount** (known as the **applicable exclusion amount** before 2011), the amount that can be transferred free from estate and gift taxation. For 2024, the basic exclusion amount was $13.61 million for an individual and $27.22 million for couples. Many transfers are likely to fall below these amounts, and hence, an A/B trust would not be necessary.

Charitable Trust

A **charitable trust** is one that benefits a qualified charity or the public in general. O.C.G.A. § 53-12-170(b) indicates the permissible charitable purposes for which trust property must be used:

(1) The relief of poverty;

(2) The advancement of education;

(3) The advancement of ethics and religion;

(4) The advancement of health;

(5) The advancement of science and the arts and humanities;

(6) The protection and preservation of the environment;

(7) The improvement, maintenance, or repair of cemeteries, other places of disposition of human remains, and memorials;

(8) The prevention of cruelty to animals;

(9) Governmental purposes; and

(10) Other similar subjects having for their object the relief of human suffering or the promotion of human civilization.

A charitable trust can be established as a living trust or a testamentary trust. It is considered a public trust since the beneficiary is not a specific ascertainable person. In addition to meeting the philanthropic goals of its creator, the charitable trust acts to reduce or eliminate the creator's tax liability.

Crummey Trust

A **Crummey trust** is a life insurance trust, transfers to which qualify for the **annual gift tax exclusion**. The annual gift tax exclusion is the amount of property that an individual may gift each year without incurring tax liability. For 2024, the annual exclusion for gifts was $18,000 for individuals and $36,000 for couples. A **life insurance trust** also called an **irrevocable life insurance trust (ILIT)** excludes the life insurance proceeds payable on the death of the grantor from federal estate taxation. At first, the IRS stated that gifts to a life insurance trust to pay premiums did not qualify for the annual gift tax exclusion. The IRS' position was that the only interest that the beneficiaries had was a future interest—a right to the proceeds when the insured died and the death proceeds were paid into the trust. However, this issue was eventually argued in *Crummey v. Commissioner*, 397 F.2d 82 (9th Cir. 1968), and the IRS lost. The court stated that whether the beneficiaries actually withdrew the gifts to the trust or not, they had the right to do so. The court held that such an election amounts to a present interest in property. This right of beneficiaries to elect to use the gift to the trust or not is referred to as **Crummey powers.**

Generation-Skipping Trust

A **generation-skipping trust** also known as a **dynasty trust** is designed to allow a gift to, as the name suggests, skip a generation. A dynasty trust can be created as a living trust or a testamentary trust. This type of trust is specifically designed to hold the amount of property that is exempt from the generation-skipping tax authorized under I.R.C. § 2601. Perhaps the gift could go directly from a grandfather to a grandson and skip a son who is already independently wealthy. The rationale for the skip may be that the gift would not substantially benefit the son but only add to a tax burden or be the target of judgment creditors that the son may have. Or, maybe the son is a spendthrift and his father seeks to protect his assets by giving them directly to his grandson via a trust. It is noteworthy that the generation-skipping trust can also be used to benefit non-family members. The only requirement is that the beneficiary is at least 37.5 years younger than the grantor of the trust.

Another important feature of the generation-skipping trust is that it traditionally circumvents the provisions of the **rule against perpetuities.** This rule has been enacted by most states, including Georgia in O.C.G.A. §§ 44-6-200 *et seq.* Exhibit 9.2 illustrates when the rule against perpetuities applies and instances when it does not. Generally, the rule against perpetuities prevents someone from controlling the disposition of his or her property for an indefinite time in the future. Instead, as O.C.G.A. § 44-6-201(a) provides, a property interest is invalid unless:

(1) When the interest is created, it is certain either to vest or to terminate within the lifetime of an individual then alive or within 21 years after the death of that individual; or

(2) The interest either vests or terminates within 360 years after its creation.

Dynasty trusts can be used to alleviate the rule against perpetuities concerns, with succeeding generations receiving distributions from the trust.

Pet Trust

A **pet trust** is a useful legal arrangement for animal lovers. A pet trust permits pet owners to provide instructions and set aside funds and other resources to care for their pets in the event of the owner's death or incapacitation. The trust may specify the identity of the desired caregiver and provide instructions for the pet's care. The instructions may get as detailed as the owner desires and may include items such as the selection of veterinary care providers, grooming services, and feeding requirements, as well as recreation and daily routines. Having a pet trust is useful because it may provide peace of mind that the pets will be cared for according to the owner's wishes, regardless of the preparation or financial capacity of those persons designated as caregivers for the pet, who may otherwise be unprepared to care for the animals.

Qualified Terminable Interest Property ("QTIP") Trust

A **qualified terminable interest property** (QTIP) **trust** is a marital trust that holds property for a surviving spouse who will not incur tax liability due to the unlimited marital deduction. A QTIP trust must provide that all income be distributed to the surviving spouse exclusively during his or her lifetime. The surviving spouse never has control of the assets owned by the QTIP trust and may not name beneficiaries of the trust property upon his or her death. Moreover, should the surviving spouse remarry, trust property may not be inherited by a subsequent spouse nor made the subject of divorce proceedings should the surviving spouse get divorced. In addition, the trust assets are protected from any creditors of the surviving spouse. Property remaining in the trust upon the death of the surviving spouse is distributed per the instructions of the trust creator.

Special Needs Trust

A **special needs trust**, also referred to as a **supplemental needs trust**, is created to enable the grantor to provide for the continuing care of a disabled person, usually a disabled child but perhaps also a spouse, other relative, or friend. The advantage of using the trust is that the beneficiary will not be disqualified from or lose eligibility for benefits such as Supplemental Security Income (SSI), Medicaid, and low-income housing assistance since the trust assets are not held directly nor controlled by the beneficiary. A special needs trust is an express trust and may be created as a living trust or a testamentary trust.

Exhibit 9.2 Rule Against Perpetuities

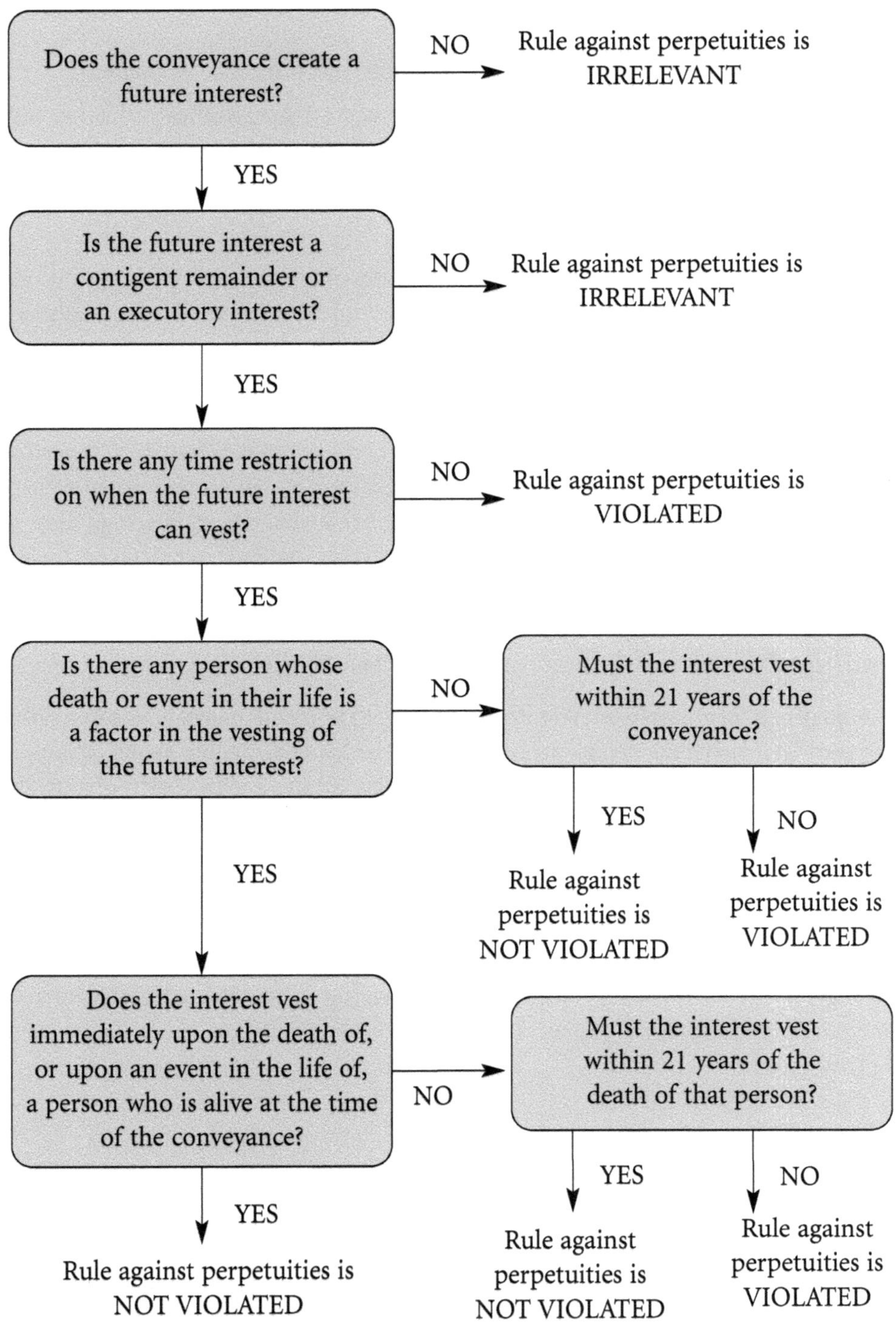

Source: LawShelf Educational Media, https://lawshelf.com

Spendthrift Trust

In Chapter 2, we mentioned that spendthrift provisions can be included in a will and a testamentary trust formed; however, a **spendthrift trust** can also be created as a living trust. A spendthrift trust is designed to avoid making distributions of property directly to irresponsible beneficiaries or their creditors. While the trustee may not be forced to make such distributions, he or she may choose to do so. It is also important to note that even the most carefully crafted spendthrift provisions may not be effective against certain creditors. For example, O.C.G.A. § 53-12-80(d) states that such provisions are invalid as to the following claims:

(1) Alimony or child support;

(2) Taxes or other governmental claims;

(3) Tort judgments;

(4) Judgments or orders for restitution as a result of a criminal conviction of the beneficiary; or

(5) Judgments for necessaries (ex. food, clothing, or shelter).

Totten Trust

Finally, we discussed totten trusts briefly in Chapter 3 when we addressed the topic of nonprobate property. A totten trust is a financial account listing a beneficiary in the event the account owner dies. The rules of the financial institution will govern the terms of trust creation, modification, and termination. Therefore, a separate trust instrument is unnecessary. This makes totten trusts relatively simple and cheap to create. Upon death, totten trust assets are paid directly to the named beneficiary and avoid probate.

Key Terms

A/B trust
annual gift tax exclusion amount
applicable exclusion amount
bypass trust
charitable trust
credit shelter trust
Crummey powers
Crummey trust
dynasty trust
exclusion amount
generation-skipping trust
Internal Revenue Code (I.R.C.)
irrevocable life insurance trust (ILIT)
life insurance trust
marital trust
pet trust
qualified terminable interest property (QTIP) trust
rule against perpetuities
special needs trust
spendthrift trust
supplemental needs trust
unified credit
unlimited marital deduction

Review Questions

1. What is an A/B trust, and why is it useful?
2. What are the two components of an A/B trust?
3. Why would someone create a charitable trust?
4. What are Crummey powers?
5. What is the concern that the rule against perpetuities addresses?
6. Why are ILITs advantageous?
7. Why is the QTIP trust popular, and what is its purpose?
8. What is the purpose of a special needs trust?
9. Why might a spendthrift trust be necessary?
10. How does one create a totten trust?

Practical Assignments

1. In this chapter, the authors mentioned that in 2024, only estates worth more than $13.61 million for an individual and $27.22 million for a couple were subject to federal estate taxes. Conduct some research on the IRS website, www.irs.gov, to determine the estate tax exemption amounts for single individuals and married couples for the last five years. Prepare a chart depicting your results and provide a citation for each source of your answers.
2. In this chapter, the authors introduced the Rule Against Perpetuities, a notoriously complex legal concept. To help you grasp this rule, complete the following steps:
    a. Research: Use a free artificial intelligence tool (such as ChatGPT, Grammarly, or Copilot) to find an alternate explanation of the Rule Against Perpetuities.
    b. Explanation Summary: Summarize the explanation in your own words. Ensure your summary highlights the key aspects of the rule, including its purpose and application.
    c. Scenario Creation: Based on your understanding, create a hypothetical scenario involving a fictional family that demonstrates how the Rule Against Perpetuities might apply. Make sure your scenario includes specific details that illustrate the rule's implications.
    d. Analysis: Provide a brief analysis of how the Rule Against Perpetuities impacts the scenario you created. Discuss any potential legal outcomes or complications that could arise.
    e. Citation: Include a citation to the source(s) you used for your explanation.

Chapter 10

Guardianships and Conservatorships

Learning Objectives

Upon completion of this chapter, you should be able to:

- Discuss issues related to guardianship and conservatorship of minors vs. adults.
- Describe the need for and duties of guardians and conservators for adults.
- Identify the qualifications required for the appointment of guardians and conservators for adults.
- Explain the procedures for the appointment of guardians and conservators for adults.
- Outline the requirements for modification and termination of guardianships and conservatorships.

Proper estate planning includes planning for incapacity. We have discussed in previous chapters that such incapacity may arise when a beneficiary under a will or trust is either disabled or a minor. In those cases, a guardian for the incapacitated person and a conservator for his or her inherited property can be nominated in a will to serve until the incapacity ends. It is noteworthy that probate and juvenile courts in Georgia have concurrent jurisdiction over the guardianship of minors. The main difference between guardianships in probate court and juvenile court is that the minor guardianship petitions pending in juvenile court also involve issues of delinquency or dependency. Generally, guardianships and conservatorships of minors end automatically by operation of law on the eighteenth birthday of the minor, or when the minor becomes emancipated.

Adults may also need guardians and conservators. A car wreck, a temporary period of sickness, or the care necessary to meet the increasing demands of a terminal illness can have devastating personal and financial consequences. As discussed in Chapter 2, one should consider long-term and short-term disability insurance to absorb or help defray the associated financial costs. Moreover, as you learned in Chapter 7, financial powers of attorney and advance directives for health care can be used to designate the individual(s) who may make critical decisions on behalf of an incapacitated adult when necessary.

However, in the event an adult is unable to make such designations due to a lack of capacity, the State of Georgia has mechanisms by which loved ones may seek authority to act on his or her behalf. An adult who, through illness or other circumstances, ceases to possess the ability to make responsible decisions, or a disabled person who reaches the age of majority, is an **incapacitated adult**. In this chapter, we will explore the procedures for adult (1) **guardianship**, which is the appointment of someone to look after the affairs of another who is unable to manage his or her own personal affairs, and (2) **conservatorship**, which is the appointment of someone to manage the property of another.

Prerequisites

It is important to note that Georgia laws outline very specific conditions that must be met before a guardian or conservator will be appointed. Related to guardianship, O.C.G.A. § 29-4-1 states, in relevant part:

(a) The court may appoint a guardian for an adult only if the court finds the adult lacks sufficient capacity to make or communicate significant responsible decisions concerning his or her health or safety.

(b) No guardian, other than a guardian ad litem, shall be appointed for an adult except pursuant to the procedures of this chapter.

(c) No guardian shall be appointed for an adult unless the appointment is in the best interest of the adult.

(d) No guardian shall be appointed for an adult within two years after the denial or dismissal on the merits of a petition for the appointment of a guardian for that adult unless the petitioner shows a significant change in the condition or circumstances of the adult.

(e)

(1) No adult shall be presumed to be in need of a guardian unless adjudicated to be in need of a guardian pursuant to this chapter.

(2) An adult shall not be presumed to be in need of a guardian solely because of a finding of criminal insanity or incompetence to stand trial or a finding of a need for treatment or services.

Almost identical prerequisites for the appointment of a conservator for adults are outlined in O.C.G.A. § 29-5-1 which states, in relevant part:

(a) The court may appoint a conservator for an adult only if the court finds the adult lacks sufficient capacity to make or communicate significant responsible decisions concerning the management of his or her property.

(b) No conservator, except a conservator for the estate of an individual who is missing or who is believed to be dead, shall be appointed for any adult except pursuant to the procedures of this chapter.

(c) No conservator shall be appointed for an adult unless the appointment is in the best interest of the adult.

(d) No conservator shall be appointed for an adult within two years after the denial or dismissal on the merits of a petition for the appointment of a conservator for that adult unless the petitioner shows a significant change in the condition or circumstances of the adult.

(e)

(1) No adult shall be presumed to be in need of a conservator unless adjudicated to be in need of a conservator pursuant to this chapter.

(2) An adult shall not be presumed to be in need of a conservator solely because of a finding of criminal insanity or incompetence to stand trial or a finding of a need for treatment or services.

What these provisions indicate is that guardianship and conservatorship apply only in limited circumstances. They are relevant when an adult can be found to lack sufficient capacity to make or communicate significant, responsible decisions concerning his or her finances, health, or safety. This lack of capacity must be established with clear and convincing evidence. In Georgia, such a determination is made by the court and the petition for appointment must be filed in the probate court in the domiciliary county of the alleged incapacitated adult for whom a guardian and/or conservator may be appointed. This incapacitated person is also known as the **proposed ward**.

Guardianship and conservatorship procedures are not meant for loved ones who you simply believe are making bad life choices. For example, suppose a mother brings a guardianship and conservatorship proceeding because her son, an otherwise healthy adult, is alleged to be an incapacitated adult since he plays video games all day, does not have a job, and spends his money frivolously. The mother will not prevail. Although some may disagree with her son's life decisions, these facts alone do not satisfy the stringent prerequisites listed above.

Guardianship

A guardianship removes from the incapacitated adult the power to enter into a contract (including marriage), consent to medical treatment, establish a residence, and bring or defend an action in court. Instead, the guardian makes those decisions for the **ward**, the person for whom the guardian has been authorized to act. The court order conferring authority for the guardian to act on behalf of the ward is referred to as **letters of guardianship**. Depending on the situation, the court may reserve certain rights for the ward. For instance, the court may preserve for the ward the ability to choose where he or she will live while all other rights of the ward are vested in the guardian.

Qualifications

O.C.G.A. § 29-4-2 sets forth the qualifications for those who may serve as a guardian.

(a) Only an individual may serve as guardian of an adult, except in the event a public guardian or the Department of Human Services is appointed pursuant to subsection (b.1) of Code Section 29-4-3.

(b) No individual may be appointed as guardian of an adult who:

  (1) Is a minor, a ward, or a protected person;

  (2) Has a conflict of interest with the adult unless the court determines that the conflict of interest is insubstantial or that the appointment would be in the adult's best interest; or

(3) Is an owner, operator, or employee of a long-term care or other caregiving institution or facility at which the adult is receiving care, unless related to the adult by blood, marriage, or adoption.

(c) No entity may be appointed as guardian of an adult which:

  (1) Has a conflict of interest with the adult unless the court determines that the conflict of interest is insubstantial or that the appointment would be in the adult's best interest; or

  (2) Is a long-term care or other caregiving institution or facility at which the adult is receiving care.

Order of Preference

Generally, the court will appoint a guardian based on the following order of preference, as outlined in O.C.G.A. § 29-4-3(b):

(1) The individual last nominated by the adult in accordance with the provisions of subsection (c) of this Code section;

(2) The spouse of the adult or an individual nominated by the adult's spouse in accordance with the provisions of subsection (d) of this Code section;

(3) An adult child of the adult or an individual nominated by an adult child of the adult in accordance with the provisions of subsection (d) of this Code section;

(4) A parent of the adult or an individual nominated by a parent of the adult in accordance with the provisions of subsection (d) of this Code section;

(5) A guardian appointed during the minority of the adult;

(6) A guardian previously appointed in Georgia or another state;

(7) A friend, relative, or any other individual;

(8) Any other person, including a volunteer to the court, found suitable and appropriate who is willing to accept the appointment; and

(9) The county guardian.

Careful consideration must be given to whether to pursue an action for guardianship. Some of the pros and cons associated with guardianship are summarized next in Exhibit 10.1.

Exhibit 10.1 Pros and Cons of Guardianship

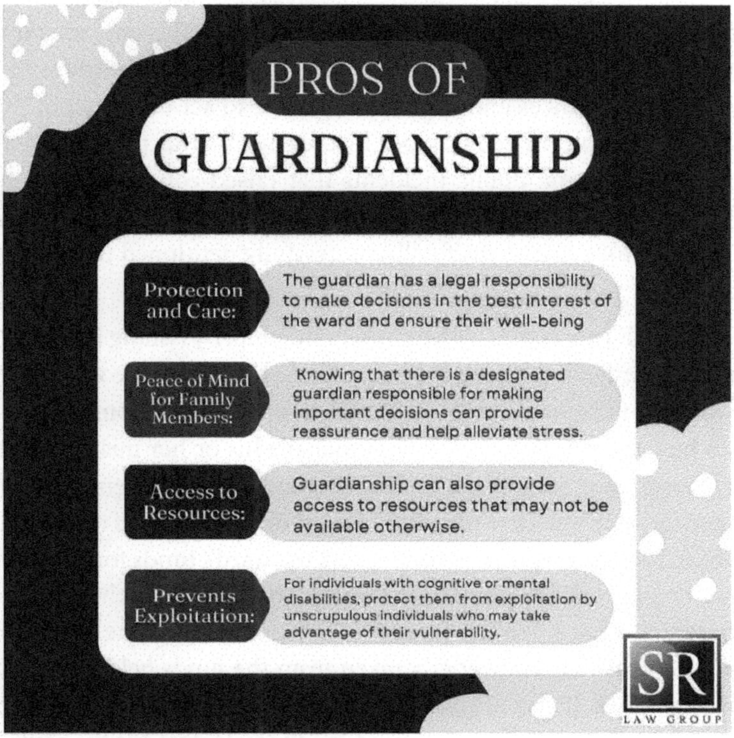

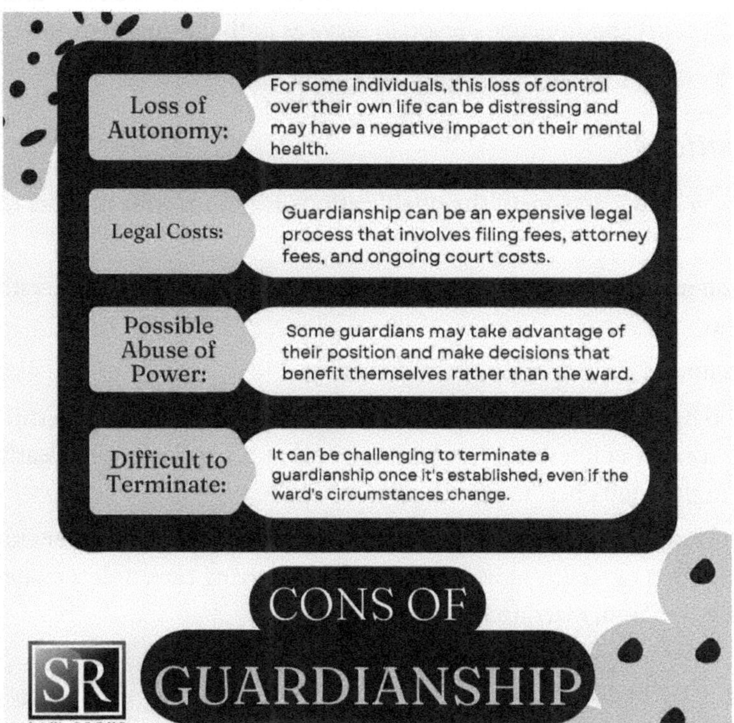

Reproduced with permission from SR Law Group, Douglasville, GA

Conservatorship

A conservatorship also requires careful consideration and is only warranted when a probate court judge determines that an individual cannot make responsible decisions regarding his or her finances and appoints someone to act on behalf of the incapacitated adult. For example, in 2008, singer Britney Spears was placed under a conservatorship following several public incidents that raised concerns about her mental health. Her father, who is also an attorney, was named her conservator and acted in that capacity until 2021, when she finally successfully petitioned the court to end the conservatorship.

Tremendous authority comes with a conservatorship. By issuing **letters of conservatorship**, the court order appointing the conservator to manage the ward's property, the court removes from the ward the power to bring or defend actions in court, to make contracts, to buy and sell property, and to manage his or her business and financial affairs. The conservator may invest the ward's funds or hold them in a financial account. The conservator must use the ward's funds for the benefit of the ward only. If the conservator can foresee a regular need to access the ward's funds for the ward's benefit, the conservator may ask the court to institute a budget for such distributions. The conservator can also file a petition for leave to encroach upon the corpus for unforeseen expenditures that can be properly taken from the funds held by the conservator without court approval. If they are two separate people, the guardian will usually advise the conservator when and if there is a need for funds to care for the ward. However, oftentimes, a court appoints one person to serve as both the guardian and conservator of the ward.

Qualifications

O.C.G.A. § 29-5-2 sets forth the qualifications for those who may serve as a conservator:

> No person may be appointed or continue to serve as conservator of the estate of an adult who:
>
> (1) Is a minor, a ward, or a protected person;
>
> (2) Who has a conflict of interest with the adult unless the court determines that the conflict of interest is insubstantial or that the appointment clearly would be in the adult's best interest; or
>
> (3) Is an owner, operator, or employee of a long-term care or other caregiving institution or facility at which the adult is receiving care, unless related to the adult by blood, marriage, or adoption.

Order of Preference

Generally, the court will appoint a conservator based on the following order of preference, as outlined in O.C.G.A. § 29-5-3(b):

(1) The person last nominated by the adult in accordance with the provisions of subsection (c) of this Code section;

(2) The spouse of the adult or a person nominated by the adult's spouse in accordance with the provisions of subsection (d) of this Code section;

(3) An adult child of the adult or a person nominated by an adult child of the adult in accordance with the provisions of subsection (d) of this Code section;

(4) A parent of the adult or a person nominated by a parent of the adult in accordance with the provisions of subsection (c) of this Code section;

(5) A conservator appointed during the minority of the adult;

(6) A conservator previously appointed in Georgia or another state;

(7) A friend, relative, or any other person; or

(8) The county guardian.

Procedure for Appointment

Guardianship and conservatorship may be sought contemporaneously within the same petition, or each can be sought separately using the same form. That form, the Petition for Letters of Guardianship/Conservatorship, is included at the end of this chapter as Exhibit 10.3. It must be filed by at least two (2) petitioners, or one petitioner may file if the petition is also supported by a medical professional (such as a psychiatrist). The petition must demonstrate that the proposed ward lacks sufficient capacity to make or communicate significant, responsible decisions concerning his or her health or safety for guardianship. For conservatorship, the petition must demonstrate that the proposed ward lacks sufficient capacity to make or communicate significant responsible decisions concerning managing his or her property.

The petition asks for considerable information including a listing of all the assets of the proposed ward and a statement attesting to the fact that the petition is filed in the proposed ward's best interest. It also calls for the names and addresses of any close relatives of the proposed ward who must be notified that the petition has been filed and is pending. Those interested relatives will also have an opportunity to attend any court hearing on the petition.

After the petition is filed, the court will examine it to make sure that it sets forth a prima facie case that the proposed ward requires a guardian and/or conservator. If the petition can move forward, the court sends a notice to the proposed ward. The court will then appoint a licensed clinical social worker or physician to examine the proposed ward. Then, the evaluating professional will file a report with the court. After reviewing that report, the court will determine whether the petition should proceed to a hearing. If the hearing is granted, the court must appoint an independent person to represent the best interests, of the proposed ward, a **guardian ad litem**. This person also serves as an investigator—the eyes and ears of the court—who will make recommendations in line with the best interests of the proposed ward. The court-appointed attorney, if any, will advocate for the proposed ward. If the petition, evaluator's report, and the report of the guardian ad litem are all in agreement, and absent any other compelling reason, the court may grant the petition without holding a hearing.

If the court determines that a hearing is necessary, the petitioner(s), the attorney for the proposed ward, if any, and the guardian ad litem must appear at the hearing. The proposed ward's attendance may be waived by his or her attorney if transportation is infeasible or for any other valid reason. After the hearing, the judge will make a determination to either deny or grant the petition. An additional requirement for conservators is to obtain a bond, which must be in the amount of the ward's personal property assets. Real property is not included in the calculation because, as a secured asset, it is self-bonding. The bond is designed to protect the ward from the conservator's intentional or accidental mismanagement of funds, if any.

Duties

The guardian and conservator must fulfill their numerous fiduciary duties in the ward's best interest and exercise reasonable care, diligence, and prudence in doing so. Like other fiduciaries, the guardian and conservator may be compensated for the performance of their duties. Among their many obligations is the duty to file regular reports with the court. The guardian must file annually a personal status report with the court related to the ward's condition, focused on his or her capacity. The conservator must file an inventory and asset management plan with the court within six (6) months of appointment. This inventory is filed once and lists what assets the conservator has received and is managing for the benefit of the ward. Thereafter, and yearly, the conservator must file a return annually. The return shows what assets came into and out of the conservatorship. Failure of the guardian and conservator to timely file these reports may result in their removal.

In general, the duties of the guardian and conservator can be summarized as indicated in Exhibit 10.2, which follows.

Exhibit 10.2 Duties of Guardians and Conservators in Georgia

Duties	Guardian	Conservator
Healthcare Decisions	✓	
Living Arrangements	✓	
Education (Minors)	✓	
Social Activities	✓	
Managing Assets		✓
Paying Debts		✓
Investing Assets		✓
Court Reporting	✓	✓
End-of-Life Decisions	✓	

Duration

Guardianships and conservatorships can be granted on an emergency basis (i.e., temporarily) or permanently. An emergency guardianship or conservatorship will only be valid for 60 days. The emergency petition is proper to be filed in a case where (1) the proposed ward's life is in imminent danger (e.g., the proposed ward is mentally unstable and refusing life-saving medical intervention) or (2) the proposed ward is in imminent danger of financial ruin (e.g., the proposed ward is being taken advantage of financially or gifting his property for no value to non-family members who are very new to his life).

A permanent guardianship or conservatorship petition should be filed with the court before the expiration of the emergency guardianship or conservatorship if one exists. Doing so will ensure that the initial order remains in place. A permanent guardianship or conservatorship petition usually takes about four to six weeks for the court to process and grant because of the more complex sequence of events that must occur in a specific, timely manner. If the need for an emergency guardianship or conservatorship is apparent and will not resolve within sixty (60) days after it is granted, it would be prudent to file the emergency and permanent petition at the same time. Depending on the circumstances, permanent guardianship or conservatorship can last for a set period (e.g., three months, six months, or a year) or indefinitely, unless the court modifies or terminates it.

Modification and Termination

As indicated, it is possible to modify and terminate guardianships and conservatorships. Under Georgia law, any interested person, including the ward, may file a petition, or the court may make its own motion for modification or termination. The requested changes to the guardianship or conservatorship would include the following: (1) adjusting the duties or powers of the guardian or conservator; (2) adjusting the powers of the ward; or, (3) making other appropriate adjustments to reflect the extent of the current capacity of the ward or other circumstances of the guardianship or conservatorship. Modification or termination may be warranted depending on the amount of evidence that has been presented to the court of a significant change in the capacity of the ward. Obviously, for a termination, sufficient proof must be provided that there is no longer a need for guardianship and/or conservatorship. Guardianship and conservatorship of an adult automatically ends when the ward dies. In addition, a conservatorship ends when a court restores the ward's rights or the ward's assets no longer need to be managed.

Exhibit 10.3 Petiton for Appointment of a Guardian/Conservator

IN THE PROBATE COURT OF ____________________ COUNTY
STATE OF GEORGIA

IN RE:)
)
______________________________,) **ESTATE NO.** __________
PROPOSED WARD)

PETITION FOR APPOINTMENT OF A
GUARDIAN AND/OR CONSERVATOR FOR A PROPOSED WARD

[NOTE: Unless there are two or more Petitioners, the affidavit beginning on page 15 must be completed by a physician, psychologist, or licensed clinical social worker and based on an examination within fifteen (15) days prior to the filing of this Petition.]

The Petition of ____,

whose relationship to the above-named Proposed Ward is______________________, whose

domicile is ____,
Street City County State Zip Code

and mailing address is ____,
Street City County State Zip Code

AND *[initial either (a) or (b) below]*

_____ (a) The Petition of ____

whose relationship to the above Proposed Ward is ______________________,

whose domicile is____,
Street City County State Zip Code

and mailing address is ____.
Street City County State Zip Code

OR

_____ (b) Attached hereto as pages 15 and 16 and made a part of this Petition is the completed affidavit of___________, a physician, psychologist licensed to practice in Georgia or licensed clinical social worker, who has examined the Proposed Ward within fifteen (15) days prior to the filing of this Petition, and shows to the Court the following:

1.

The Proposed Ward ____
[Full name of Proposed Ward] First *Middle* *Last*

whose age is __________, date of birth is ______________________________,

Social Security Number is ______________________, domicile is ______________

____
Street *City* *County* *State* *Zip Code*

presently located at ____,
Street *City* *County* *State* *Zip Code*

which is a ______________________________________ and can be contacted at
[type of facility, if applicable]

telephone number: __________________.

2.

(a) Will the Proposed Ward be moved within the next three (3) days? *[Select One]* ☐ Yes ☐ No

(b) Is the Proposed Ward a citizen of a foreign country? *[Select One]* ☐ Yes ☐ No

If you answer "Yes" to (a) and/or (b), provide the necessary information below:

(a) The following is the address where the Proposed Ward is anticipated to be moved:

____
Street *City* *County* *State* *Zip Code* *Telephone Number*

(b) The Proposed Ward is a citizen of a foreign country, said country being: ________________ (if a guardianship or conservatorship is granted, pursuant to The Vienna Convention, the Probate Court must notify the consul).

3.

(a) Is a guardianship necessary because the Proposed Ward lacks sufficient capacity to make or communicate significant responsible decisions concerning his or her health or safety? *[Select One]* ☐ Yes ☐ No

(b) Is a conservatorship necessary because the Proposed Ward lacks sufficient capacity to make or communicate significant responsible decisions concerning the management of his or her property? *[Select One]* ☐ Yes ☐ No

If you answer "Yes" to (a) and/or (b), provide the facts that support the claim of the need for a guardian/conservator (continued on next page):

[NOTE: The Petition cannot be granted unless sufficient facts are presented that support the allegation that the appointment of a guardian and/or conservator is necessary. While an attached physician's, psychologist's, or social worker's affidavit is permissible, the Petition MUST specifically provide sufficient facts to support the granting of this Petition.]

4.

(a) It is in the best interest of the Proposed Ward for the following individual to be appointed guardian: ______________________________

(b) It is in the best interest of the Proposed Ward for the following individual to be appointed conservator: ____________________________

5.

The foreseeable duration of the Proposed Ward's incapacity is__________________ and the Court should allow the Proposed Ward to retain the following rights and powers:

6.

[NOTE: The law requires notice to be given to the spouse, if any, and to all living children whose addresses are known, if any. If there are no living adult children whose addresses are known, then list at least two (2) adults in the following order of priority: lineal descendants of the Proposed Ward; parents and siblings of the Proposed Ward; and friends of the Proposed Ward. In determining the persons to whom notice is required to be given according to the foregoing rules, the Petitioner(s) should not be counted as persons receiving notice. The "Notice of Filing of Petition for Guardianship and/or Conservatorship" will be sent to these parties and not the entire Petition.]

Pursuant to law, the names, addresses, telephone numbers, and relationships of the persons to be notified are as follows:

Name	*Age (if under 18)*	*Address*	*Relationship*

7.

(a) Was an individual nominated to serve under a living will, durable power of attorney for healthcare, or other instrument that deals with the management of the person of the Proposed Ward in the event of incapacity, prior to the filing of this Guardianship Petition? *[Select One]* ☐ Yes ☐ No

If you answer "Yes" to (a), provide the name(s), address(es), and relationship(s) to the Proposed Ward, if any, indicate the nature of his/her/their interest, and whether he/she/they are willing to act or have failed to act under said appointment and attach the document as an exhibit to this Petition:

(b) Was an individual nominated in writing to serve as guardian by the Proposed Ward, or any other individual such as a spouse, adult child, or parent, to care for the Proposed Ward either because of or in the event of incapacity? *[Select One]* ☐ Yes ☐ No

If you answer "Yes" to (b), provide the name(s), address(es), and relationship(s) to the Proposed Ward, if any, indicate the nature of his/her/their interest, whether he/she/they are willing to act under said appointment, and whether the individual(s) is/are an owner, operator, or employee of a caregiving institution in which the Proposed Ward currently is receiving care and attach the document as an exhibit to this Petition:

(c) Was an order relating to cardiopulmonary resuscitation issued by the Proposed Ward or another individual addressing end of life decisions and/or life sustaining procedures? *[Select One]* ☐ Yes ☐ No

If you answer "Yes" to (c), provide the name(s), address(es), and relationship(s) to the Proposed Ward, if any, indicate the nature of his/her/their interest, whether he/she/they are willing to act under said appointment, and attach the document as an exhibit to this Petition:

(d) Was a trust created for or by the Proposed Ward? *[Select One]* ☐ Yes ☐ No

If you answer "Yes" to (d), provide the name(s), address(es), and relationship(s) to the Proposed Ward (if any) of the Trustee; indicate the nature of the Ward's interest in the Trust, whether the Trustee(s) is/are willing to act under said appointment, and attach the document as an exhibit to this Petition:

(e) Was any other document created which gave another individual authority to act on the Proposed Ward's behalf either by the Proposed Ward or someone else? *[Select One]* ☐ Yes ☐ No

If you answer "Yes" to (e), provide the name(s), address(es), and relationship(s) to the Proposed Ward, if any, indicate the nature of his/her/their interest, whether he/she/they are willing to act under said appointment, and attach the document as an exhibit to this Petition:

(f) Does another person have the authority to act on behalf of the Proposed Ward? *[Select One]* ☐ Yes ☐ No

If you answer "Yes" to (f), provide the name(s), address(es), and relationship(s) to the Proposed Ward, if any, indicate the nature of his/her/their interest, whether he/she/they are willing to act under said appointment, and attach the document as an exhibit to this Petition:

8.

Does anyone named above, or the proposed guardian(s)/conservator(s) have a financial conflict of interest with the Proposed Ward? *[Select One]* ☐ Yes ☐ No

[Note: A conflict of interest may exist if the proposed conservator is co-owner of real property or a joint account with the Proposed Ward.]

If you answer "Yes," list the nature of the conflict of interest:

9.

(a) On behalf of the Proposed Ward, a Petition for Emergency Guardianship and/or Conservatorship was filed. *[Select One]* ☐ Yes ☐ No

If you answer "Yes" to (a), provide the filing date of the Petition for Emergency Guardianship and/or Conservatorship and the name of the County and State in which it was filed:

____

(b) On behalf of the Proposed Ward, an Emergency Guardianship and/or Conservatorship was created. *[Select One]* ☐ Yes ☐ No

If you answer "Yes" to (b), list the full name and address of the person(s) appointed as Emergency Guardian(s) and/or Conservator(s):

Emergency Guardian(s): ______________________________,
(Full name) First Middle Last

____
Street City County State Zip Code

Emergency Conservator(s): ______________________________,
(Full name) First Middle Last

____
Street City County State Zip Code

(c) On behalf of the Proposed Ward, a Petition for Permanent Guardianship and/or Conservatorship was filed. *[Select One]* ☐ Yes ☐ No

If you answer "Yes" to (c), provide the filing date of the Petition for Guardianship and/or Conservatorship and the name of the County and State in which it was filed:

(d) On behalf of the Proposed Ward, a Petition for Permanent Guardianship and/or Conservatorship was created. *[Select One]* ☐ Yes ☐ No

If you answer "Yes" to (d), list the full name and address of the person(s) appointed as Guardian(s) and/or Conservator(s):

Guardian(s): ____,
(Full name) *First* *Middle* *Last*

____
Street *City* *County* *State* *Zip Code*

Conservator(s): ____,
(Full name) *First* *Middle* *Last*

____
Street *City* *County* *State* *Zip Code*

(e) On behalf of the Proposed Ward, a Petition for Permanent Guardianship and/or Conservatorship was denied. *[Select One]* ☐ Yes ☐ No

If you answer "Yes" to (e), provide the reason the Petition for Guardianship and/or Conservatorship was denied and whether any change of circumstances has occurred with the Proposed Ward:

10.

ASSETS, INCOME, OTHER SOURCES OF FUNDS, LIABILITIES, AND EXPENSES OF PROPOSED WARD

REAL PROPERTY

[Indicate if property is jointly owned and, if so, with whom]

	Description	County	State	Joint Owner, if any	**Approximate Equity:**
Parcel 1:					$
Parcel 2:					$
Parcel 3:					$

INCOME FROM ALL SOURCES

Yearly Total:

Social Security per year:	$
SSI *[Supplemental Security Income]* per year:	$
Retirement benefits per year:	$
VA benefits per year:	$
Other income per year (e.g., alimony, annuity, or trust distributions):	$
Interest, dividend, or investment income:	$
Yearly Total of All Income:	$ 0.00

PERSONAL AND INTANGIBLE PROPERTY

[Indicate if property is jointly owned and, if so, with whom]

(1) Checking/Savings/Money Market/Certificates of Deposit/ Liquid Accounts:

Bank/Financial Institution/Broker	Account Number	Joint Owner, if any	
			$
			$
			$
			$

(2) Stocks/Bonds/Investments (including retirement and profit-sharing accounts):

(a) Held by Brokers:

Brokerage Firm/Institution	Account Number	Joint Owner, if any	
			$
			$
			$
			$

(b) Privately Held:

Company/Issuer Number of Shares Joint Owner, if any

____ $____________
____ $____________

(3) Automobiles

Year/Make/Model V.I.N. Joint Owner, if any

____ $____________
____ $____________

(4) Other assets of significant value:

Description Joint Owner, if any

____ $____________
____ $____________

Total Value of Personal and Intangible Property: $ 0.00

DEBTS AND OTHER LIABILITIES

PERSONAL AND INTANGIBLE PROPERTY

The Proposed Ward has the following debts and/or liabilities: **Approximate Balance:**

(1) Secured Debts

Obligor/Payee Collateral Joint Owner, if any

____ $____________
____ $____________
____ $____________

(2) Unsecured Debts

Obligor/Payee Account Number Joint Owner, if any

____ $____________
____ $____________
____ $____________

Total Debts and Other Liabilities of Proposed Ward: $ 0.00

AVERAGE MONTHLY LIABILITIES AND EXPENSES

<u>Household</u>:
Care Facility/Rent/Mortgage Payments: $____________
Property Taxes/Insurance: $____________
Utilities/Lawn Care/Pest Control: $____________
Miscellaneous Household Food: $____________
Total Credit Account and Other Debt Payments: $____________
Other *[specify]* ________________________: $____________

Automotive/Transportation:

Fuel and Repairs:	$______
Tags, License Fees, Insurance:	$______
Bus/Train/Taxi Fares:	$______

Minors or Other Dependents of Proposed Ward:

Childcare:	$______
School Tuition/Supplies/Expenses/Lunches:	$______
Clothing/Diapers/Grooming/Hygiene:	$______
Medical/Dental/Prescription:	$______

Other Insurance:

Health:	$______
Life/Disability:	$______
Other *[specify]* ____________:	$______

Proposed Ward's Other Expenses:

Laundry/Clothing/Grooming/Hygiene:	$______
Medical/Dental/Prescriptions/Medications:	$______
Entertainment/Vacations/Subscriptions/Dues:	$______
Personal Caretakers/Cleaning Personnel:	$______
Total Expenses:	$ 0.00

PAYMENTS TO CREDITORS

Is the Proposed Ward behind on any debt payments? *[Select One]* ☐ Yes ☐ No

If so, payee and amount: ____________ $______

SUMMARY

(1) Average Monthly Income: $______

(2) Average Monthly Expenses: $ 0.00

11.

A guardian ad litem should be appointed because the following additional powers pursuant to O.C.G.A. §§ 29-4-23 (b) and/or 29-5-23 (b) and (c) are requested, with the reasons for seeking such powers:

12.

Was the Proposed Ward physically present in another state at least six (6) consecutive months during the year preceding the filing of this Petition? *[Select One]* ☐ Yes ☐ No

If you answer "Yes," list below the address, county, and state in which the Proposed Ward resided during the preceding year.

____;
Street *City* *County* *State* *Zip Code*

Did the Proposed Ward live alone? *[Select One]* ☐ Yes ☐ No

If you answer "No," list below the name(s) and address(es) of those individuals with whom the ward resided.

____,
(Full name) *First* *Middle* *Last*

____;
Street *City* *County* *State* *Zip Code*

____,
(Full name) *First* *Middle* *Last*

____;
Street *City* *County* *State* *Zip Code*

If you answer "Yes," list the names and addresses of the friends or family members living in that area. List the two individuals in the closest degree of kinship to the Proposed Ward who live in that area, not previously listed. Include the individuals' full names and complete addresses:

____,
(Full name) *First* *Middle* *Last*

____;
Street *City* *County* *State* *Zip Code*

____,
(Full name) *First* *Middle* *Last*

____;
Street *City* *County* *State* *Zip Code*

13.

This Court has jurisdiction to hear this action under Georgia law, and particularly under Chapters 4, 5, and 11 of Title 29 because:

14.

Additional Data: *[Where full particulars are lacking, state here the reasons for any such omission.]*

15.

It is in the best interest of the Proposed Ward that the within nominated guardian and/or conservator be appointed.

WHEREFORE, Petitioner(s) pray(s):

1. that service be perfected as required by law;
2. that the Court appoint legal counsel and an evaluator for the Proposed Ward and order an evaluation as required by law;
3. that upon receipt of the evaluation report, the Court order a hearing to determine the need for a guardian and/or conservator for the Proposed Ward; and
4. that a guardian and/or conservator be appointed for the Proposed Ward.

______________________ Signature of First Petitioner	______________________ Signature of Second Petitioner, if any
______________________ Printed Name	______________________ Printed Name
______________________ ______________________ Mailing Address	______________________ ______________________ Mailing Address
______________________ Telephone Number	______________________ Telephone Number

Signature of Attorney: ______________________

Printed name of Attorney: ______________________

Address: ______________________

____

Telephone Number: ______________________ State Bar # ______________

VERIFICATION

GEORGIA, ________________________ COUNTY

Personally appeared before me the undersigned Petitioner(s) who, after being duly sworn, state(s) that the facts set forth in the foregoing Petition for the Appointment of a Guardian and/or Conservator for a Proposed Ward (and the attached Exhibit(s)) are true and correct.

Sworn to and subscribed before me this
_____ day of ______________, 20___.

____
Signature of First Petitioner

____
NOTARY/CLERK OF PROBATE COURT
My Commission Expires ____________

____
Printed Name of First Petitioner

Sworn to and subscribed before me this
_____ day of ______________, 20___.

____
Signature of Second Petitioner

____
NOTARY/CLERK OF PROBATE COURT
My Commission Expires ____________

____
Printed Name of Second Petitioner

Source: https://www.fultonprobatega.org/207/Guardianship-Conservatorship-of-an-Adult

Key Terms

conservatorship
guardian ad litem
guardianship
incapacitated adult
letters of conservatorship
letters of guardianship
proposed ward
ward

Review Questions

1. What is the difference between guardianship and conservatorship for minors versus adults?
2. When may it be necessary for an adult to have a guardian or conservator?
3. What are the prerequisites for the appointment of a guardian for an adult in Georgia?
4. Are the prerequisites the same for the appointment of a conservator for an adult in Georgia? If not, how do they differ?
5. Who may serve as a guardian? A conservator?
6. What is the court's order of preference when appointing a guardian? A conservator?
7. How long will a guardianship or conservatorship last?
8. What is the purpose of an emergency guardianship?
9. Can guardianships and conservatorships be modified? If so, when and how?
10. When is the termination of a guardianship or conservatorship warranted? Who may request termination?

Practical Assignment

Conduct some research in Georgia case law and locate a case involving a guardian or conservator who has breached his or her duty. Brief the case and provide the following information in your case brief.

1. Case name and citation: The name of the case and where the case can be found
2. Facts: A summary of what happened in the case
3. Procedural history: What happened when the case was brought to trial and appealed
4. Issue: The question the court is asked to answer
5. Rule: The rule of law that the court applies to the case
6. Holding: The court's decision on the issue
7. Reasoning: The process the court used to reach its decision

Chapter 11

Personal Representatives

Learning Objectives

Upon completion of this chapter, you should be able to:

- Explain the need for a personal representative.
- Name and describe the duties of each type of personal representative.
- Discuss the forms and procedure for appointing a personal representative.
- Determine how a personal representative is compensated.
- Identify the circumstances that call for the resignation or removal of a personal representative.

O.C.G.A. § 53-1-2(12) indicates that "personal representative" is a generic umbrella term used to refer to "any administrator, administrator with the will annexed, county administrator, or executor." In previous chapters, we have discussed the testator's nomination of personal representatives in the will and the role of an executor. In this chapter, we will reiterate this information concerning executors for comparison. Moreover, we will explore the various types of administrators and their respective roles in settling a decedent's estate. Finally, we will discuss compensation, resignation, and removal of personal representatives.

Executors

To begin, O.C.G.A. § 53-6-2 makes reference to an **executor de son tort**, which is someone acting as a personal representative of the decedent without having the requisite authority to do so. In other words, the decedent did not nominate an executor in his or her will, or the person(s) named failed to qualify, and the court has yet to appoint an administrator. So, this individual stepped in and started to settle the decedent's unrepresented estate without first obtaining court permission. For example, suppose George dies intestate, and his eldest daughter, Louise, immediately starts taking his property for herself and her children. In this case, Louise would be considered an executor de son tort, since she did not have the proper authority to act as the administrator of her father's estate. Per the above-referenced statute, the executor de son tort (in this case, Louise) will be doubly liable to creditors and heirs or beneficiaries for such wrongful intermeddling or conversion.

What is permissible, according to O.C.G.A. § 53-6-10, is for a testator to nominate a personal representative in his or her will. This personal representative nominated in a will is more specifically referred to as the executor. An executor must carry out the testator's wishes under the will and settle the testator's estate. As you will learn in Chapter 12, handling the estate will involve several tasks, including, but not limited to: petitioning to have the will admitted to probate; locating the decedent's property; paying off creditors; filing final income and estate tax returns; and distributing any remaining property from the estate to beneficiaries under the will.

However, to serve as an executor, the nominee must first qualify to serve in this capacity. Under Georgia law, this means that the nominee must accept the nomination and petition the court to probate the will and to issue **letters testamentary**. Letters testamentary represent written proof of the executor's authority to act on behalf of the decedent. To qualify, the nominee must not be (1) adjudged **unfit**, that is, incapable of carrying out the duties associated with the role, or (2) under the age of majority, which is 18 in the State of Georgia. If the nominee meets these criteria, then the executor will receive letters testamentary. If the nominee fails to meet these criteria, then a successor executor named in the will may qualify. If the successor(s) fail(s) to qualify, then the estate will be deemed unrepresented and the probate court will need to appoint an administrator for the estate.

The Council of Probate Court Judges of Georgia has included standard forms of all necessary probate documents on its website: www.gaprobate.gov. You will find the form of petition to probate a will included next as Exhibit 11.1. Thereafter, in Exhibit 11.2, you will find a form of the letters testamentary which will be issued if the court grants the nominated executor the authority to act.

Administrators

As we discussed previously, when someone dies intestate or dies testate, but the estate is unrepresented, then the court must appoint a personal representative. An individual appointed by the court in this regard is more specifically referred to as an administrator. According to O.C.G.A. § 53-6-30, in the event there is a need to act expeditiously to protect the best interests of the estate, the court will appoint a **temporary administrator**, who will administer and preserve the estate until a permanent replacement is appointed.

O.C.G.A. § 53-6-20 states that for an intestate estate, the normal procedure to appoint an administrator is for the heirs of the decedent to unanimously select someone, or for the court to appoint an administrator when no unanimous selection is made. The court will appoint the individual to serve in the following order of preference:

Exhibit 11.1 Petition to Probate Will

IN THE PROBATE COURT OF ______________________COUNTY
STATE OF GEORGIA

IN RE: ESTATE OF	)	
	)	
______________________________,	)	**ESTATE NO. ___________**
DECEASED	)	

PETITION TO PROBATE WILL IN COMMON FORM

The petition of ____
[Full name(s) of petitioner(s)] First Middle Last

whose physical address(es) is/are ____
Street City County State Zip Code

and mailing address(es) is/are ____
Street City County State Zip Code

shows the Court the following:

1.

____
[Full name of decedent] First Middle Last

whose place of domicile was ____
Street City County State Zip Code

departed this life on _____________, 20___.

2.

While alive, decedent duly made and published a last will and testament dated ____, (along with codicil(s) dated ____), which is herewith offered for probate in common form as the decedent□s □will.□___________________________ is/are named as executor(s).

3.

Listed below are all of decedent□s heirs, the age or majority status, address, and relationship to the decedent set opposite the name of each:

Name	*Age (or over 18)*	*Address*	*Relationship*

4.

Required: *[Provide sufficient factual information to enable the Court to conclude that all of the heirs of the decedent are included and that there are no heirs of similar or closer degree according to O.C.G.A. □53-2-1. Provide the names of any deceased heirs, the name and address of his or her personal representative, if any, and include the date of death for each. [See instructions for further clarification.] Also, state here all pertinent facts that may govern the method of giving notice to any person and that may determine whether a guardian ad litem should be appointed for any person. If any heirs listed above are cousins, grandchildren, nephews, or nieces of the decedent, indicate the deceased ancestor through whom they are related to the decedent. If any executor nominated in the will has a priority equal to or higher than the propounder but will not qualify, indicate the name and reasons.]*

5.

[Initial one]

________ (a) To the knowledge of the petitioner(s), no other proceedings with respect to this estate are pending, or have been completed, in any other probate court in this State or any other state.

________ (b) The probate of another purported will of the decedent is pending in the State of ______________________________, in the __________________________ County ________________________ Court. The name(s) and address(es) of the propounder(s) and the names, addresses and ages or majority status of the beneficiaries under the other purported will to whom notice is required under O.C.G.A. □53-5-22 (b) are listed on the attachment hereto, as □Exhibit ____,□which is expressly made a part hereof, as if fully set forth herein.

________ (c) An administration is pending in the State of ____________________________, in the _________________________ County _______________________ Court. The name and address of each petitioner, and the name and address of any appointed administrator is listed on the attachment hereto, as □Exhibit ____,□which is expressly made a part hereof, as if fully set forth herein.

6.

[Initial all that apply; however, please note that this form may not be appropriate if the Petitioner(s) is/are seeking the appointment of a testamentary guardian, which requires notice to the relatives of the decedent□s minor child(ren) pursuant to O.C.G.A. □29-2-4.]

At the time of the decedent□s death, and at this time, the decedent left (a) minor child(ren) and the will names a testamentary conservator.

________ (a) The will names a testamentary conservator of (a) minor child(ren) of the decedent. At the time of the decedent□s death, he/she had (a) minor child(ren) and there is/are no court-appointed conservator(s); the following individual(s) is/are named as testamentary conservator(s) in the decedent□s will:

Name Address

____

____

________ (b) The will names a testamentary conservator of (a) minor child(ren) of the decedent. At the time of the decedent□s death, he/she had (a) minor child(ren) and there is/are a court-appointed conservator(s), who is/are identified as follows: *[If named testamentary conservator(s) and court-appointed conservator(s) are different.]*

Name Address

____

____

Additional Data: *[Where full particulars are lacking, state here the reason for any such omission.]*

WHEREFORE, petitioner(s) pray(s):
1. Leave to prove said will (and codicil(s)) in common form;
2. That due and legal notice be given as required by the Court;
3. That said will be admitted to record on proper proof;
4. That letters of testamentary conservatorship issue, if applicable;
5. That letters testamentary issue; and
6. That this Court order such other relief as may be proper under the circumstances.

____
Signature of Petitioner

____
Printed Name

____

____
Mailing Address

____
Telephone Number

Signature of Attorney: ____

Printed Name of Attorney: ____

Address: ____

____

____

Telephone Number: ________________ State Bar #______________________

VERIFICATION

GEORGIA, _________________ COUNTY

Personally appeared before me the undersigned petitioner(s) who, after being duly sworn, state(s) that the facts set forth in the foregoing Petition to Probate Will in Common Form (and the attached exhibit(s)) are true and correct.

Sworn to and subscribed before me this

______ day of ________________, 20_____

____
Signature of Petitioner

____
NOTARY/CLERK OF PROBATE COURT

My Commission Expires: ______________

____
Printed Name of Petitioner

Source: https://gaprobate.gov/standard-forms/

Exhibit 11.2 Letters Testamentary

IN THE PROBATE COURT OF _______________COUNTY
STATE OF GEORGIA

IN RE: ESTATE OF	)	
	)	
_____________________________,	)	**ESTATE NO. ____________**
DECEASED	)	

LETTERS TESTAMENTARY

[Relieved of Filing Returns]

At a regular term of the probate court, the last will and testament dated ___________________________ (and codicil(s) dated ___________________________), of the above-named decedent, who was domiciled in this county at the time of his or her death or who was domiciled in another state but owned property in this county at the time of his or her death, was legally proven in common form to be the decedent□s will and was admitted to record by order, and it was further ordered that _________________________, named as executor(s) in said will, be allowed to qualify, and that upon so doing, letters testamentary be issued to such executor(s).

THEREFORE, the executor(s), having taken the oath of office and complied with all the necessary prerequisites of the law, is/are legally authorized to discharge all the duties and exercise all the powers of executor(s) under the will of said decedent, according to the Decedent□s Will and the law.

Given under my hand and official seal, the _____ day of __________________, 20____.

____
Judge of the Probate Court

The following must be signed if the judge does not sign the original of this document:

Issued by: *[Seal]*

____
Clerk of the Probate Court

GPCSF 4 Eff. July 2021

Source: https://gaprobate.gov/standard-forms/

(1) The surviving spouse, unless an action for divorce or separate maintenance was pending between the deceased intestate and the surviving spouse at the time of death;

(2) One or more other heirs of the intestate or the person selected by the majority in interest of them;

(3) Any other eligible person;

(4) Any creditor of the estate; or

(5) The county administrator.

Note that the Code also provides for what will happen in the event an heir is not **sui juris**, meaning having full legal rights and not under the power or guardianship of another person. In such a case, his or her legal guardian may consent to the nomination of an administrator. For example, if one of the heirs is a minor, then his or her legal guardian will have to participate in the nomination process on the minor's behalf.

In any event, whether the administrator is selected unanimously by the heirs or appointed by the court, the individual named will receive **letters of administration**. These letters will serve as evidence of his or her appointment and authority to act on behalf of the estate.

Additionally, as stated earlier, an administrator may be needed even when a decedent is testate. O.C.G.A. § 53-6-13 indicates instances when this may be necessary:

(1) No executor is nominated in the will;

(2) The nominated executor has not reached the age of majority, to serve until the disability ceases;

(3) The executor dies, resigns, or otherwise becomes disqualified to serve; or

(4) A testate estate is unrepresented for any other reason.

In these cases, the court will appoint an **administrator with the will annexed**, meaning the court is appointing a personal representative and the decedent's will is present. According to O.C.G.A. § 53-1-2(2), an administrator with the will annexed is "any person, other than an executor, appointed and qualified to administer a testate estate, including a testate estate already partially administered and from any cause unrepresented." This administrator with the will annexed may be unanimously selected by the beneficiaries per O.C.G.A. § 53-6-14(b) or nominated by the court in the order of preference outlined in O.C.G.A. § 53-6-20 above. Upon qualification, the appointee will receive **letters of administration with the will annexed**, as evidence of his or her authority to act on behalf of the estate.

This brings us to the final category of administrator mentioned in O.C.G.A. § 53-1-2(12): the **county administrator**. We referred to the county administrator earlier in the list of possible court appointees from O.C.G.A. § 53-6-20. This is the last person in the order of priority for those the court may appoint in the event a decedent is intestate or a testate estate is unrepresented. If no one of a higher priority comes forward to serve as administrator, a public official, the county administrator, will be appointed to administer the decedent's estate. Upon qualification, this appointee will receive letters of administration as evidence of his or her authority.

You will find a form of the petition for letters of administration included as Exhibit 11.3. Following immediately thereafter, in Exhibit 11.4, you will find a form of the letters of administration which will be issued if the court grants the authority to an administrator to act on behalf of a decedent.

Compensation

Under O.C.G.A. § 53-6-60(a), a personal representative may be compensated for the many duties he or she performs on behalf of the estate. The nature of such compensation may be outlined in: (1) the decedent's will; (2) a contract entered into between the personal representative and the decedent before the decedent's death; or (3) a contract signed by all the beneficiaries of a testate estate or all the heirs of an intestate estate and the personal representative. In the absence of such written documents, the personal representative is entitled to compensation following the fee schedule set forth in O.C.G.A. § 53-6-60(b) and included in Appendix A for your review.

According to O.C.G.A. § 53-6-61, in addition to compensation, "Personal representatives shall be allowed reasonable expenses incurred in the administration of the estate, including without limitation expenses for travel, the expenses and premiums incurred in securing a bond, and the expenses of counsel and other agents." In other words, if necessary, a personal representative may hire attorneys, investigators, accountants, tax professionals, and others who may assist in settling the decedent's estate. Such costs will be covered by the estate.

Resignation and Removal

A personal representative who has completed all tasks and settled the estate may resign after getting the court's approval, as you will learn in the next chapter. Additionally, a personal representative who has not yet settled a decedent's estate, but no longer wants to serve in this capacity, may voluntarily petition the court to resign from his or her position and for a successor to be appointed. Per O.C.G.A. § 53-7-56(a)(3), the court will likely grant such a petition if the personal representative can demonstrate satisfactorily that:

(1) The personal representative is unable to continue serving due to age, illness, infirmity, or other good cause;

(2) Greater burdens have developed upon the office of personal representative than those that were contemplated or should have been contemplated when the personal representative was qualified and the additional burdens would work a hardship upon the personal representative;

(3) Disagreement exists between one or more of the beneficiaries or heirs and the personal representative in respect to the personal representative's man-

agement of the estate, which disagreement and conflict appear deleterious to the estate;

(4) The resignation of the personal representative will result in or permit substantial financial benefit to the estate;

(5) The resigning personal representative is one of two or more acting personal representatives and the other personal representatives will continue in office with no adversity to the estate contemplated; or

(6) The resignation would not be disadvantageous to the estate.

Generally, it is difficult to remove a personal representative from office. However, if the beneficiaries or heirs can demonstrate that the representative has breached or is threatening to breach his or her fiduciary duties, removal is a possibility. A breach of duty may include mismanagement of estate funds, conflicts of interest, failure to perform required tasks, and so forth. According to O.C.G.A. § 53-7-54(a), a beneficiary or heir may bring a cause of action for the above-referenced breaches and seek the following as possible remedies:

(1) To recover damages;

(2) To compel the performance of the personal representative's or temporary administrator's duties;

(3) To enjoin the commission of a breach of fiduciary duty;

(4) To compel the redress of a breach of fiduciary duty by payment of money or otherwise;

(5) To appoint another personal representative or temporary administrator to take possession of the estate property and administer the estate;

(6) To remove the personal representative or temporary administrator; and

(7) To reduce or deny compensation to the personal representative or temporary administrator.

An excellent example of an executor's breach of his fiduciary duty and the remedies available can be found in *In re: Estate of Arnsdorff*, 273 Ga. App. 612 (2005). A copy of that opinion follows as Exhibit 11.5. In that case, the Georgia Court of Appeals affirmed the probate court's decision removing Fred Clark as an executor of John Arnsdorff Jr.'s estate and ordering Clark to forfeit $79,000 in commissions and fees received and costs incurred as executor and attorney for the estate. The Court held that Clark "demonstrated a general pattern of inattention to his basic duties as executor." *Id.* at 615. The Court reasoned that (1) the record showed that the attorney filed a purported estate accounting six inches thick, which was prepared by the staff and with which the attorney showed little familiarity; (2) the attorney delayed a distribution to St. Paul's Evangelical Church (the beneficiary who brought the removal action) by trying to force the church to create a trust, which was not required by the decedent's will; (3) the attorney filed an erroneous tax return that had to be amended as well as took a deduction the attorney knew was improper; and (4) the attorney incurred unnecessary expenses and fees by showing the decedent's house when the will did not require the sale of the house.

Finally, Exhibit 11.6, which follows, is a form of petition for discharge of a personal representative and Exhibit 11.7 is a sample order for discharge that a judge may sign in response to such a petition.

Exhibit 11.3 Petition for Letters of Administration

IN THE PROBATE COURT OF ____________________ COUNTY
STATE OF GEORGIA

IN RE: ESTATE OF)
)
_______________________________,) **ESTATE NO.** ___________
DECEASED)

PETITION FOR LETTERS OF ADMINISTRATION

The petition of ____
[Full name(s) of petitioner(s)] First Middle Last
whose physical address(es) is/are ____,
Street City County State Zip Code
and mailing address(es) is/are ____,
Street City County State Zip Code
shows to the Court the following:

1.

____,
[Full name of decedent] First Middle Last

whose place of domicile was ____,
Street City County State Zip Code
departed this life on ____________________, 20____, intestate.

2.

The Decedent died intestate *[i.e., without making a valid last will and testament]*.

3.

Listed below are all of the decedent□s heirs at law, with age or majority status, address, and relationship to the decedent set opposite the name of each:

Name *Age (or over 18)* *Address* *Relationship*
____
____
____
____
____
____
____
____

4.

Required: *[Provide sufficient factual information to enable the Court to conclude that all of the heirs of the decedent are included and that there are no heirs of the same or closer degree according to O.C.G.A. § 53-2-1. Provide the names of any deceased heirs, the name and address of his or her personal representative, if any, and include the date of death for each (see instructions for further clarification). Also, state here all pertinent facts that may govern the method of giving notice to any person and that may determine whether or not a guardian ad litem should be appointed for any person. If any heirs listed above are cousins, grandchildren, nephews or nieces of the decedent, indicate the deceased ancestor through whom they are related to the decedent.]*

5.

Under the law, it is necessary that said estate be administered and ____ should be appointed administrator(s) by reason of:

[Initial one]

______ (a) being unanimously selected by all the heirs *[This alternative does not apply if the surviving spouse is the sole heir and an action for divorce or separate maintenance was pending at the time of decedent's death.]*;

______ (b) being the surviving spouse where no action for divorce or separate maintenance was pending at the time of decedent's death;

______ (c) being (an) heir(s) and not the surviving spouse;

______ (d) having been selected by a majority in interest of the heirs;

______ (e) being (an) eligible person(s) as defined by O.C.G.A. § 53-6-1;

______ (f) being (a) creditor(s) of the decedent (evidence of the indebtedness is attached);

______ (g) being the county administrator.

6.

To the knowledge of the petitioner(s), no other proceedings with respect to this estate are pending, or have been completed, in any other probate court in this or any other state.

7.

The decedent passed leaving an estate of real property located in ___________________ _______________ County(ies), Georgia *[List real property that is located in another state and/or country]* having a total fair market value of approximately $ _________________.

The decedent passed leaving personal property as follows *[Provide approximate value]*:

☐	(a) Cash/bank accounts/certificates of deposit:	$ _______________
☐	(b) Stocks/bonds/brokerage accounts:	$ _______________
☐	(c) Other assets of significant value *[List assets]*:	$ _______________
	_____________________________	
	_____________________________	

APPROXIMATE TOTAL VALUE OF PERSONAL PROPERTY $ 0.00

8.

[Petitioner(s) MUST initial one]

_______ (a) All heirs have consented to the waiver of bond, waiver of reports, waiver of statements, and/or grant of certain powers contained in O.C.G.A. § 53-12-261 to the administrator(s). Therefore, the petitioner(s) hereby move(s) the Court to publish notice of the filing of the petition and tender(s) with this petition publication fees. ***[This only applies if all heirs have properly selected, acknowledged, and consented to this option.]***

_______ (b) The identities and/or addresses of all heirs are not known. Therefore, the petitioner(s) hereby move(s) the Court to publish notice of the filing of the petition, and tender(s) with this petition publication fees.

_______ (c) Notice of this petition need not be published because the petitioner(s) has/have listed all heirs at law and their addresses, and petitioner(s) is/are not requesting a waiver of bond, waiver of reports, waiver of statements, or the grant of powers contained in O.C.G.A. § 53-12-261.

9.

Additional data: *[Where full particulars are lacking, state here the reasons for any such omission.]*

WHEREFORE, petitioner(s) pray(s):

1. Service be perfected; and
2. that if no good cause is shown to the contrary, ________________________________
be appointed administrator(s) of the estate of said decedent.

____
Signature of Petitioner

____
Printed Name

____

____
Mailing Address

____
Telephone Number

Signature of Attorney: ________________________________

Printed Name of Attorney: ________________________________

Address: ________________________________

____

Telephone Number: ________________ State Bar #________________

VERIFICATION

GEORGIA, _________________ COUNTY

Personally appeared before me the undersigned petitioner(s) who, after being duly sworn, state(s) that the facts set forth in the foregoing petition for letters of administration (and the attached exhibit(s)) are true and correct.

Sworn to and subscribed before me this
______ day of ______________, 20_____

____
Signature of Petitioner

____
NOTARY/CLERK OF PROBATE COURT

____
Printed Name of Petitioner

My Commission Expires: _______________

Source: https://gaprobate.gov/standard-forms/

Exhibit 11.4 Letters of Administration

IN THE PROBATE COURT OF ____________________ COUNTY
STATE OF GEORGIA

IN RE: ESTATE OF	)	
	)	
______________________________,	)	**ESTATE NO.** __________
DECEASED	)	

LETTERS OF ADMINISTRATION
[Bond waived and/or certain powers granted]

At a regular term of probate court, this Court granted an order allowing ________________________________ to qualify as administrator(s) of the above-named decedent, who was domiciled in this county at the time of his or her death or was domiciled in another state but owned property in this county at the time of his or her death, and that upon so doing, letters of administration be issued to such personal representative(s).

THEREFORE, the said administrator(s), having taken the oath of office and complied with all necessary prerequisites of the law, is/are legally authorized to discharge all the duties and exercise all powers of personal representative(s), according to Georgia law. In addition this Court:

[Initial all that apply]

______ (a) ***POWERS GRANTED*****:** Grants to the administrator(s) all of the powers contained in O.C.G.A. § 53-12-261, except the administrator(s) shall not be authorized to bind the estate by any warranty in any conveyance or contract in violation of O.C.G.A. § 53-8-14 (a).

______ (b) ***REPORTS WAIVED*****:** Grants to the administrator(s) the specific power to serve without making and filing inventory, and without filing any annual or other returns or reports to any court.

______ (c) ***BOND WAIVED*****:** Waives the specific requirement to post bond.

______ (d) ***STATEMENTS WAIVED*****:** Grants to the administrator(s) the specific power to serve without furnishing to the heirs statements of receipts and disbursements.

IN TESTIMONY WHEREOF, I have hereunto affixed my signature as judge of the probate court of said county and the seal of this office this ____ day of ____________, 20____.

____
Judge of the Probate Court

The following must be signed if the judge does not sign the original of this document:

Issued by: *[Seal]*

____
Clerk of the Probate Court

GPCSF 3 Eff. July 2021

Source: https://gaprobate.gov/standard-forms/

Exhibit 11.5 In re Estate of Arnsdorff

In re Estate of Arnsdorff, 615 S.E.2d 758, 273 Ga.App. 612 (Ga. App. 2005)

273 Ga. App. 612
615 S.E.2d 758
In re ESTATE OF ARNSDORFF.
No. A05A0049.
Court of Appeals of Georgia.
May 9, 2005.
Reconsideration Denied June 13, 2005.

Page 759

Thomas J. Mahoney, Jr., Ranitz, Mahoney & Mahoney, Savannah, for appellant.

J. Hamrick Gnann, Jr., Gannam & Gnann, Tracy A. O'Connell, Ellis, Painter, Ratterree & Adams, L.L.P., Savannah, for appellee.

RUFFIN, Chief Judge.

St. Paul's Evangelical Lutheran Church ("St. Paul's") filed a Petition to Remove Executor, seeking to remove Fred S. Clark ("Clark") as executor of the estate of John Daniel Arnsdorff, Jr. (the "Estate") and to deny him compensation. After a hearing, the probate court granted St. Paul's petition and ordered Clark to forfeit over 79,000 in commissions and fees he had received and costs he had incurred as executor and attorney for the Estate. Clark appeals, arguing that the trial court erred in removing him and that it lacked authority to order repayment. For the following reasons, we affirm.

Clark was appointed executor of the Estate on September 27, 1999. Over a year later, St. Paul's, which is a beneficiary under Arnsdorff's will, petitioned the probate court to order Clark to provide **[273 Ga. App. 613]** an accounting of the Estate's assets. The trial court held a hearing on the petition and issued an order requiring Clark to:

> file in this Court a Final Accounting of all receipts and disbursements of said estate, together with supporting vouchers [or] receipts and disbursements, within 30 days of the date of this order. Said accounting shall be in a format compatible with the official form used by this Court for accountings.

In response, Clark filed a stack of documents which he characterized as an "accounting."[1] St. Paul's then filed a petition to remove Clark as executor. Both parties presented evidence and testimony at a hearing on the petition. Subsequently, the trial court issued findings of fact and conclusions of law in an order dated June 26, 2003, from which Clark appeals.

In re Estate of Arnsdorff, 615 S.E.2d 758, 273 Ga.App. 612 (Ga. App. 2005)

1. Initially, we address Clark's contention that the trial court erred in dismissing him as executor of the Estate. In reviewing a probate court's order removing an executor, we apply an abuse of discretion standard.[2] A probate court has discretion to remove an executor

[u]pon the petition of any person having an interest in the estate or whenever it appears to the probate court that good cause may exist to revoke the letters of a personal representative or impose other sanctions....[3]

Thus, "the relevant question in reviewing a removal order is whether the trial court had grounds to conclude that there was `good cause' for the removal."[4] We will not set aside the trial court's findings of fact unless the findings are clearly erroneous.[5]

Here the record supports the trial court's finding that the "accounting" Clark was charged with providing was actually prepared

Page 760

by Clark's office staff. Clark only briefly reviewed the six inches of documents gathered by those staff members. The "accounting" was not in a format compatible with the official form used by the probate **[273 Ga. App. 614]** court for accountings, as directed by the Court's order. The accounts and entries therein were not reconciled and contained errors in excess of 267,000. Two certified public accountants testified that the "accounting" as submitted by Clark required hours of additional work on their part in order to understand the financial condition of the Estate.

The record also showed that Clark filed an erroneous tax return on behalf of the Estate, which had to be amended, and Clark himself testified that he took a tax deduction knowing it was improper when he took it. When the improper deduction was questioned by a representative of St. Paul's, Clark suggested that the remedy was to wait for the statute of limitation to run on contesting the return, and then to distribute the funds in question. Clark also filed the federal estate tax return late, without seeking an extension.

Under the circumstances, the testimony and evidence in the record clearly support the conclusion that there was good cause shown to remove Clark as executor.[6] Therefore, the trial court did not abuse its discretion in ordering Clark's removal.

2. Clark asserts that the trial court erred in finding that he did not properly disclose the conflict of interest created by Clark serving as drafter of the will, executor and attorney for the Estate. We need not reach this issue

In re Estate of Arnsdorff, 615 S.E.2d 758, 273 Ga.App. 612 (Ga. App. 2005)

because, as discussed above, the trial court had good cause to remove Clark as executor regardless of whether Clark made full disclosure of the conflict to his client.

3. Finally, Clark argues that the trial court erred in ordering him to forfeit commissions paid to him as executor. Specifically, Clark contends that the trial court lacked legal authority to order such forfeiture. We disagree.

Our analysis is governed by two principles of law. First, the trial court is authorized to deny compensation to an executor who breaches his fiduciary duty to the estate or its beneficiaries.[7] Second, an executor cannot be reimbursed for costs and expenses of litigation caused by his own misconduct.[8] Applying these two principles, it is clear that the trial court properly ordered Clark to forfeit the sums paid to him.

(a) An executor "is a fiduciary who, in addition to the specific duties imposed by law, is under a general duty to settle the estate as expeditiously and with as little sacrifice of value as is reasonable **[273 Ga. App. 615]** under all of the circumstances."[9] The Georgia Code further provides that:

[i]f a personal representative ... commits a breach of fiduciary duty ..., a beneficiary of a testate estate ... shall have a cause of action: (1) To recover damages; ... (6) To remove the personal representative ...; and (7) To reduce or deny compensation to the personal representative....[10]

The record shows that Clark, as executor, paid himself 69,782.50 in fees from the Estate. His services to the Estate included probating the will, arranging the funeral, compiling the assets, and arranging for their distribution. The record also reflects, however, that Clark caused unnecessary delay and expense to the Estate throughout his time as executor. He personally handled the sale of Mr. Arnsdorff's house, including showing it to prospective buyers, although the will did not require that the house be sold. The trial court was authorized to conclude that this unnecessary expenditure of time was detrimental to the value of the Estate and a breach of fiduciary duty.

Clark delayed distributing funds to St. Paul's because he wanted St. Paul's to create a trust in which to hold the funds; however,

Page 761

the will did not require such a trust, Clark had already distributed some funds without requiring a trust, and the trust which Clark drafted (at expense to the Estate) was not appropriate. Clark's only explanation for his

In re Estate of Arnsdorff, 615 S.E.2d 758, 273 Ga.App. 612 (Ga. App. 2005)

actions, which prevented settlement of the Estate and caused it additional expense, was that matters between St. Paul's and him had gotten "adversarial." The trial court was authorized to find Clark's behavior unreasonable and a breach of his fiduciary duty.

Clark also demonstrated a general pattern of inattention to his basic duties as executor. A tax return prepared by Clark had to be redone at additional expense to the Estate because of his mistakes. The accounting Clark provided was disorganized and contained mathematical errors, resulting in St. Paul's having to pay an accountant to do additional work to determine the condition of the Estate.

The record supports the trial court's finding that Clark's handling of the Estate was generally unsatisfactory and resulted in "an unreasonable prolongation of the administration of the estate and postponed final distribution without justifiable cause." Clearly, the trial court concluded that Clark's actions throughout his time as executor were in breach of his fiduciary duty and, thus, he was not **[273 Ga. App. 616]** entitled to compensation for any of his work.[11] Because Clark's numerous breaches of fiduciary duty pervaded his work as executor, the trial court was authorized to order that Clark forfeit commissions paid to him as executor.

(b) Moreover, Clark is not entitled to recover for his time or costs incurred in defending himself against the charges brought against him as executor. "[F]raud or misconduct on the part of an administrator giving rise to a suit against him by an heir would not authorize a charge against the estate for attorneys fees to defend the suit."[12] Much of the time for which Clark billed the Estate was spent defending himself against St. Paul's petition for an accounting and motion to remove him as executor. Indeed, more than half of Clark's fees were incurred after he was ordered to make the accounting in September 2001, although the Estate's assets were liquidated and either distributed or ready for distribution by that date, and Clark performed no further services to benefit the Estate. Clark also charged the Estate 9,564.75 for costs associated with opposing the petition for accounting. Because Clark's own misconduct caused the proceedings for an accounting and to remove him as executor, the trial court did not abuse its discretion in ordering Clark to repay all fees and expenses incurred in defending himself in these actions.[13]

Judgment affirmed.

JOHNSON, P.J., and BARNES, J., concur.

In re Estate of Arnsdorff, 615 S.E.2d 758, 273 Ga.App. 612 (Ga. App. 2005)

Notes:

1. According to the trial court's order, the stack of documents was "approximately 6 inches thick." The order also noted that the accounting, which had been prepared by persons other than Clark, was neither verified nor attested to by Clark as the executor. Clark testified that his review of the lengthy accounting was extremely brief.

2. See *In re Estate of Moriarty,* 262 Ga.App. 241, 242(2), 585 S.E.2d 182 (2003); *In re Estate of Dunn,* 236 Ga.App. 211, 214(3), 511 S.E.2d 575 (1999).

3. See OCGA § 53-7-55.

4. See *In re Estate of Davis,* 243 Ga.App. 58, 63(1), 532 S.E.2d 169 (2000).

5. See *Fowler v. Cox,* 264 Ga.App. 880, 882, 592 S.E.2d 510 (2003).

6. See id.

7. See OCGA § 53-7-54(a).

8. See *In re Estate of Garmon,* 254 Ga.App. 84, 87(2), 561 S.E.2d 216 (2002).

9. OCGA § 53-7-1(a).

10. OCGA § 53-7-54(a).

11. This case is distinguishable from *Bryan v. Granade,* 257 Ga. 219, 357 S.E.2d 92 (1987), in which the Supreme Court held that an attorney's misconduct as administrator of an estate would not bar him from recovering fees for services rendered in litigation prior to his becoming administrator. The court in *Bryan* found that the attorney's litigation work was "distinct and severable" from his later duties as administrator. Id. at 221, 357 S.E.2d 92. In contrast, all work for which Clark seeks compensation is related to his duties as executor.

12. *Chester v. Bouchillon,* 253 Ga. 175, 177(4), 317 S.E.2d 525 (1984).

13. See *Garmon,* supra at 87, 561 S.E.2d 216; *Ray v. Beneventi,* 229 Ga. 209, 213(3), 190 S.E.2d 514 (1972).

Exhibit 11.6 Petition for Discharge of Personal Representative

IN THE PROBATE COURT OF ________________________ COUNTY
STATE OF GEORGIA

IN RE: ESTATE OF)
)
______________________________,) **ESTATE NO. _______________**
DECEASED)

PETITION FOR DISCHARGE OF PERSONAL REPRESENTATIVE

The petition of ____, as (executor(s))(administrator(s))(temporary administrator(s)) of the above-referenced estate, shows:

1.

Petitioner(s)

[Initial one]:

______ (a) has/have fully administered the estate of the decedent.

______ (b) was/were allowed to resign without fully administering said estate.

______ (c) has/have completely discharged all duties as temporary administrator(s).

2.

Listed below are all of the heirs of the intestate decedent or beneficiaries of the testate decedent, or persons who succeeded to the interest of any heir or beneficiary who died after the decedent died:

Name	*Age (or over 18)*	*Address*	*Relationship*

[If discharge is sought solely from office and not from office and all liability, STRIKE paragraphs 3 and 4 below.]

3.

Required: *[If the decedent died intestate (without a will), make a definitive statement with sufficient factual information to enable the Court to conclude that all of the heirs of the decedent are included and that there are no heirs of similar or closer degree according to O.C.G.A. □53-2-1. Provide the names of any deceased heirs and include the date of death for each (see instructions for further clarification). Also, state here all pertinent facts that may govern the method of giving notice to any party and that may determine whether or not a guardian ad litem should be appointed for any party. If any heirs listed above are cousins, grandchildren, nephews, or nieces of the decedent, please indicate the deceased ancestor through whom they are related to the decedent.]*

4.

Of those named in paragraph 2 above, it is not necessary to notify the following heirs or beneficiaries (a) who have relieved the personal representative of all liability and as to each of whom a copy of the writing(s) granting such relief is/are attached hereto; or (b) with respect to whom the personal representative has been relieved of all further liability in (a settlement of accounts)(an intermediate report)(other binding proceeding) pursuant to an order of this Court dated ________________________________ and hereby incorporated herein as follows:

5.

The following heirs or beneficiaries are represented or should be represented by a guardian *[State names of heir/beneficiary and guardian, if one has already been appointed, and reason guardian needed/appointed]*:

6.

All claims against the estate have been paid (except for the following that have not been paid for the reasons set forth below) *[Provide names and addresses for service]*:

7.

[Initial one]:

____ All necessary (inventories)(and)(returns) have been filed.

____ Petitioner was relieved of filing (inventories)(and)(returns).

8.

Additional Data: *[Where full particulars are lacking, state here the reasons for any such omission.]*

WHEREFORE, petitioner(s) pray(s):

[Initial one]

______ (a) to be discharged solely from office and, therefore, pray(s) that notice issue and be published one time in the official county newspaper with copies thereof being mailed by First-Class Mail to the creditors named in paragraph 6 above and that an order issue discharging the petitioner(s) from office.

OR

______ (b) to be discharged from office and all liability and, therefore, pray(s) that notice issue and be served and published as required by law and that an order issue releasing and discharging the petitioner(s) from office and from all liability.

____
Signature of Petitioner

____
Printed Name

____
Mailing Address
____

____
Telephone Number

Signature of Attorney: ______________________________

Printed Name of Attorney: ______________________________

Address:

Telephone Number: ______________ State Bar #______________

VERIFICATION

GEORGIA, ___________________________ COUNTY

Personally appeared before me the undersigned petitioner(s) who after being duly sworn, state(s) that the facts set forth in the foregoing petition for discharge of personal representative (and the attached exhibit(s)) are true and correct.

Sworn to and subscribed before me this
______day of________________, 20____.

____
Signature of Petitioner

____
NOTARY/CLERK OF PROBATE COURT
My Commission Expires: ________________

____
Printed Name of Petitioner

Source: https://gaprobate.gov/standard-forms/

Exhibit 11.7 Order Granting Petition for Discharge of Personal Representative

IN THE PROBATE COURT OF _________________________ COUNTY
STATE OF GEORGIA

IN RE: ESTATE OF	)	
	)	
________________________________,	)	**ESTATE NO.** _________________
DECEASED	)	

FINAL ORDER

The foregoing petition for discharge of ______________________________ as _____________________________________ was filed. The Court finds that no objection has been filed and all requirements of law have been fulfilled.

ACCORDINGLY, IT IS ORDERED that petitioner(s) be, and is/are hereby, discharged

[Initial one]

_____ (a) solely from office; or

_____ (b) from office and all liability.

SO ORDERED this _______________ day of _________________, 20____.

____
Judge of the Probate Court

GPCSF 33 Eff. July 2021

Source: https://gaprobate.gov/standard-forms/

Key Terms

administrator with the will annexed
county administrator
executor de son tort
letters of administration
letters of administration with the will
annexed
letters testamentary
sui juris
temporary administrator
unfit

Review Questions

1. What is an executor de son tort? How is it different from an executor nominated in a will?
2. What are letters testamentary, and how does the executor obtain them?
3. Why might a temporary administrator be necessary?
4. When will an administrator be appointed for a testate decedent?
5. When will an administrator be appointed for an intestate decedent?
6. What are letters of administration, and how do they differ from letters testamentary?
7. What is a county administrator, and when might one be necessary in the administration process?
8. Is a personal representative entitled to compensation? If so, how is it determined?
9. For what reasons may a personal representative resign?
10. Why might a personal representative be removed?

Practical Assignment

Take a look at the hypothetical that is included in Appendix C of this textbook. Answer the following questions based on the facts presented there.

1. Who do you suppose William should nominate as the executor of his will?
2. Who should be nominated as the successor executor?
3. If William dies intestate, who is a court likely to appoint as his administrator?
4. Who is likely to be appointed as the successor administrator?

Be sure to provide a detailed justification for each of the above answers.

Chapter 12

Estate Administration

Learning Objectives

Upon completion of this chapter, you should be able to:

- Define basic terminology and concepts associated with estate administration.
- Outline the steps in the probate process.
- Identify court and tax forms necessary for the administration of estates.

Exhibit 12.1 Probate Defined

Usually, the death of a loved one brings tremendous emotional and physical stress for those left behind. A family member or close friend may face tough decisions including making final arrangements and wrapping up their loved one's affairs. Therefore, it is critical for the legal team to advise clients to attempt to make the process as easy as possible for those who will survive them. As they plan their estates, clients should advise one or more trusted family members or friends of their final wishes, so they are informed and not surprised. Moreover, they should let their loved ones know where their important documents are located and how to access them. As mentioned previously, all these documents should be left in one place: either in a fireproof, waterproof safe or lockbox at home or in a safe deposit box. In either case, it is best to ensure that a trusted individual can easily find the documents in the event of the decedent's death. Some documents that clients should gather for safekeeping include, but are not limited to, the following, which will prove helpful to effective estate administration:

- originally signed will or trust;
- originals of advance directive and financial power of attorney;
- funeral/burial contracts or arrangements;
- tax returns for the past three years;
- copies of any military discharge papers;
- copies of bank and brokerage statements, and statements from other financial accounts for the last calendar year;
- deeds for real property and titles for personal property;
- life insurance policies;
- information regarding death benefits from current and previous employers;
- list of creditors and account numbers;
- birth certificate, social security card, and benefit information; and
- marriage/divorce papers, if any.

Once the family member or friend has access to these documents and the death certificate for the decedent, he or she will be well-equipped to make funeral and other arrangements according to the decedent's stated wishes. If a will is found, it must be filed promptly with the appropriate probate court. The court will then validate, or **prove**, the will. Once the will is proved and admitted to probate, the administration process described in this chapter may begin. Exhibit 12.2 below outlines the basic steps that occur thereafter, usually in the order described.

Exhibit 12.2 Steps for Estate Administration

Step 1	Obtain authority from probate court
Step 2	Ascertain assets of the deceased
Step 3	Determine and notify interested parties
Step 4	Apply for employer identification number for the estate
Step 5	Publish notice to debtors and creditors
Step 6	Prepare applicable tax returns
Step 7	Pay debts and expenses of administration
Step 8	Sell estate property, if necessary Make distributions to heirs or beneficiaries
Step 9	File reports with court
Step 10	Close the estate

Step One: Obtain Court Authority

As a preliminary matter, to be officially recognized as the estate's personal representative, one must seek authority from the probate court in the county in which the deceased was domiciled at the time of his or her death. As we discussed in Chapter 11, the term "personal representative" refers broadly to either an executor nominated by a testator in his or her will or an administrator appointed by the probate court. We described previously that various types of petitions may be filed to obtain the requisite authority to probate the decedent's estate, and the petition must be served on all beneficiaries or heirs of the decedent. Hence, it may prove prudent for the potential personal representative to hire legal counsel. A probate attorney can help determine the correct petition so that he or she can timely receive the authorization necessary to manage the affairs of the deceased. As we will illustrate, legal counsel and the advice of other professionals will be critical to the personal representative throughout the probate process.

In Chapter 11, we also discussed that, to act on behalf of an estate, one must obtain letters of administration if the decedent died intestate or letters testamentary if the decedent died testate. These court orders may be referred to simply as "letters." The letters will grant the authority to a personal representative to act in a legal capacity to administer the estate. Early in the process, the personal representative may conduct estate business by presenting the letters to financial institutions. The personal representative's activities may include gaining access to the deceased's accounts, opening a bank account in the estate's name, and filing a death claim through the deceased's life insurance company.

Before formally taking on the role, the personal representative must take an oath committing to fairly and properly administering the estate. In doing so, a fiduciary relationship is established and the executor or administrator may be held personally liable if he or she mismanages the affairs of the estate. Acting as a personal representative of an estate is a serious responsibility that should not be taken lightly. As discussed previously, some wills may require that the personal representative be bonded or the testator may waive this requirement. Even if there is no will, the court will likely require a bond if the estate has assets. The bond is required just in case the personal representative mismanages the estate funds. As indicated previously, the bond acts as a protection for the estate beneficiaries or heirs and creditors in the event of the personal representative's wrongdoing. The amount of the bond will depend on the value of the estate. Generally, the bonding company will inquire into the credit score and financial condition of the personal representative to determine the premium rate. If the applicant has a lower credit score, he or she is likely to be quoted a higher cost. If he or she is approved, the bonding company will require a premium to be paid yearly. This premium is properly an estate expense for which the personal representative may be reimbursed.

Step Two: Ascertain Assets

After obtaining the necessary authority, the personal representative must locate, secure, and preserve all of the decedent's property. This includes personal property (such as clothes, money, cars, and so forth) and real property (located inside and outside of the domiciliary state). If the deceased was working, special considerations are to be made to obtain the last paycheck; or, if the deceased was a business owner, the personal representative must seize control of any equipment and assets of that business.

Then, the personal representative needs to make a comprehensive list of estate assets called an **inventory**. He or she may want to employ the assistance of the legal team and the decedent's financial advisors to prepare this inventory. Per O.C.G.A. § 53-7-30, the personal representative must file an inventory of estate property within six (6) months of taking the oath of office. The format that the inventory must take will vary from county to county within the State of Georgia. Therefore, it is best to contact the clerk of court or check the website of the domiciliary probate court to ensure that one is using the proper form. Exhibit 12.3, which follows, is the current inventory form for Fulton County.

Step Three: Notify Interested Parties

Beneficiaries or heirs of the decedent's estate must be notified of their interests therein. If the deceased has a will, his or her beneficiaries will be named in that document and the legal team can assist the personal representative in notifying those individuals of their respective interests in the decedent's estate. Additional investigation and research will be necessary to determine the proper heirs when the decedent dies intestate, or the will fails for some reason.

As we discussed in Chapter 4, in the instances of intestacy or will failure, Georgia's laws of intestate succession control to determine the rightful heirs also known as heirs-at-law. In the event the decedent was married or had children, this may be a fairly easy task. However, it may become more complex for many different reasons. For example, the personal representative may need to seek out counsel if the decedent is survived by children who have not been legitimated. **Legitimation** is the process by which children born out of wedlock secure the same rights as children born to a married couple. In this scenario, it would be imperative for the personal representative to seek legal counsel to help determine the true heirs of the decedent's estate.

In cases where the deceased is intestate and has no spouse or children, Georgia law dictates that any property will be distributed in the following order: parents, siblings, grandparents, uncles and aunts, and then to more distant relatives. Each category takes to the exclusion of the next. For instance, suppose Mary never married, had no children, and both parents predeceased her. At the time of her death, Mary had only one

Exhibit 12.3 Inventory Form for Personal Representative

FULTON COUNTY

INVENTORY- PERSONAL REPRESENTATIVE

Probate Court
136 Pryor Street SW, Suite C-230
Atlanta, Georgia, 30303
404-613-4070

STATE OF GEORGIA, FULTON COUNTY

ESTATE NO. ____________________

INVENTORY

TO THE HONORABLE JUDGE OF THE PROBATE COURT OF SAID STATE AND COUNTY:

The following is a true and complete inventory of the estate, both real and personal.

Decedent: ______________________ Personal Representative: ______________________

	ITEM	APPROXIMATE VALUE
REAL ESTATE	Address	
Parcel One:	____________________	__________
Parcel Two:	____________________	__________
Parcel Three:	____________________	__________
Parcel Four:	____________________	__________

TOTAL APPROXIMATE VALUE OF REAL ESTATE __________

PERSONAL PROPERTY

Bank Accounts (give name of financial institution and account number): APPROXIMATE VALUE

Savings:	____________________	__________
	____________________	__________
Checking:	____________________	__________
	____________________	__________

Certificates of deposit (give name of institution and amount only):

____________________	__________
____________________	__________

Stocks (give no. of shares of each company), Bonds (give face amount), and other securities:	APPROXIMATE VALUE
______________________________	__________
______________________________	__________
______________________________	__________

Vehicles (automobiles, trucks, boats, etc.)

______________________________	__________
______________________________	__________
______________________________	__________

Other personal property and personal effects:

______________________________	__________
______________________________	__________
______________________________	__________

TOTAL APPROXIMATE VALUE OF PERSONAL PROPERTY: __________

This inventory contains a true statement of all the property of the decedent within my knowledge. A copy of this inventory has been mailed by first class mail to each beneficiary or heir of the estate pursuant to O.C.G.A. §53-7-30.

If any beneficiary or heir has waived the right to receive the inventory, as provided in Code Section 53-7-32, their name is set forth as follows:

______________________________	______________________________
Signature of Attorney representing fiduciary, if any	Personal Representative
Ordered recorded in the minutes of the court.	Sworn to and subscribed before me this
This _____ day of ____________, 20_____.	This _____ day of ____________, 20_____.
______________________________	______________________________
Judge of the Probate Court	Notary Public or Clerk of Probate Court

Source: https://fultoncountyga.gov/-/media/forms/probate-court-forms/probate-court-form-04inventorypersonal-representative-decedents-estate-fixed-4.ashx

Exhibit 12.4 Heirs Determination Worksheet

HEIRS
DETERMINATION WORKSHEET

A. Name of Decedent: ______________________
Date of Death: ______________________
County of Domicile: ______________________
Address: ______________________
____

B. Name of Proposed Petitioner: ______________________
Address: ______________________
____

3. **List of heirs (Spouse and Blood Relatives Only):**

(a) Name of decedent's surviving spouse, if any (NOTE: Do <u>not</u> list a person from which the decedent was divorced at time of decedent's death):

____

(2) If a person is named in (a) immediately above and that person has died since the decedent, show the date of death of the person named in 1(a):

____

(3) (This question relates only to the right to serve as administrator.) If there was a surviving spouse who is still alive, was an action for divorce or separate maintenance pending between the decedent and the surviving spouse at the time of decedent's death? ____________

<u>NOTE</u>: IF THERE WAS A SURVIVING SPOUSE AND THERE ARE NO CHILDREN OR DESCENDANTS OF CHILDREN WHO SURVIVED THE DECEDENT, YOU MAY STOP.

1. (a) Children of decedent born in wedlock or legally adopted by decedent:

Living Children		Deceased Children	
<u>Name</u>	<u>Age</u>	<u>Name</u>	<u>DOD</u>

Revised 03/22/01

(b) Children of decedent born out of wedlock:

Living Children		Deceased Children	
Name	Age	Name	DOD

NOTE: IF ALL OF THE CHILDREN OF DECEDENT ARE ALIVE, YOU MAY STOP.

1. Grandchildren of the decedent:

Living Grandchildren

Name	Age	Parent's Name

Deceased Grandchildren

Name	DOD	Parent's Name

NOTE: IF ALL OF THE GRANDCHILDREN OF THE DECEDENT ARE ALIVE, YOU MAY STOP.

1. Great-grandchildren of the decedent:

Revised 03/22/01

Living Great-grandchildren

Name	Age	Parent's Name

Deceased Great-grandchildren

Name	DOD	Parent's Name

NOTE: IF ALL OF THE GREAT-GRANDCHILDREN OF THE DECEDENT ARE ALIVE, YOU MAY STOP. IF THERE ARE ANY DECEASED GREAT-GRANDCHILDREN, YOU MUST ATTACH AN ADDITIONAL SHEET FOR THEIR CHILDREN.

1. Mother and father of the decedent:

	Name	Age	Date of Death, if Deceased
Mother:	______________________	________	
	______________________		
Father:	______________________	________	
	______________________		

NOTE: IF ANY PARENT IS ALIVE, YOU MAY STOP.

2. Brothers and Sisters of the Decedent:

Living Brothers and Sisters		Deceased Brothers and Sisters	
Name	Age	Name	DOD

NOTE: IF ALL OF THE BROTHERS AND SISTERS OF THE DECEDENT ARE ALIVE, YOU MAY STOP.

Revised 03/22/01

1. Nieces and nephews of the decedent:

Living Nieces and Nephews

Name	Age	Parent's Name

Deceased Nieces and Nephews

Name	DOD	Parent's Name

<u>NOTE</u>: IF ALL OF THE NIECES AND NEPHEWS OF THE DECEDENT ARE ALIVE, YOU MAY STOP.

1. Great-nieces and nephews of the decedent:

Living great-nieces and nephews

Name	Age	Parent's Name

Revised 03/22/01

Deceased great-nieces and nephews

Name DOD Parent's Name

______________________________ ______________________________
______________________________ ______________________________
______________________________ ______________________________
______________________________ ______________________________
______________________________ ______________________________
______________________________ ______________________________

NOTE:IF ALL OF THE GREAT-NIECES AND GREAT-NEPHEWS OF THE DECEDENT ARE ALIVE, YOU MAY STOP.

1. Grandparents of the decedent:

NameAgeDate of Death, if Deceased

Mother's Mother: ______________________________

Mother's Father: ______________________________

Father's Mother:: ______________________________

Father's Father: ______________________________

NOTE: IF ANY GRANDPARENT OF THE DECEDENT IS ALIVE, YOU MAY STOP.

2. Aunts and uncles of the decedent:

Living aunts and uncles

Name Age Parent's Name

______________________________ ______________________________
______________________________ ______________________________
______________________________ ______________________________
______________________________ ______________________________
______________________________ ______________________________
______________________________ ______________________________

Deceased aunts and uncles

Revised 03/22/01

Name	DOD	Parent's Name

NOTE: IF ALL OF THE AUNTS AND UNCLES OF THE DECEDENT ARE ALIVE, YOU MAY STOP.

1. First Cousins of the decedent who are alive:

Name	Age	Parent's Name

NOTE: IF ANY FIRST COUSINS ARE ALIVE, YOU MAY STOP.

12. The more remote degrees of kinship are determined by counting the number of steps in the chain from the claimant to the closest common ancestor of the claimant and the decedent, and from said ancestor back to the decedent. The sum of the two chains is the degree of kinship. The surviving relatives who have the lowest sum are in the nearest degree and thus inherit the estate equally.

Revised 03/22/01

Source: https://www.cherokeega.com/Probate-Court/_resources/documents/Heirs%20Determination%20Worksheet.pdf

sibling named Martha and 10 uncles. In this scenario, Mary's sole heir is Martha. It does not matter that Mary had 10 uncles. Under Georgia law, Martha, the sibling, takes to the exclusion of those 10 uncles. The **heir determination worksheet** that appears as Exhibit 12.4 may be helpful to the personal representative seeking to determine the decedent's proper heirs-at-law.

Step Four: Apply for Employer Identification Number (EIN)

For tax purposes, the decedent is separate from his or her estate. While they are alive, individuals filing personal income taxes do so using their social security numbers. As you will learn later in this chapter and the next, one of the obligations of a personal representative is to file tax returns on behalf of the estate. Therefore, a personal representative must apply to the Internal Revenue Service (IRS) for a **taxpayer identification number (TIN)**, which is more commonly referred to as an **employer identification number (EIN)**, for the estate. The EIN operates like a separate social security number for use by the estate, which is a taxable entity.

Applying for an EIN is a simple process. Form SS-4 Application for Employer Identification Number can be filed with the IRS online, by fax, by mail, or by telephone. The current version of that form is included next as Exhibit 12.5.

Step Five: Publish Notice to Debtors and Creditors

Another responsibility of the personal representative is to publish a notice to the decedent's debtors and creditors to inform them of his or her death. Regarding debtors, the personal representative will need to take the necessary steps to recover any property that is owed to the decedent, to include the same in the calculation of estate assets. Again, the advice of financial advisors and accountants may be helpful in this process as well as in assessing the liabilities of the decedent and the validity of creditor claims against the estate. Related to creditors, the personal representative may look through the decedent's recent mail or order credit reports to identify those who may assert that the decedent or the estate owes them money.

Debtors and creditors must receive notice of the decedent's death within sixty (60) days of the personal representative's appointment. This notice must be published for four consecutive weeks in the newspaper designated for legal notices in the county in which the deceased was domiciled. Creditors will have three months from the date of the fourth publication to make known their claims on the estate. Each court has its own rules related to what should be contained in the notice to debtors and creditors. To give you some idea of the possible content, Henry County's current form of notice to debtors and creditors is included next as Exhibit 12.6.

Exhibit 12.5 Form SS-4

Form **SS-4** (Rev. December 2023) Department of the Treasury Internal Revenue Service

Application for Employer Identification Number

(For use by employers, corporations, partnerships, trusts, estates, churches, government agencies, Indian tribal entities, certain individuals, and others.)
See separate instructions for each line. Keep a copy for your records.
Go to *www.irs.gov/FormSS4* for instructions and the latest information.

OMB No. 1545-0003

EIN

Type or print clearly.

1 Legal name of entity (or individual) for whom the EIN is being requested

2 Trade name of business (if different from name on line 1)

3 Executor, administrator, trustee, "care of" name

4a Mailing address (room, apt., suite no. and street, or P.O. box)

5a Street address (if different) (Don't enter a P.O. box.)

4b City, state, and ZIP code (if foreign, see instructions)

5b City, state, and ZIP code (if foreign, see instructions)

6 County and state where principal business is located

7a Name of responsible party

7b SSN, ITIN, or EIN

8a Is this application for a limited liability company (LLC) (or a foreign equivalent)? . . . . ☐ Yes ☐ No

8b If 8a is "Yes," enter the number of LLC members . . . .

8c If 8a is "Yes," was the LLC organized in the United States? . . . . ☐ Yes ☐ No

9a **Type of entity** (check only one box). **Caution:** If 8a is "Yes," see the instructions for the correct box to check.

- ☐ Sole proprietor (SSN) ____________
- ☐ Partnership
- ☐ Corporation (enter form number to be filed) ____________
- ☐ Personal service corporation
- ☐ Church or church-controlled organization
- ☐ Other nonprofit organization (specify) ____________
- ☐ Other (specify)
- ☐ Estate (SSN of decedent) ____________
- ☐ Plan administrator (TIN) ____________
- ☐ Trust (TIN of grantor) ____________
- ☐ Military/National Guard
- ☐ State/local government
- ☐ Farmers' cooperative
- ☐ Federal government
- ☐ REMIC
- ☐ Indian tribal governments/enterprises

Group Exemption Number (GEN) if any

9b If a corporation, name the state or foreign country (if applicable) where incorporated — State — Foreign country

10 **Reason for applying** (check only one box)

- ☐ Started new business (specify type) ____________
- ☐ Hired employees (Check the box and see line 13.)
- ☐ Compliance with IRS withholding regulations
- ☐ Other (specify)
- ☐ Banking purpose (specify purpose) ____________
- ☐ Changed type of organization (specify new type) ____________
- ☐ Purchased going business
- ☐ Created a trust (specify type) ____________
- ☐ Created a pension plan (specify type) ____________

11 Date business started or acquired (month, day, year). See instructions.

12 Closing month of accounting year

13 Highest number of employees expected in the next 12 months (enter -0- if none). If no employees expected, skip line 14.

Agricultural	Household	Other

14 If you expect your employment tax liability to be $1,000 or less in a full calendar year **and** want to file Form 944 annually instead of Forms 941 quarterly, check here. (Your employment tax liability will generally be $1,000 or less if you expect to pay $5,000 or less, $6,536 or less if you're in a U.S. territory, in total wages.) If you don't check this box, you must file Form 941 for every quarter. ☐

15 First date wages or annuities were paid (month, day, year). **Note:** If applicant is a withholding agent, enter date income will first be paid to nonresident alien (month, day, year) . . . .

16 Check **one** box that best describes the principal activity of your business.

- ☐ Health care & social assistance
- ☐ Wholesale—agent/broker
- ☐ Construction
- ☐ Rental & leasing
- ☐ Transportation & warehousing
- ☐ Accommodation & food service
- ☐ Wholesale—other
- ☐ Retail
- ☐ Real estate
- ☐ Manufacturing
- ☐ Finance & insurance
- ☐ Other (specify)

17 Indicate principal line of merchandise sold, specific construction work done, products produced, or services provided.

18 Has the applicant entity shown on line 1 ever applied for and received an EIN? ☐ Yes ☐ No
If "Yes," write previous EIN here

Third Party Designee

Complete this section **only** if you want to authorize the named individual to receive the entity's EIN and answer questions about the completion of this form.

Designee's name — Designee's telephone number (include area code)

Address and ZIP code — Designee's fax number (include area code)

Under penalties of perjury, I declare that I have examined this application, and to the best of my knowledge and belief, it is true, correct, and complete.

Applicant's telephone number (include area code)

Name and title (type or print clearly)

Applicant's fax number (include area code)

Signature — Date

For Privacy Act and Paperwork Reduction Act Notice, see separate instructions. Cat. No. 16055N Form **SS-4** (Rev. 12-2023)

Form SS-4 (Rev. 12-2023) Page 2

Do I Need an EIN?

File Form SS-4 if the applicant entity doesn't already have an EIN but is required to show an EIN on any return, statement, or other document.[1] See also the separate instructions for each line on Form SS-4.

IF the applicant...	AND...	THEN...
started a new business	doesn't currently have (nor expect to have) employees	complete lines 1, 2, 4a–8a, 8b–c (if applicable), 9a, 9b (if applicable), 10–14, and 16–18.
hired (or will hire) employees, including household employees	doesn't already have an EIN	complete lines 1, 2, 4a–6, 7a–b, 8a, 8b–c (if applicable), 9a, 9b (if applicable), and 10–18.
opened a bank account	needs an EIN for banking purposes only	complete lines 1–5b, 7a–b, 8a, 8b–c (if applicable), 9a, 9b (if applicable), 10, and 18.
changed type of organization	either the legal character of the organization or its ownership changed (for example, you incorporate a sole proprietorship or form a partnership)[2]	complete lines 1–18 (as applicable).
purchased a going business[3]	doesn't already have an EIN	complete lines 1–18 (as applicable).
created a trust	the trust is other than a grantor trust or an IRA trust[4]	complete lines 1–18 (as applicable).
created a pension plan as a plan administrator[5]	needs an EIN for reporting purposes	complete lines 1, 3, 4a–5b, 7a–b, 9a, 10, and 18.
is a foreign person needing an EIN to comply with IRS withholding regulations	needs an EIN to complete a Form W-8 (other than Form W-8ECI), avoid withholding on portfolio assets, or claim tax treaty benefits[6]	complete lines 1–5b, 7a–b (SSN or ITIN as applicable), 8a, 8b–c (if applicable), 9a, 9b (if applicable), 10, and 18.
is administering an estate	needs an EIN to report estate income on Form 1041	complete lines 1–7b, 9a, 10–12, 13–17 (if applicable), and 18.
is a withholding agent for taxes on nonwage income paid to an alien (that is, individual, corporation, or partnership, etc.)	is an agent, broker, fiduciary, manager, tenant, or spouse who is required to file Form 1042, Annual Withholding Tax Return for U.S. Source Income of Foreign Persons	complete lines 1, 2, 3 (if applicable), 4a–5b, 7a–b, 8a, 8b–c (if applicable), 9a, 9b (if applicable), 10, and 18.
is a state or local agency	serves as a tax reporting agent for public assistance recipients under Rev. Proc. 80-4, 1980-1 C.B. 581[7]	complete lines 1, 2, 4a–5b, 7a–b, 9a, 10, and 18.
is a single-member LLC (or similar single-member entity)	needs an EIN to file Form 8832, Entity Classification Election, for filing employment tax returns and excise tax returns, or for state reporting purposes[8], or is a foreign-owned U.S. disregarded entity and needs an EIN to file Form 5472, Information Return of a 25% Foreign-Owned U.S. Corporation or a Foreign Corporation Engaged in a U.S. Trade or Business	complete lines 1–18 (as applicable).
is an S corporation	needs an EIN to file Form 2553, Election by a Small Business Corporation[9]	complete lines 1–18 (as applicable).

[1] For example, a sole proprietorship or self-employed farmer who establishes a qualified retirement plan, or is required to file excise, employment, alcohol, tobacco, or firearms returns, must have an EIN. A partnership, corporation, REMIC (real estate mortgage investment conduit), nonprofit organization (church, club, etc.), or farmers' cooperative must use an EIN for any tax-related purpose even if the entity doesn't have employees.

[2] However, don't apply for a new EIN if the existing entity only (a) changed its business name, (b) elected on Form 8832 to change the way it is taxed (or is covered by the default rules), or (c) terminated its partnership status because at least 50% of the total interests in partnership capital and profits were sold or exchanged within a 12-month period. The EIN of the terminated partnership should continue to be used. See Regulations section 301.6109-1(d)(2)(iii).

[3] Don't use the EIN of the prior business unless you became the "owner" of a corporation by acquiring its stock.

[4] However, grantor trusts that don't file using Optional Method 1 and IRA trusts that are required to file Form 990-T, Exempt Organization Business Income Tax Return, must have an EIN. For more information on grantor trusts, see the Instructions for Form 1041.

[5] A plan administrator is the person or group of persons specified as the administrator by the instrument under which the plan is operated.

[6] Entities applying to be a Qualified Intermediary (QI) need a QI-EIN even if they already have an EIN. See Rev. Proc. 2000-12.

[7] See also *Household employer agent* in the instructions. **Note:** State or local agencies may need an EIN for other reasons, for example, hired employees.

[8] See *Disregarded entities* in the instructions for details on completing Form SS-4 for an LLC.

[9] An existing corporation that is electing or revoking S corporation status should use its previously assigned EIN.

Source: https://www.irs.gov

Exhibit 12.6 Form of Notice to Debtors and Creditors

__________________ **Notice will appear in print on Fridays for 4 consecutive weeks**

NOTICE TO DEBTORS AND CREDITORS

STATE OF GEORGIA, COUNTY OF HENRY. All creditors of the estate of ____, Estate number 20___-ES-____, deceased, late of Henry County, Georgia are hereby notified to render their demands by filing same with the Probate Court of Henry County, 99 Sims Street, McDonough, Georgia 30253, according to law, and all persons indebted to said Estate are required to make immediate payment to the undersigned.

This the _______ day of _________________, 20___.

____
Signature of Administrator / Executor / Attorney
(circle one)

____
Printed Name (of party to receive creditor claims)

____
Address

____
City, State, Zip Code

Please return tearsheet to:
Henry County Probate Court
99 Sims Street
McDonough, Georgia 30253
(770) 288-7600

DO NOT RECORD

Publication Fee: $60.00, check or money order made payable to Henry County Probate Court

Notice to Debtors and Creditors Form
Henry County Probate Court – Rev. 1/23/24

Source: https://www.henrycountyprobatecourt.com/Portals/0/2024%20-%20Notice%20to%20Debtors%20and%20Creditors %20Form.pdf

Step Six: Prepare Applicable Tax Returns

As noted earlier, filing tax returns is another of the duties a personal representative must perform. In Chapter 13, we will explore in greater depth the numerous tax considerations and returns related to estate planning. Nonetheless, we will note here that it may prove prudent for the personal representative to consult a tax attorney or accountant who specializes in estate taxation for assistance with these complex matters to ensure that returns are submitted accurately and in a timely fashion.

Step Seven: Pay Debts and Expenses of Administration

Yet another duty of the personal representative is to pay bills on behalf of the decedent and the estate. Once the validity of a debt or expense has been established, the personal representative must pay it promptly based on the following order of priority outlined in O.C.G.A. § 53-7-40:

(1) Year's support for the family;

(2) Funeral expenses, whether or not the decedent leaves a surviving spouse, in an amount which corresponds with the circumstances of the decedent in life. If the estate is solvent, the personal representative is authorized to provide a suitable protection for the grave;

(3) Other necessary expenses of administration;

(4) Reasonable expenses of the decedent's last illness;

(5) Unpaid taxes or other debts due the state or the United States;

(6) Judgments, secured interests, and other liens created during the lifetime of the decedent, to be paid according to their priority of lien. Secured interests and other liens on specific property shall be preferred only to the extent of such property; and

(7) All other claims.

There are a few important things to note related to the list above. First, some tax claims may have a higher priority than a year's support, in which case they must be paid first. Second, claims higher in priority may exhaust the assets of the estate so that lower priority claims may not be paid. For instance, a year's support claim may wipe out all estate assets, and no funds will be available to anyone else. Third, claims within the same class are not necessarily similarly treated. For example, suppose a decedent had three credit cards (A, B, and C) on which he owed a total of $10,000 at the time of his death; however, only $5,000 remains in his estate after the personal representative paid higher priority claims. In this scenario, the funds will not be split equally among creditors—A, B, and C—even though they are members of the same class. Instead, each credit card company will be entitled to recover a portion of the remaining assets

($5,000), in a share that corresponds to the percentage of the total debt the decedent owed to that creditor. Exhibit 12.7, which follows, illustrates the breakdown of how payments would be allocated.

Exhibit 12.7 Sample Distribution to Creditors

	Amount Owed	% of Total Debt	Calculations	Total Recovery
Creditor A	$5,000	50%	50% of $5000	$2,500
Creditor B	$3,000	30%	30% of $5000	$1500
Creditor C	$2,000	20%	20% of $5000	$1000
Total Credit Card Debt	$10,000			
Assets Remaining	$5,000			

Step Eight: Sell Estate Property and Make Distributions

If it is necessary and in the best interests of the estate, the personal representative may liquidate estate assets. He or she may do so to fulfill the wishes of the testator under the will or to pay estate creditors and/or taxes. The personal representative may organize an estate sale or auction or hire a real estate agent and an estate sale professional for assistance with these matters.

After all creditor's claims, funeral expenses, expenses of the last illness, personal administration expenses, and taxes (amongst other expenses) are paid, the heirs or beneficiaries are entitled to receive their distributions from the remaining estate as either set forth under the will or per Georgia's laws of intestate succession. The personal representative should take extreme care to ensure that distributions are made to the proper persons in the correct proportion.

Step Nine: File Reports with the Court

Throughout this administration process, the personal representative must be mindful not to neglect the reporting requirements to the probate court. In Chapter 11, we noted that one of the grounds for termination of a personal representative is his or her failure to timely file necessary documents. As mentioned earlier in this chapter, the personal representative is responsible to prepare and file an initial inventory of assets to the court within six (6) months of being appointed. In addition, each year, the personal representative must provide a status report to the probate court called an **annual return**. It is due within sixty (60) days of the anniversary date of the personal representative's appointment. Courts differ concerning the substantive requirements for the annual return. Therefore, to determine the proper form to use, the personal rep-

Exhibit 12.8 Annual Return

Return for the Estate of ______________________________, (Deceased)

(Ward)

Estate No. ____________ Reporting Period: ____________ to ________

(Conservator's) (Personal Representative's) Name: ______________________________

Beginning Balance: *If this is the first return, use for a beginning balance the figures you listed on the inventory as the amount of funds in all bank accounts, certificates of deposit, stocks, bonds, or other securities. If this is not the first return, your beginning balance on this return should be the ending balance on the previous return.*

Date		Amount
	Beginning Balance: see above instructions for method of calculation	$
Date	**Receipts** into the estate including interest earned; proceeds from sale of assets; social security; pension, etc.; itemize by category - use the second page of this form if necessary:	Amount
Line A	subtotal from second page	
	Total receipts	$
TOTAL	**BEGINNING BALANCE PLUS TOTAL RECEIPTS**	$
Date	**Disbursements**: itemize by category any distributions made to heirs, beneficiaries, or on behalf of wards. **If this is a decedent's estate,** you must specify the payee and amount paid to them. **If this is a conservatorship,** you must categorize disbursements by type, e.g. Autilities,@ or Anursing home,@ etc. Use the second page of this form if necessary	Amount
Line B	subtotal from second page	
	Total disbursements	$
TOTAL	**balance on hand**: beginning balance plus total receipts less total disbursements	$

Please attach original bank documents showing ending balance and title of account.

I have compared the original vouchers with the items listed on the return and certify that this return is correct.

____

Personal Representative/Conservator

It is ordered that this return be allowed this _____ day of ______________, 20______

____

Personal Representative/Conservator

____

Tammy S. Brown, Judge
Probate Court of Barrow County

Sworn to me this ________ day of ______________, 20________ .

____

Notary Public or Clerk of Court

Estate No. ______________________________

Date	**Receipts** into the estate:	Amount
		$
LINE A	**Subtotal for all receipts; transfer to front of page**	$

Date	**Disbursements**: itemize by category; any distributions made to heirs or beneficiaries should specify the payee and amount paid to them:	Amount
LINE B	**Subtotal for all disbursements; transfer to front of page**	$

Name of Financial Institution or asset	Account Number(s)	Value listed on attached original documentation

Total balance on hand as shown by attached bank documentation: $______________________

Please attach original bank documents showing ending balance and title of account.

Instructions for Completing Annual Returns

1. For Computation of Beginning Balance:

a. ***If this is the first return****, use for a beginning balance the* total approximate value of liquid personal property *as you listed on the inventory.*

b. *If this is* ***not*** *the first return, your beginning balance on this return must be the ending balance on the previous return.*

2. A Receipts@ section:

a. **Decedent Estates - list:**

$ interest earned / unrealized gains
$ social security payments payable while decedent was alive
$ pension payments payable while decedent was alive
$ proceeds from sale of assets (sale after probate court approval, if powers not granted)
$ *itemize by category and use the second page of this form if necessary*

b. **Conservator Estates - list:**

$ interest earned / unrealized gains
$ proceeds from sale of assets after probate court approval
$ disability payments
$ IRA distributions
$ Workers= Compensation
$ Social Security (Adult Conservators Only)
$ pension
$ inheritances
$ annuity payments
$ *itemize by category and use the second page of this form if necessary*

3. A Disbursements@ section:

a. **Decedent Estates**:

$ list disbursements to beneficiaries or heirs at law with the payee and amount paid SPECIFIED.
$ debts may be itemized by type, e.g. Afuneral, burial@
$ show unrealized losses as disbursements
$ use the second page of this form if necessary
$ Note: you must file the certificate of mailing of inventory or annual return, signed by all personal representatives in front of a notary, listing the names and addresses of the recipients of the report.

b. **Conservator Estates**:

$ you must categorize disbursements by type
$ for adult Conservators ONLY, categories could include Autilities,@ or Anursing home,@ etc. (minor's funds should never be spent for expenses that the parent is responsible for providing, e.g. rent, utilities, food, etc. without specific order of the probate court)
$ no disbursements over $200.00 may be titled A miscellaneous@ or Aassorted costs@
$ show unrealized losses as disbursement
$ use the second page of this form if necessary

4. Don't Forget!

$ all personal representatives / conservators must sign, in front of a notary or the probate clerk
$ most recent original bank statement(s) verifying the account balance and title of the account must be filed with the return
$ filing fees ($30.00 Estate or $30.00 Conservator) payable to the Barrow County Probate Court, must be transmitted with the return. Mail to Barrow County Probate Court, 652 Barrow Park Dr, Ste. D, Winder, GA 30680

IN THE PROBATE COURT OF BARROW COUNTY

STATE OF GEORGIA

CERTIFICATE OF MAILING OF ANNUAL/FINAL RETURN

IN RE: ____________________ **DOCKET NO.** ____________

Personal Representative/Conservator:____

The undersigned certifies that, on this date, a copy of annual/final return of the above estate/conservatorship was provided by first-class mail with adequate postage attached to the parties required to receive the same as provided by law. These include:

- **The heirs of intestate estates or beneficiaries of a testate estate, and surety (bonding company) if any. O.C.G.A. §53-7-68**
- **In adult conservatorships, the surety (bonding company) the ward, and the guardian (if any). O.C.G.A. §29-5-60**
- **In minor conservatorships, the surety (bonding company) and the guardian. If there is no guardian OR if the conservator and the guardian are the same person, a copy must also be provided to the minor. O.C.G.A. §29-4-60**

The parties provided with notice in compliance with the above are as follows (add additional pages, if necessary):

NAME:	**ADDRESS:**
____________________	____________________
____________________	____________________
____________________	____________________
____________________	____________________
____________________	____________________
____________________	____________________

____________________	____________________
Personal Representative of Estate	**Personal Representative of Estate**
Address:______________	**Address:**______________
____________________	____________________
Telephone:______________	**Telephone:**______________

Sworn to and subscribed before me
this ______ day of ______________, 20_____.

____

Notary Public or Clerk of the Probate Court

Source: https://www.barrowga.org/347/Annual-Return-Form-PDF

resentative should either contact the clerk of court or check the website of the county's probate court for guidance. Take a look at Barrow County's current form of annual return, which appears as Exhibit 12.8.

Once the personal representative has paid all of the aforementioned debts and expenses, then he or she must file with the probate court a **final accounting** in a form similar to the annual return. It must include a more comprehensive disclosure of the various debts collected and expenses paid on behalf of the decedent, copies of the tax returns filed, and a proposal for distribution of the remaining estate assets to the decedent's beneficiaries or heirs.

Step Ten: Close the Estate

Finally, after the personal representative has disbursed the remaining estate assets to beneficiaries or heirs, he or she may close the estate. To complete the estate administration process, the personal representative must file a **petition for discharge** with the probate court and receive a discharge order. Until that point, the personal representative remains personally liable for the estate. Interested parties receive notice of the petition for discharge and during the time of the court's consideration, they have an opportunity to raise any objections to the discharge. If the court is satisfied that the personal representative has fulfilled his or her obligations completely, then the court will issue an **order for discharge**. The order for discharge formally closes the estate and releases the personal representative from liability. The current Georgia forms of Petition for Discharge and Order for Discharge were included in Chapter 11 as Exhibits 11.6 and 11.7, respectively.

Currently, the entire probate process takes about a year or a year and a half in the State of Georgia. However, the estate administration may last longer if it is a large and complex estate, if there are a significant number of heirs or beneficiaries, or if there are disputes that arise among heirs or beneficiaries. One notable example in the State of Georgia was when singer James Brown died on Christmas Day in 2006. His estate was valued at over $100 million at the time of his death, including royalties, properties, and other assets. While James Brown had a valid will that left a substantial portion of his estate to a charitable trust, it was extremely vague. As a result, his numerous children and grandchildren and an ex-wife fought over the estate for over 15 years. That case serves as yet another cautionary tale of why careful estate planning is vital.

Key Terms

annual return
employer identification number (EIN)
final accounting
heir determination worksheet
inventory
legitimation
order for discharge
petition for discharge
prove
taxpayer identification number (TIN)

Review Questions

1. What is the significance of the oath that the personal representative takes before formally beginning his or her role?
2. What is an inventory, and why is it necessary?
3. As part of the probate process, who should be notified of the decedent's death? Why?
4. Under what circumstances is an heir determination worksheet valuable?
5. What is an EIN? Why is it necessary as part of the estate administration process?
6. List and describe the tax documents mentioned in this chapter that the personal representative may need to file on behalf of the decedent and the estate.
7. In your own words, describe the order in which debts and expenses of the estate must be paid.
8. What is an annual return, and why is it necessary?
9. What is the procedure for closing an estate?
10. When is the personal representative released from liability for the estate?

Practical Assignment

Find a case or a news story about a lawyer's breach of his or her duties in administering a client's estate. Answer the following questions related to the same:

1. How did the lawyer come to represent the estate?
2. In what way(s) did the lawyer breach his or her ethical duties to the client? Be specific.
3. Did the lawyer commit any crimes in breaching his or her duties? If so, describe them.

Be sure to provide a direct link to or a citation for the case or news story about which you will be writing.

Chapter 13

Tax Considerations

Learning Objectives

Upon completion of this chapter, you should be able to:

- Explain gift and estate taxes.
- Identify the difference between a deduction and a credit.
- Identify credits that may apply to lower estate tax liability.
- Recognize tax forms needed for estate administration purposes.

General Tax Considerations

As we have discussed previously, a primary objective of estate planning is to avoid tax liability. It is prudent for the personal representative to consult a qualified estate tax attorney or accountant to assist with navigating tax considerations for the estate. We have discussed the various taxes that may be imposed, including gift and estate taxes. The estate tax is also referred to as either a **death tax** or an **inheritance tax**. The main difference is that estate taxes are paid directly by the estate before the property is transferred while inheritance taxes are usually those paid by the person who inherits assets from the estate. It is noteworthy that at this writing, the State of Georgia has no state estate tax per O.C.G.A. § 48-12-1(a). Therefore, one only has to consult the Internal Revenue Code to determine the estate tax due under federal law.

Per our discussion in Chapter 12, when someone dies, it is essential to advise the IRS that the taxpayer is no longer living and that the personal representative has been appointed to administer the decedent's estate. Doing so will allow the personal representative to deal directly with the IRS concerning the decedent's and the estate's tax matters. A current version of the form that is used for this purpose, IRS Form 56 Notice Concerning Fiduciary Relationship, is included at the end of this chapter as Exhibit 13.2. Filing this form will put the IRS on notice that any future correspondence related to the tax liability of the decedent and his or her estate should be directed to the personal representative.

In addition, the personal representative must submit several important tax documents to the IRS. He or she must file IRS Form 2848 Power of Attorney and Declaration of Representative related to the duties as the agent of the decedent. This form will give the personal representative the authority to act before the IRS for tax purposes on behalf of the decedent and his or her estate. The current version of Form 2848 is included at the end of this chapter as Exhibit 13.3.

Personal Income Tax Returns

Among the forms the personal representative must file are final personal income tax returns at the state and federal levels for the year of the decedent's death. The obligation to file income tax returns is not relieved by a taxpayer's death. Therefore, if Martha passes away and has income above the yearly minimum income threshold during the year of her death, then the personal representative for Martha's estate is obligated to file the regular state and federal income tax returns on her behalf, just as if Martha were alive and able to file her own taxes. These returns will be due on or about the 15th day of April, in the year following the decedent's death. It will cover the period of January 1 until the date of the decedent's death. If the decedent was married at the time of death, joint returns may be necessary. Moreover, if the deceased taxpayer has returns from previous years that were not filed, the personal representative will need to file those. Related to the decedent's final personal income taxes, generally, the personal representative will use IRS Form 1040 and Georgia Department of Revenue Form 500. Copies of the current versions of these forms are included at the end of this chapter as Exhibits 13.4 and 13.5, respectively. Note also that extensions to file for personal income tax returns and the others described in this chapter are possible.

Estate Income Tax Returns

Additionally, the personal representative may need to file estate income tax returns if the estate is open longer than a year and meets a certain income threshold. In most instances, estates may be opened, administered, and closed without generating any income. However, there are some cases where estates gain substantial income and may need to remain open for an extended duration. For example, certain celebrities have made considerable money after death. Some, like Elvis Presley, have earned more in death than in life. In most cases, especially when there has been no prior planning, the estate controls and manages those earnings. Currently, the estate, as the legal successor in interest to the individual, is responsible for paying taxes on the income received so long as that income exceeds $600 per year. Deductions are available for administration expenses. Just as with individual income tax returns, estate income tax returns must be filed and the applicable income taxes must be paid on or about April 15 of each year. Generally, for these tax returns, it is IRS Form 1041 and Georgia Department of Revenue Form 501 that the personal representative must file. Copies of the current versions of these forms are included at the end of this chapter as Exhibits 13.6 and 13.7, respectively.

Estate Tax Returns

It is important to note that while Georgia does not have a state estate tax, the personal representative may need to file the federal form to cover any federal taxes imposed on the estate based on its value as of the date of the taxpayer's death. The amount of taxation will be calculated according to a formula contained in Chapter 11 of the Internal Revenue Code. As indicated earlier, in 2024, only estates worth more than $13.61 million for an individual and $27.22 million for a couple were subject to federal estate taxes. At the end of 2025, the estate and gift tax exemptions are set to sunset or expire and, unless extended, the limits may be cut by more than half. In either case, the personal representative should consult with professionals to determine the estate value. If necessary, the personal representative will use IRS Form 706 United States Estate (and Generation-Skipping Transfer) Tax Return to report estate taxes (and certain generation-skipping transfer taxes which we will discuss later in this chapter). It is due within nine months of the date of the decedent's death. A copy of the current Form 706 is included at the end of this chapter as Exhibit 13.8.

Calculating Estate Taxes

As discussed previously, the estate tax does not apply to estates that have a value that is less than the exclusion amount listed above. To calculate the tax liability for estates worth more than the exclusion amount, several steps are necessary.

Step 1: Calculate the gross estate

First, one must determine the total value of all non-exempt estate assets, which is referred to as the **gross estate**. These may include cash, real property, securities, and other assets. In Chapter 3, we discussed nonprobate property, which is exempt from the gross estate. As a reminder, in Georgia, the following are not considered part of the gross estate: (1) property owned by joint tenancy; (2) property in a living trust; (3) life insurance with a named beneficiary; (4) retirement/pension accounts with a named beneficiary; and (5) life estates.

Step 2: Subtract deductions to arrive at taxable estate

Second, once the gross estate is calculated, certain deductions are allowed. A **deduction** is an amount that may be subtracted from the gross estate. For example, mortgages and debt, administration expenses of the estate, and losses during estate administration are all allowable deductions. The most common allowable deductions are the marital deduction and gifts to charity. An estate is entitled to a marital deduction if there is a surviving spouse and the decedent leaves all or a part of his or her estate to that surviving spouse. The amount left to the surviving spouse that can be inherited free from estate and gift tax liability is the unlimited marital deduction. A **charitable deduction** is allowed for the amount of money that the estate has donated to a qualifying charity that is free from estate and gift tax liability. The gross estate minus exclusions, expenses, and deductions amounts to the **taxable estate.**

Step 3: Multiply the taxable estate by the applicable estate tax rate

The third step in the estate tax calculation process is to take the taxable estate and multiply it by the applicable estate tax rate. I.R.C. § 2001(c) outlines the current rates:

Exhibit 13.1 Applicable Estate Tax Rates

If the amount with respect to which the tentative tax to be computed is:	**The tentative tax is:**
Not over $10,000	18 percent of such amount.
Over $10,000 but not over $20,000	$1,800, plus 20 percent of the excess of such amount over $10,000.
Over $20,000 but not over $40,000	$3,800, plus 22 percent of the excess of such amount over $20,000.
Over $40,000 but not over $60,000	$8,200 plus 24 percent of the excess of such amount over $40,000.
Over $60,000 but not over $80,000	$13,000, plus 26 percent of the excess of such amount over $60,000.
Over $80,000 but not over $100,000	$18,200, plus 28 percent of the excess of such amount over $80,000.
Over $100,000 but not over $150,000	$23,800, plus 30 percent of the excess of such amount over $100,000.
Over $150,000 but not over $250,000	$38,800, plus 32 percent of the excess of such amount over $150,000.
Over $250,000 but not over $500,000	$70,800, plus 34 percent of the excess of such amount over $250,000.
Over $500,000 but not over $750,000	$155,800, plus 37 percent of the excess of such amount over $500,000.
Over $750,000 but not over $1,000,000	$248,300, plus 39 percent of the excess of such amount over $750,000.
Over $1,000,000	$345,800, plus 40 percent of the excess of such amount over $1,000,000.

Source: http://uscode.house.gov/view.xhtml?req=granuleid:USC-prelim-title26-section2001&num=0&edition=prelim

Step 4: Subtract any credits

Fourth, after that computation, the product of Step 3 is reduced by any applicable credits. A **credit** is defined as any amount of money that can be used to offset tax liability. For example, you will remember that the unified credit is the credit given against the federal estate tax after the death of the taxpayer. In addition, although Georgia has no estate tax, in states that do have it, a credit is available to estates for the amount paid for the state estate tax due.

Step 5: Arrive at estate taxes due

Finally, once all available credits are applied, one arrives at the amount of the estate taxes that are due.

Gift Tax Returns

As stated previously, a gift tax is a tax on the transfer of property during the donor's lifetime that is greater than the annual gift tax exclusion. It must be a complete gift, meaning that the donor retains no control whatsoever over the property gifted. The excess gift is reported on IRS Form 709 United States Gift (and Generation-Skipping Transfer) Tax Return, which, as the name implies, is also the form used to report certain other generation-skipping transfer taxes not included on Form 706. According to I.R.C. § 2502(c), the gift tax is paid by the donor and not by the person receiving the gift. As indicated earlier, in 2024, the annual exclusion for gifts was $18,000 and $36,000 per couple. That means that one could give up to $18,000 per recipient and avoid incurring the gift tax. Even if a donor makes a gift under the annual gift exclusion amount, it may still be prudent to file a gift tax return in the year a gift is made to later claim the unified credit for the total amount of lifetime gifts. A copy of the current Form 709 is included at the end of this chapter as Exhibit 13.9.

Generation-Skipping Transfer Tax Returns

Finally, we discussed generation-skipping trusts, also known as dynasty trusts, in Chapter 9. The **generation-skipping transfer tax** is a tax imposed on outright gifts or transfers in trust that are above the exemption amount and made to or for the benefit of unrelated persons who are more than 37.5 years younger than the donor or to related persons more than one generation younger than the donor, such as grandchildren. As indicated previously, the exemption amount for 2024 was $13.61 million for an individual and $27.22 million for a couple. For those who have made applicable transfers above these amounts, the generation-skipping transfer tax can be reported on either Form 706 or 709, Exhibits 13.8 and 13.9, respectively, depending on the type of transfer.

Exhibit 13.2 Form 56 Notice Concerning Fiduciary Relationship

Form **56**
(Rev. November 2022)
Department of the Treasury
Internal Revenue Service

Notice Concerning Fiduciary Relationship

(Internal Revenue Code Sections 6036 and 6903)

Go to *www.irs.gov/Form56* for instructions and the latest information.

OMB No. 1545-0013

Part I Identification

Name of person for whom you are acting (as shown on the tax return)	Identifying number	**Decedent's social security no.**

Address of person for whom you are acting (number, street, and room or suite no.)

City or town, state, and ZIP code (If a foreign address, see instructions.)

Fiduciary's name

Address of fiduciary (number, street, and room or suite no.)

City or town, state, and ZIP code	Telephone number (optional)
	( )

Section A. Authority

1 Authority for fiduciary relationship. Check applicable box:

a ☐ Court appointment of testate estate (valid will exists)
b ☐ Court appointment of intestate estate (no valid will exists)
c ☐ Court appointment as guardian or conservator
d ☐ Fiduciary of intestate estate
e ☐ Valid trust instrument and amendments
f ☐ Bankruptcy or assignment for the benefit of creditors
g ☐ Other. Describe: ____________

2a If box 1a, 1b, or 1d is checked, enter the date of death: ____________
b If box 1c, 1e, 1f, or 1g is checked, enter the date of appointment, taking office, or assignment or transfer of assets: ____________

Section B. Nature of Liability and Tax Notices

3 Type of taxes (check all that apply): ☐ Income ☐ Gift ☐ Estate ☐ Generation-skipping transfer ☐ Employment ☐ Excise ☐ Other (describe): ____________

4 Federal tax form number (check all that apply): **a** ☐ 706 series **b** ☐ 709 **c** ☐ 940 **d** ☐ 941, 943, 944 **e** ☐ 1040 or 1040-SR **f** ☐ 1041 **g** ☐ 1120 **h** ☐ Other (list): ____________

5 If your authority as a fiduciary does not cover all years or tax periods, check here . . . . ☐ and list the specific years or periods within your authority: ____________

For Paperwork Reduction Act and Privacy Act Notice, see separate instructions. Cat. No. 16375I Form **56** (Rev. 11-2022)

Form 56 (Rev. 11-2022) Page 2

Part II Revocation or Termination of Notice

Section A—Total Revocation or Termination

6 Check this box if you are revoking or terminating all prior notices concerning fiduciary relationships on file with the Internal Revenue Service for the same tax matters and years or periods covered by this notice concerning fiduciary relationship . . ☐

Reason for termination of fiduciary relationship. Check applicable box:

a ☐ Court order revoking fiduciary authority

b ☐ Certificate of dissolution or termination of a business entity

c ☐ Other. Describe:

Section B—Partial Revocation

7a Check this box if you are revoking earlier notices concerning fiduciary relationships on file with the Internal Revenue Service for the same tax matters and years or periods covered by this notice concerning fiduciary relationship . . . . ☐

b Specify to whom granted, date, and address, including ZIP code.

Section C—Substitute Fiduciary

8 Check this box if a new fiduciary or fiduciaries have been or will be substituted for the revoking or terminating fiduciary and specify the name(s) and address(es), including ZIP code(s), of the new fiduciary(ies) . . . . ☐

Part III Court and Administrative Proceedings

Name of court (if other than a court proceeding, identify the type of proceeding and name of agency)		Date proceeding initiated	
Address of court		Docket number of proceeding	
City or town, state, and ZIP code	Date	Time ☐ a.m. ☐ p.m.	Place of other proceedings

Part IV Signature

Please Sign Here

Under penalties of perjury, I declare that I have examined this document, including any accompanying statements, and to the best of my knowledge and belief, it is true, correct, and complete.

Fiduciary's signature	Title, if applicable	Date

Form **56** (Rev. 11-2022)

Source: www.irs.gov

Exhibit 13.3 Form 2848 Power of Attorney and Declaration of Representative

Check Form for Common Errors & Reminders

Form **2848**
(Rev. January 2021)
Department of the Treasury
Internal Revenue Service

Power of Attorney and Declaration of Representative

► **Go to *www.irs.gov/Form2848* for instructions and the latest information.**

OMB No. 1545-0150

For IRS Use Only
Received by:
Name ______
Telephone ______
Function ______
Date / /

Part I Power of Attorney

Caution: A separate Form 2848 must be completed for each taxpayer. Form 2848 will not be honored for any purpose other than representation before the IRS.

1 Taxpayer information. Taxpayer must sign and date this form on page 2, line 7.

Taxpayer name and address | Taxpayer identification number(s) | Daytime telephone number | Plan number (if applicable)

hereby appoints the following representative(s) as attorney(s)-in-fact:

2 Representative(s) must sign and date this form on page 2, Part II.

Name and address — CAF No. ______ PTIN ______ Telephone No. ______ Fax No. ______
Check if to be sent copies of notices and communications ☐ — Check if new: Address ☐ Telephone No. ☐ Fax No. ☐

Name and address — CAF No. ______ PTIN ______ Telephone No. ______ Fax No. ______
Check if to be sent copies of notices and communications ☐ — Check if new: Address ☐ Telephone No. ☐ Fax No. ☐

Name and address — CAF No. ______ PTIN ______ Telephone No. ______ Fax No. ______
(**Note:** IRS sends notices and communications to only two representatives.) — Check if new: Address ☐ Telephone No. ☐ Fax No. ☐

Name and address — CAF No. ______ PTIN ______ Telephone No. ______ Fax No. ______
(**Note:** IRS sends notices and communications to only two representatives.) — Check if new: Address ☐ Telephone No. ☐ Fax No. ☐

to represent the taxpayer before the Internal Revenue Service and perform the following acts:

3 Acts authorized (you are required to complete line 3). Except for the acts described in line 5b, I authorize my representative(s) to receive and inspect my confidential tax information and to perform acts I can perform with respect to the tax matters described below. For example, my representative(s) shall have the authority to sign any agreements, consents, or similar documents (see instructions for line 5a for authorizing a representative to sign a return).

Description of Matter (Income, Employment, Payroll, Excise, Estate, Gift, Whistleblower, Practitioner Discipline, PLR, FOIA, Civil Penalty, Sec. 4980H Shared Responsibility Payment, etc.) (see instructions)	Tax Form Number (1040, 941, 720, etc.) (if applicable)	Year(s) or Period(s) (if applicable) (see instructions)

4 Specific use not recorded on the Centralized Authorization File (CAF). If the power of attorney is for a specific use not recorded on CAF, check this box. See *Line 4. Specific Use Not Recorded on CAF* in the instructions . . . . ► ☐

5a Additional acts authorized. In addition to the acts listed on line 3 above, I authorize my representative(s) to perform the following acts (see instructions for line 5a for more information): ☐ Access my IRS records via an Intermediate Service Provider;
☐ Authorize disclosure to third parties; ☐ Substitute or add representative(s); ☐ Sign a return; ______

☐ Other acts authorized: ______

For Privacy Act and Paperwork Reduction Act Notice, see the instructions. Cat. No. 11980J Form **2848** (Rev. 1-2021)

Form 2848 (Rev. 1-2021) Page **2**

b **Specific acts not authorized.** My representative(s) is (are) not authorized to endorse or otherwise negotiate any check (including directing or accepting payment by any means, electronic or otherwise, into an account owned or controlled by the representative(s) or any firm or other entity with whom the representative(s) is (are) associated) issued by the government in respect of a federal tax liability.

List any other specific deletions to the acts otherwise authorized in this power of attorney (see instructions for line 5b): ____________

____

6 **Retention/revocation of prior power(s) of attorney.** The filing of this power of attorney automatically revokes all earlier power(s) of attorney on file with the Internal Revenue Service for the same matters and years or periods covered by this form. If you **do not** want to revoke a prior power of attorney, check here . . . . ▶ ☐

YOU MUST ATTACH A COPY OF ANY POWER OF ATTORNEY YOU WANT TO REMAIN IN EFFECT.

7 **Taxpayer declaration and signature.** If a tax matter concerns a year in which a joint return was filed, each spouse must file a separate power of attorney even if they are appointing the same representative(s). If signed by a corporate officer, partner, guardian, tax matters partner, partnership representative (or designated individual, if applicable), executor, receiver, administrator, trustee, or individual other than the taxpayer, I certify I have the legal authority to execute this form on behalf of the taxpayer.

▶ IF NOT COMPLETED, SIGNED, AND DATED, THE IRS WILL RETURN THIS POWER OF ATTORNEY TO THE TAXPAYER.

Signature ____________ Date ____________ Title (if applicable) ____________

Print name ____________ Print name of taxpayer from line 1 if other than individual ____________

Part II Declaration of Representative

Under penalties of perjury, by my signature below I declare that:

- I am not currently suspended or disbarred from practice, or ineligible for practice, before the Internal Revenue Service;
- I am subject to regulations in Circular 230 (31 CFR, Subtitle A, Part 10), as amended, governing practice before the Internal Revenue Service;
- I am authorized to represent the taxpayer identified in Part I for the matter(s) specified there; and
- I am one of the following:

a Attorney—a member in good standing of the bar of the highest court of the jurisdiction shown below.
b Certified Public Accountant—a holder of an active license to practice as a certified public accountant in the jurisdiction shown below.
c Enrolled Agent—enrolled as an agent by the IRS per the requirements of Circular 230.
d Officer—a bona fide officer of the taxpayer organization.
e Full-Time Employee—a full-time employee of the taxpayer.
f Family Member—a member of the taxpayer's immediate family (spouse, parent, child, grandparent, grandchild, step-parent, step-child, brother, or sister).
g Enrolled Actuary—enrolled as an actuary by the Joint Board for the Enrollment of Actuaries under 29 U.S.C. 1242 (the authority to practice before the IRS is limited by section 10.3(d) of Circular 230).
h Unenrolled Return Preparer—Authority to practice before the IRS is limited. An unenrolled return preparer may represent, provided the preparer (1) prepared and signed the return or claim for refund (or prepared if there is no signature space on the form); (2) was eligible to sign the return or claim for refund; (3) has a valid PTIN; and (4) possesses the required Annual Filing Season Program Record of Completion(s). ***See Special Rules and Requirements for Unenrolled Return Preparers in the instructions for additional information.***
k Qualifying Student or Law Graduate—receives permission to represent taxpayers before the IRS by virtue of his/her status as a law, business, or accounting student, or law graduate working in a LITC or STCP. See instructions for Part II for additional information and requirements.
r Enrolled Retirement Plan Agent—enrolled as a retirement plan agent under the requirements of Circular 230 (the authority to practice before the Internal Revenue Service is limited by section 10.3(e)).

▶ IF THIS DECLARATION OF REPRESENTATIVE IS NOT COMPLETED, SIGNED, AND DATED, THE IRS WILL RETURN THE POWER OF ATTORNEY. REPRESENTATIVES MUST SIGN IN THE ORDER LISTED IN PART I, LINE 2.

Note: For designations d–f, enter your title, position, or relationship to the taxpayer in the "Licensing jurisdiction" column.

Designation—Insert above letter **(a–r).**	Licensing jurisdiction (State) or other licensing authority (if applicable)	Bar, license, certification, registration, or enrollment number (if applicable)	Signature	Date

Form **2848** (Rev. 1-2021)

Source: www.irs.gov

Exhibit 13.4 IRS Form 1040 U.S. Individual Income Tax Return

Form **1040** Department of the Treasury—Internal Revenue Service
U.S. Individual Income Tax Return **2024** OMB No. 1545-0074 IRS Use Only—Do not write or staple in this space.

For the year Jan. 1–Dec. 31, 2024, or other tax year beginning ____________, 2024, ending ____________, 20____ See separate instructions.

Your first name and middle initial	Last name	**Your social security number**
If joint return, spouse's first name and middle initial	Last name	**Spouse's social security number**
Home address (number and street). If you have a P.O. box, see instructions.	Apt. no.	**Presidential Election Campaign** Check here if you, or your spouse if filing jointly, want $3 to go to this fund. Checking a box below will not change your tax or refund. ☐ **You** ☐ **Spouse**
City, town, or post office. If you have a foreign address, also complete spaces below.	State / ZIP code	
Foreign country name	Foreign province/state/county / Foreign postal code	

Filing Status
Check only one box.
☐ Single ☐ Head of household (HOH)
☐ Married filing jointly (even if only one had income)
☐ Married filing separately (MFS) ☐ Qualifying surviving spouse (QSS)
If you checked the MFS box, enter the name of your spouse. If you checked the HOH or QSS box, enter the child's name if the qualifying person is a child but not your dependent: ____________
☐ If treating a nonresident alien or dual-status alien spouse as a U.S. resident for the entire tax year, check the box and enter their name (see instructions and attach statement if required): ____________

Digital Assets At any time during 2024, did you: (a) receive (as a reward, award, or payment for property or services); or (b) sell, exchange, or otherwise dispose of a digital asset (or a financial interest in a digital asset)? (See instructions.) ☐ **Yes** ☐ **No**

Standard Deduction **Someone can claim:** ☐ You as a dependent ☐ Your spouse as a dependent
☐ Spouse itemizes on a separate return or you were a dual-status alien

Age/Blindness **You:** ☐ Were born before January 2, 1960 ☐ Are blind **Spouse:** ☐ Was born before January 2, 1960 ☐ Is blind

Dependents (see instructions):
If more than four dependents, see instructions and check here . . ☐

(1) First name Last name	(2) Social security number	(3) Relationship to you	(4) Check the box if qualifies for (see instructions): Child tax credit	Credit for other dependents
			☐	☐
			☐	☐
			☐	☐
			☐	☐

Income

Attach Form(s) W-2 here. Also attach Forms W-2G and 1099-R if tax was withheld.
If you did not get a Form W-2, see instructions.

1a	Total amount from Form(s) W-2, box 1 (see instructions)	1a	
b	Household employee wages not reported on Form(s) W-2	1b	
c	Tip income not reported on line 1a (see instructions)	1c	
d	Medicaid waiver payments not reported on Form(s) W-2 (see instructions)	1d	
e	Taxable dependent care benefits from Form 2441, line 26	1e	
f	Employer-provided adoption benefits from Form 8839, line 29	1f	
g	Wages from Form 8919, line 6	1g	
h	Other earned income (see instructions)	1h	
i	Nontaxable combat pay election (see instructions) 1i		
z	Add lines 1a through 1h	1z	
2a	Tax-exempt interest . . . 2a ____ b Taxable interest	2b	
3a	Qualified dividends . . . 3a ____ b Ordinary dividends	3b	
4a	IRA distributions . . . 4a ____ b Taxable amount	4b	
5a	Pensions and annuities . . 5a ____ b Taxable amount	5b	
6a	Social security benefits . . 6a ____ b Taxable amount	6b	
c	If you elect to use the lump-sum election method, check here (see instructions) ☐		
7	Capital gain or (loss). Attach Schedule D if required. If not required, check here ☐	7	
8	Additional income from Schedule 1, line 10	8	
9	Add lines 1z, 2b, 3b, 4b, 5b, 6b, 7, and 8. This is your **total income**	9	
10	Adjustments to income from Schedule 1, line 26	10	
11	Subtract line 10 from line 9. This is your **adjusted gross income**	11	
12	**Standard deduction or itemized deductions** (from Schedule A)	12	
13	Qualified business income deduction from Form 8995 or Form 8995-A	13	
14	Add lines 12 and 13	14	
15	Subtract line 14 from line 11. If zero or less, enter -0-. This is your **taxable income**	15	

Attach Sch. B if required.

Standard Deduction for—
- Single or Married filing separately, $14,600
- Married filing jointly or Qualifying surviving spouse, $29,200
- Head of household, $21,900
- If you checked any box under *Standard Deduction*, see instructions.

For Disclosure, Privacy Act, and Paperwork Reduction Act Notice, see separate instructions. Cat. No. 11320B Form **1040** (2024)

Form 1040 (2024) Page **2**

Tax and Credits	16	**Tax** (see instructions). Check if any from Form(s): **1** ☐ 8814 **2** ☐ 4972 **3** ☐		16
	17	Amount from Schedule 2, line 3		17
	18	Add lines 16 and 17		18
	19	Child tax credit or credit for other dependents from Schedule 8812		19
	20	Amount from Schedule 3, line 8		20
	21	Add lines 19 and 20		21
	22	Subtract line 21 from line 18. If zero or less, enter -0-		22
	23	Other taxes, including self-employment tax, from Schedule 2, line 21		23
	24	Add lines 22 and 23. This is your **total tax**		24
Payments	25	Federal income tax withheld from:		
	a	Form(s) W-2	25a	
	b	Form(s) 1099	25b	
	c	Other forms (see instructions)	25c	
	d	Add lines 25a through 25c		25d
If you have a qualifying child, attach Sch. EIC.	26	2024 estimated tax payments and amount applied from 2023 return		26
	27	Earned income credit (EIC)	27	
	28	Additional child tax credit from Schedule 8812	28	
	29	American opportunity credit from Form 8863, line 8	29	
	30	Reserved for future use	30	
	31	Amount from Schedule 3, line 15	31	
	32	Add lines 27, 28, 29, and 31. These are your **total other payments and refundable credits**		32
	33	Add lines 25d, 26, and 32. These are your **total payments**		33
Refund	34	If line 33 is more than line 24, subtract line 24 from line 33. This is the amount you **overpaid**		34
	35a	Amount of line 34 you want **refunded to you.** If Form 8888 is attached, check here ☐		35a
Direct deposit? See instructions.	b	Routing number	**c** Type: ☐ Checking ☐ Savings	
	d	Account number		
	36	Amount of line 34 you want **applied to your 2025 estimated tax**	36	
Amount You Owe	37	Subtract line 33 from line 24. This is the **amount you owe.** For details on how to pay, go to *www.irs.gov/Payments* or see instructions		37
	38	Estimated tax penalty (see instructions)	38	

Third Party Designee Do you want to allow another person to discuss this return with the IRS? See instructions ☐ **Yes.** Complete below. ☐ **No**

Designee's name | Phone no. | Personal identification number (PIN)

Sign Here Under penalties of perjury, I declare that I have examined this return and accompanying schedules and statements, and to the best of my knowledge and belief, they are true, correct, and complete. Declaration of preparer (other than taxpayer) is based on all information of which preparer has any knowledge.

Your signature	Date	Your occupation	If the IRS sent you an Identity Protection PIN, enter it here (see inst.)
Spouse's signature. If a joint return, **both** must sign.	Date	Spouse's occupation	If the IRS sent your spouse an Identity Protection PIN, enter it here (see inst.)
Phone no.	Email address		

Joint return? See instructions. Keep a copy for your records.

Paid Preparer Use Only

Preparer's name	Preparer's signature	Date	PTIN	Check if: ☐ Self-employed
Firm's name			Phone no.	
Firm's address			Firm's EIN	

Go to *www.irs.gov/Form1040* for instructions and the latest information. Form **1040** (2024)

Source: www.irs.gov

Exhibit 13.5 Georgia Form 500 Individual Income Tax Return

2500404116

Please print your numbers like this in black or blue ink: 9 8 7 6 5 4 3 2 1 0

Georgia Form 500 (Rev. 08/01/24)
Individual Income Tax Return
Georgia Department of Revenue
2024 (Approved web2 version)

Page 1

Fiscal Year Beginning ☐☐-☐☐-☐☐☐☐ STATE ISSUED ☐☐

Fiscal Year Ending ☐☐-☐☐-☐☐☐☐ YOUR DRIVER'S LICENSE/STATE ID

1. YOUR FIRST NAME | MI | YOUR SOCIAL SECURITY NUMBER

LAST NAME (For Name Change See IT-511 Tax Booklet) | SUFFIX

SPOUSE'S FIRST NAME | MI | SPOUSE'S SOCIAL SECURITY NUMBER

LAST NAME | SUFFIX

DEPARTMENT USE ONLY

2. ADDRESS (NUMBER AND STREET or P.O. BOX) (Use 2nd address line for Apt, Suite or Building Number) ☐ CHECK IF ADDRESS HAS CHANGED

3. CITY (Please insert a space if the city has multiple names) | STATE | ZIP CODE

(COUNTRY IF FOREIGN)

4. Enter your Residency Status with the appropriate number .... Residency Status 4. ☐

1. FULL-YEAR RESIDENT 2. PART-YEAR RESIDENT ☐☐-☐☐-☐☐☐☐ TO ☐☐-☐☐-☐☐☐☐ 3. NONRESIDENT

Omit Lines 9 thru 14 and use Form 500 Schedule 3 if you are a part-year or nonresident filer.

5. Enter Filing Status with appropriate letter (See IT-511 Tax Booklet) .... Filing Status 5. ☐

A. Single
B. Married filing jointly
C. Married filing separately (Spouse's social security number must be entered above)
D. Head of household or Qualifying surviving spouse

6a. Your Date of Birth ☐☐-☐☐-☐☐☐☐ 6b. Spouse's Date of Birth ☐☐-☐☐-☐☐☐☐

7a. Number of Qualified Dependents* ☐☐ 7b. Number of Unborn Dependents ☐☐ 7c. Total Number of Dependents ☐☐

*Enter details on Line 7d., and DO NOT include yourself, spouse and/or your unborn dependents. See IT-511 Tax Booklet.

All Pages (1-5) are required for processing

Georgia Form 500
Individual Income Tax Return
Georgia Department of Revenue
2024 **Page 2**

2500404126

YOUR SOCIAL SECURITY NUMBER

7d. Qualified Dependents. (If you have more than 4 dependents, attach a list of additional dependents).

First Name, MI.	Last Name
Social Security Number	Relationship to You
First Name, MI.	Last Name
Social Security Number	Relationship to You
First Name, MI.	Last Name
Social Security Number	Relationship to You
First Name, MI.	Last Name
Social Security Number	Relationship to You

INCOME COMPUTATIONS

If amount on line 8, 9, 10, 13 or 15 is negative, use the minus sign (-). Example -3456.

8. Federal adjusted gross income (From Federal Form 1040) .... 8. ___ , ___ , ___ . 00
(Do not use FEDERAL TAXABLE INCOME) If the amount on Line 8 is $40,000 or more, or your gross income is less than your W-2s you must include a copy of your Federal Form 1040 Pages 1, 2, and Schedule 1.

9. Adjustments from Form 500 Schedule 1 (See IT-511 Tax Booklet) .... 9. ___ , ___ , ___ . 00

10. Georgia adjusted gross income (Net total of Line 8 and Line 9) .... 10. ___ , ___ , ___ . 00

11. Standard Deduction (Do not use FEDERAL STANDARD DEDUCTION) .... 11. ___ , ___ . 00
(See IT-511 Tax Booklet)

Enter $12,000 if the filing status from Line 5 is A, C, or D. If the filing status is B, enter $24,000.
Use EITHER Line 11 OR Line 12c. (Do not write on both lines).

12. Total Itemized Deductions used in computing Federal Taxable Income. If you use itemized deductions, **you must include Federal Schedule A.**

a. Federal Itemized Deductions (Schedule A- Form 1040) .... 12a. ___ , ___ , ___ . 00

b. Less adjustments: (See IT-511 Tax Booklet) .... 12b. ___ , ___ , ___ . 00

c. Georgia Total Itemized Deductions .... 12c. ___ , ___ , ___ . 00

13. Subtract either Line 11 or Line 12c from Line 10; enter balance .... 13. ___ , ___ , ___ . 00

All Pages (1-5) are required for processing

Georgia Form 500
Individual Income Tax Return
Georgia Department of Revenue
2024

Page 3

2500404136

YOUR SOCIAL SECURITY NUMBER

14. Enter the number from Line 7c [ ] Multiply by $4,000 .... 14. .00

15a. Income before GA NOL (Line 13 less Line 14 or Schedule 3, Line 14) .... 15a. .00

15b. Georgia NOL utilized (Cannot exceed Line 15a or the amount after applying the 80% limitation, see IT-511 Tax Booklet for more information)... 15b. .00

15c. Georgia Taxable Income (Subtract Line 15b from Line 15a) .... 15c. .00

16. Tax (Multiply Line 15c by 5.39%. Round to the nearest dollar) .... 16. .00

17. Low Income Credit 17a. [ ] 17b. [ ] .... 17c. .00

18. Other State(s) Tax Credit (Include a copy of the other state(s) return) .... 18. .00

19. Georgia Resident Itemizer Tax Credit **(See IT-511 Tax Booklet)** .... 19. .00

20. Credits used from IND-CR Summary Worksheet .... 20. .00

21. **Total Credits Used from Schedule 2 Georgia Tax Credits (must be filed electronically)** 21. .00

22. Total Credits Used (sum of Lines 17-21) cannot exceed Line 16 .... 22. .00

23. Balance (Subtract Line 22 from Line 16) if zero or less than zero, enter zero.... 23. .00

INCOME STATEMENT DETAILS Only enter income on which Georgia tax was withheld. Enter income from W-2s, 1099s, and G2-As on Line 4 GA Wages/Income. For other income statements complete Line 4 using the income reported from **Form G2-RP Line 12** or **13**; **Form G2-LP Line 11**, or for **Form G2-FL enter zero**.

(INCOME STATEMENT A)

1. WITHHOLDING TYPE:
   ☐ W-2 ☐ G2-A ☐ G2-LP
   ☐ 1099 ☐ G2-FL ☐ G2-RP
2. EMPLOYER/PAYER FEDERAL ID NUMBER (FEIN) ☐ SSN ☐
3. EMPLOYER/PAYER STATE WITHHOLDING ID
4. GA WAGES / INCOME .00
5. GA TAX WITHHELD .00

(INCOME STATEMENT B)

1. WITHHOLDING TYPE:
   ☐ W-2 ☐ G2-A ☐ G2-LP
   ☐ 1099 ☐ G2-FL ☐ G2-RP
2. EMPLOYER/PAYER FEDERAL ID NUMBER (FEIN) ☐ SSN ☐
3. EMPLOYER/PAYER STATE WITHHOLDING ID
4. GA WAGES / INCOME .00
5. GA TAX WITHHELD .00

(INCOME STATEMENT C)

1. WITHHOLDING TYPE:
   ☐ W-2 ☐ G2-A ☐ G2-LP
   ☐ 1099 ☐ G2-FL ☐ G2-RP
2. EMPLOYER/PAYER FEDERAL ID NUMBER (FEIN) ☐ SSN ☐
3. EMPLOYER/PAYER STATE WITHHOLDING ID
4. GA WAGES / INCOME .00
5. GA TAX WITHHELD .00

PLEASE COMPLETE INCOME STATEMENT DETAILS ON PAGE 4.

All Pages (1-5) are required for processing

Georgia Form 500
Individual Income Tax Return
Georgia Department of Revenue
2024

2500404146

YOUR SOCIAL SECURITY NUMBER

Page 4

(INCOME STATEMENT D)
1. WITHHOLDING TYPE: ☐ W-2 ☐ G2-A ☐ G2-LP ☐ 1099 ☐ G2-FL ☐ G2-RP
2. EMPLOYER/PAYER FEDERAL ID NUMBER (FEIN) ☐ SSN ☐
3. EMPLOYER/PAYER STATE WITHHOLDING ID
4. GA WAGES / INCOME .00
5. GA TAX WITHHELD .00

(INCOME STATEMENT E)
1. WITHHOLDING TYPE: ☐ W-2 ☐ G2-A ☐ G2-LP ☐ 1099 ☐ G2-FL ☐ G2-RP
2. EMPLOYER/PAYER FEDERAL ID NUMBER (FEIN) ☐ SSN ☐
3. EMPLOYER/PAYER STATE WITHHOLDING ID
4. GA WAGES / INCOME .00
5. GA TAX WITHHELD .00

(INCOME STATEMENT F)
1. WITHHOLDING TYPE: ☐ W-2 ☐ G2-A ☐ G2-LP ☐ 1099 ☐ G2-FL ☐ G2-RP
2. EMPLOYER/PAYER FEDERAL ID NUMBER (FEIN) ☐ SSN ☐
3. EMPLOYER/PAYER STATE WITHHOLDING ID
4. GA WAGES / INCOME .00
5. GA TAX WITHHELD .00

24. **Georgia Income Tax Withheld on Wages and 1099s** .... 24. .00
(Enter Tax Withheld Only and include W-2s and/or 1099s)

25. **Other Georgia Income Tax Withheld** .... 25. .00
(Must include G2-A, G2-FL, G2-LP and/or G2-RP)

26. Estimated Tax paid for 2024 and Form IT-560 .... 26. .00

27. Schedule 2B Refundable Tax Credits........ 27. .00
(Cannot be claimed unless filed electronically)

28. Total prepayment credits (Add Lines 24, 25, 26 and 27)........ 28. .00

29. If Line 23 exceeds Line 28, subtract Line 28 from Line 23 and enter balance due........ 29. .00

30. If Line 28 exceeds Line 23, subtract Line 23 from Line 28 and enter overpayment .... 30. .00

31. **Amount to be credited to 2025 ESTIMATED TAX** .... 31. .00

32. Georgia Wildlife Conservation Fund **(No gift of less than $1.00)**........ 32. .00

33. Georgia Fund for Children and Elderly **(No gift of less than $1.00)**........ 33. .00

34. Georgia Cancer Research Fund **(No gift of less than $1.00)**........ 34. .00

35. Georgia Land Conservation Program **(No gift of less than $1.00)**........ 35. .00

36. Georgia National Guard Foundation **(No gift of less than $1.00)**........ 36. .00

37. Dog & Cat Sterilization Fund **(No gift of less than $1.00)**........ 37. .00

38. Saving the Cure Fund **(No gift of less than $1.00)**........ 38. .00

39. Realizing Educational Achievement Can Happen (REACH) Program .... 39. .00
(No gift of less than $1.00)

All Pages (1-5) are required for processing

Georgia Form 500
Individual Income Tax Return
Georgia Department of Revenue
2024 Page 5

2500404156

YOUR SOCIAL SECURITY NUMBER

40. Public Safety Memorial Grant **(No gift of less than $1.00)** .... 40. , .00

41. Disabled Veterans' Scholarship Fund **(No gift of less than $1.00)** .... 41. , .00

42. Form 500 UET **(Estimated tax penalty)** ☐ 500 UET exception attached .... 42. , , .00

43. Penalty: Late Payment and/or Late Filing .... 43. , , .00

44. Interest .... 44. , , .00

45. **(If you owe)** Add Lines 29, 32 through 44 .... 45. , , .00
MAKE CHECK PAYABLE TO GEORGIA DEPARTMENT OF REVENUE,
Mail To: GEORGIA DEPARTMENT OF REVENUE PROCESSING CENTER,
PO BOX 740399 ATLANTA, GA 30374-0399

46. **(If you are due a refund)** Subtract the sum of Lines 31 thru 44 from Line 30
THIS IS YOUR REFUND .... 46. , , .00
Refund Due Mail To: GEORGIA DEPARTMENT OF REVENUE PROCESSING CENTER,
PO BOX 740392 ATLANTA, GA 30374-0392

If you do not enter Direct Deposit information or if you are a first time filer you will be issued a paper check.

46a. **Direct Deposit (U.S. Accounts Only)** **Type: Checking** ☐ **Savings** ☐

Routing Number **Account Number**

Mail pages 1-5 and any applicable schedules, forms, documentation. DO NOT staple pages.
I/We declare under the penalties of perjury that I/we have examined this return (including accompanying schedules and statements) and to the best of my/our knowledge and belief, it is true, correct, and complete. If prepared by a person other than the taxpayer(s), this declaration is based on all information of which the preparer has knowledge.

Taxpayer's Signature ☐ (Check box if deceased) Spouse's Signature ☐ (Check box if deceased)

Taxpayer's Date of Death Spouse's Date of Death

Taxpayer's Signature Date Taxpayer's Phone Number Spouse's Signature Date

By providing my e-mail address I am authorizing the Georgia Department of Revenue to electronically notify me at the below e-mail address regarding any updates to my account(s).

Taxpayer's E-mail Address

☐ I authorize DOR to discuss this return with the named preparer.

Signature of Preparer Preparer's Phone Number

Name of Preparer Other Than Taxpayer Preparer's FEIN

Preparer's Firm Name Preparer's SSN/PTIN/SIDN

All Pages (1-5) are required for processing

Exhibit 13.6 IRS Form 1041 U.S. Income Tax Return for Estates and Trusts

Form **1041** Department of the Treasury—Internal Revenue Service
U.S. Income Tax Return for Estates and Trusts
Go to *www.irs.gov/Form1041* for instructions and the latest information.
2024 OMB No. 1545-0092

A Check all that apply:
- ☐ Decedent's estate
- ☐ Simple trust
- ☐ Complex trust
- ☐ Qualified disability trust
- ☐ ESBT (S portion only)
- ☐ Grantor type trust
- ☐ Bankruptcy estate—Ch. 7
- ☐ Bankruptcy estate—Ch. 11
- ☐ Pooled income fund

For calendar year 2024 or fiscal year beginning , 2024, and ending , 20

Name of estate or trust (If a grantor type trust, see the instructions.)

Name and title of fiduciary

Number, street, and room or suite no. (If a P.O. box, see the instructions.)

City or town, state or province, country, and ZIP or foreign postal code

C Employer identification number

D Date entity created

E Nonexempt charitable and split-interest trusts, check applicable box(es). See instructions.
- ☐ Described in sec. 4947(a)(1). Check here if not a private foundation . . ☐
- ☐ Described in sec. 4947(a)(2)

B Number of Schedules K-1 attached (see instructions)

F Check applicable boxes: ☐ Initial return ☐ Final return ☐ Amended return ☐ Net operating loss carryback ☐ Change in trust's name ☐ Change in fiduciary ☐ Change in fiduciary's name ☐ Change in fiduciary's address

G Check here if the estate or filing trust made a section 645 election . . . . ☐ Trust TIN

Income	1	Interest income	1	
	2a	Total ordinary dividends	2a	
	b	Qualified dividends allocable to: (1) Beneficiaries ______ (2) Estate or trust ______		
	3	Business income or (loss). Attach Schedule C (Form 1040)	3	
	4	Capital gain or (loss). Attach Schedule D (Form 1041)	4	
	5	Rents, royalties, partnerships, other estates and trusts, etc. Attach Schedule E (Form 1040)	5	
	6	Farm income or (loss). Attach Schedule F (Form 1040)	6	
	7	Ordinary gain or (loss). Attach Form 4797	7	
	8	Other income. List type and amount	8	
	9	**Total income.** Combine lines 1, 2a, and 3 through 8	9	
Deductions	10	Interest. Check if Form 4952 is attached ☐	10	
	11	Taxes	11	
	12	Fiduciary fees. If only a portion is deductible under section 67(e), see instructions	12	
	13	Charitable deduction (from Schedule A, line 7)	13	
	14	Attorney, accountant, and return preparer fees. If only a portion is deductible under section 67(e), see instructions	14	
	15a	Other deductions (attach schedule). See instructions for deductions allowable under section 67(e)	15a	
	b	Net operating loss deduction. See instructions	15b	
	16	Add lines 10 through 15b	16	
	17	Adjusted total income or (loss). Subtract line 16 from line 9 17		
	18	Income distribution deduction (from Schedule B, line 15). Attach Schedules K-1 (Form 1041)	18	
	19	Estate tax deduction including certain generation-skipping taxes (attach computation)	19	
	20	Qualified business income deduction. Attach Form 8995 or 8995-A	20	
	21	Exemption	21	
	22	Add lines 18 through 21	22	
Tax and Payments	23	Taxable income. Subtract line 22 from line 17. If a loss, see instructions	23	
	24	**Total tax** (from Schedule G, Part I, line 9)	24	
	25	Current year net 965 tax liability paid from Form 965-A, Part II, column (k) (see instructions)	25	
	26	**Total payments** (from Schedule G, Part II, line 19)	26	
	27	Estimated tax penalty. See instructions	27	
	28	**Tax due.** If line 26 is smaller than the total of lines 24, 25, and 27, enter amount owed	28	
	29	**Overpayment.** If line 26 is larger than the total of lines 24, 25, and 27, enter amount overpaid	29	
	30	Amount of line 29 to be: **a Credited to 2025** ; **b Refunded**	30	

Sign Here
Under penalties of perjury, I declare that I have examined this return, including accompanying schedules and statements, and to the best of my knowledge and belief, it is true, correct, and complete. Declaration of preparer (other than taxpayer) is based on all information of which preparer has any knowledge.

Signature of fiduciary or officer representing fiduciary | Date | EIN of fiduciary if a financial institution

May the IRS discuss this return with the preparer shown below? See instructions. ☐ Yes ☐ No

Paid Preparer Use Only

Preparer's name	Preparer's signature	Date	Check ☐ if self-employed	PTIN
Firm's name			Firm's EIN	
Firm's address			Phone no.	

For Paperwork Reduction Act Notice, see the separate instructions. Cat. No. 11370H Form **1041** (2024)

Form 1041 (2024) Page 2

Schedule A **Charitable Deduction.** Don't complete for a simple trust or a pooled income fund.

1	Amounts paid or permanently set aside for charitable purposes from gross income. See instructions	1	
2	Tax-exempt income allocable to charitable contributions. See instructions	2	
3	Subtract line 2 from line 1	3	
4	Capital gains for the tax year allocated to corpus and paid or permanently set aside for charitable purposes	4	
5	Add lines 3 and 4	5	
6	Section 1202 exclusion allocable to capital gains paid or permanently set aside for charitable purposes. See instructions	6	
7	**Charitable deduction.** Subtract line 6 from line 5. Enter here and on page 1, line 13	7	

Schedule B **Income Distribution Deduction**

1	Adjusted total income. See instructions			1	
2	Adjusted tax-exempt interest			2	
3	Total net gain from Schedule D (Form 1041), line 19, column (1). See instructions			3	
4	Enter amount from Schedule A, line 4 (minus any allocable section 1202 exclusion)			4	
5	Capital gains for the tax year included on Schedule A, line 1. See instructions			5	
6	Enter any gain from page 1, line 4, as a negative number. If page 1, line 4, is a loss, enter the loss as a positive number			6	
7	**Distributable net income.** Combine lines 1 through 6. If zero or less, enter -0-			7	
8	If a complex trust, enter accounting income for the tax year as determined under the governing instrument and applicable local law	8			
9	Income required to be distributed currently			9	
10	Other amounts paid, credited, or otherwise required to be distributed			10	
11	Total distributions. Add lines 9 and 10. If greater than line 8, see instructions			11	
12	Enter the amount of tax-exempt income included on line 11			12	
13	Tentative income distribution deduction. Subtract line 12 from line 11			13	
14	Tentative income distribution deduction. Subtract line 2 from line 7. If zero or less, enter -0-			14	
15	**Income distribution deduction.** Enter the smaller of line 13 or line 14 here and on page 1, line 18			15	

Schedule G **Tax Computation and Payments** (see instructions)

Part I — Tax Computation

1	**Tax:**				
a	Tax on taxable income. See instructions	1a			
b	Tax on lump-sum distributions. Attach Form 4972	1b			
c	Alternative minimum tax (from Schedule I (Form 1041), line 54)	1c			
d	Amount from Form 4255, Part I, line 3, column (q)	1d			
e	**Total.** Add lines 1a through 1d			1e	
2a	Foreign tax credit. Attach Form 1116	2a			
b	General business credit. Attach Form 3800	2b			
c	Credit for prior year minimum tax. Attach Form 8801	2c			
d	Bond credits. Attach Form 8912	2d			
e	**Total credits.** Add lines 2a through 2d			2e	
3	Subtract line 2e from line 1e. If zero or less, enter -0-			3	
4	Tax on the ESBT portion of the trust (from ESBT Tax Worksheet, line 17). See instructions			4	
5	Net investment income tax from Form 8960, line 21			5	
6a	Amount from Form 4255, Part I, line 3, column (r)			6a	
b	Recapture tax from Form 8611			6b	
c	Other recapture taxes:			6c	
7	Household employment taxes. Attach Schedule H (Form 1040)			7	
8	Other taxes and amounts due			8	
9	**Total tax.** Add lines 3 through 8. Enter here and on page 1, line 24			9	

Form **1041** (2024)

Form 1041 (2024) Page 3

Schedule G **Tax Computation and Payments** (see instructions) *(continued)*

Part II — Payments

10	Current year's estimated tax payments and amount applied from preceding year's return	**10**	
11	Estimated tax payments allocated to beneficiaries (from Form 1041-T)	**11**	
12	Subtract line 11 from line 10	**12**	
13	Tax paid with Form 7004. See instructions	**13**	
14	Federal income tax withheld. If any is from Form(s) 1099, check here ☐	**14**	
15	Current year net 965 tax liability from Form 965-A, Part I, column (f) (see instructions)	**15**	
16	Payments from Form 2439	**16**	
17	Payments from Form 4136	**17**	
18a	Elective payment election amount from Form 3800	**18a**	
b	Other credits or payments (see instructions)	**18b**	
19	**Total payments.** Add lines 12 through 18b. Enter here and on page 1, line 26	**19**	

Other Information

		Yes	No
1	Did the estate or trust receive tax-exempt income? If "Yes," attach a computation of the allocation of expenses. Enter the amount of tax-exempt interest income and exempt-interest dividends . . . . . $		
2	Did the estate or trust receive all or any part of the earnings (salary, wages, and other compensation) of any individual by reason of a contract assignment or similar arrangement?		
3	At any time during calendar year 2024, did the estate or trust have an interest in or a signature or other authority over a bank, securities, or other financial account in a foreign country? See the instructions for exceptions and filing requirements for FinCEN Form 114. If "Yes," enter the name of the foreign country		
4	During the tax year, did the estate or trust receive a distribution from, or was it the grantor of, or transferor to, a foreign trust? If "Yes," the estate or trust may have to file Form 3520. See instructions		
5	Did the estate or trust receive, or pay, any qualified residence interest on seller-provided financing? If "Yes," see the instructions for the required attachment		
6	If this is an estate or a complex trust making the section 663(b) election, check here. See instructions ☐		
7	To make a section 643(e)(3) election, attach Schedule D (Form 1041), and check here. See instructions ☐		
8	If the decedent's estate has been open for more than 2 years, attach an explanation for the delay in closing the estate, and check here ☐		
9	Are any present or future trust beneficiaries skip persons? See instructions		
10	Was the trust a specified domestic entity required to file Form 8938 for the tax year? See the Instructions for Form 8938		
11a	Did the estate or trust distribute S corporation stock for which it made a section 965(i) election?		
b	If "Yes," did each beneficiary enter into an agreement to be liable for the net tax liability? See instructions		
12	Did the estate or trust either make a section 965(i) election or enter into a transfer agreement as an eligible section 965(i) transferee for S corporation stock held on the last day of the tax year? See instructions		
13	At any time during the tax year, did the estate or trust (a) receive (as a reward, award, or payment for property or services); or (b) sell, exchange, or otherwise dispose of a digital asset (or a financial interest in a digital asset)? See instructions		
14	**ESBTs only.** Does the ESBT have a nonresident alien grantor? If "Yes," see instructions		
15	**ESBTs only.** Did the S portion of the trust claim a qualified business income deduction? If "Yes," see instructions		

Form **1041** (2024)

Source: www.irs.gov

Exhibit 13.7 Georgia Form 501 Fiduciary Income Tax Return

2500804111

Georgia Form 501 (Rev. 07/11/24)
Fiduciary Income Tax Return
2024 (Approved web2 version)

Page 1

Fiscal Year Beginning ☐☐-☐☐-☐☐☐☐
Fiscal Year Ending ☐☐-☐☐-☐☐☐☐

☐ Change in Trust or Estate Name
☐ Change in Fiduciary
☐ Change of Address

☐ Grantor Trust
☐ Trust is a Qualified Funeral Trust
☐ Estate is a Bankruptcy Estate
☐ 500 UET Exception Attached

Department Use Only

Enter your Residency Status with the appropriate number 1. Full-Year 2. Part Year ________ to ________ 3. Nonresident ☐

A. Federal Employer ID No.	Name of Estate or Trust		Date of Creation of Trust
B. Date of Decedent's Death	Name of Fiduciary	Title of Fiduciary	Telephone No.

C. Address of Fiduciary (Number and Street)			(Apt., Suite or Building Number)
City	State	Zip Code	Country

Schedule 1 - Computation of Tax		
1. Income of fiduciary (Adjusted total income from attached Form 1041)	1.	
2. Adjustments: (List of all items in Schedule 2, Page 3)	2.	
3. **Total (Net total of Lines 1 and 2)**	3.	
4. Beneficiaries' Share of Income (Total of Schedule 3)	4.	
5. **Balance (Line 3 less Line 4)**	5.	
6. Exemptions: ☐ 6a. Trust $1350 ☐ 6b. Estate $2700	6.	
7a. Georgia Taxable Income before GA NOL (Line 5 less Line 6 or Line 14, Schedule 4)	7a.	
7b. Georgia NOL utilized (cannot exceed Line 7a or the amount after applying the 80% limitation, see instructions for more information)	7b.	
7c. Net taxable income of fiduciary (Line 7a less Line 7b)	7c.	
8. **Total tax**	8.	
9. Credits used 9a. Other state(s) tax credit used (Include a copy of the other state(s) tax return)	9a.	
9b. **Schedule 5 credits (cannot be claimed unless filed electronically)**	9b.	
9c. Total Credits used (9a plus 9b cannot exceed Line 8)	9c.	
10. **Tax less credit used (Net total of Line 8 less Line 9c, if 0 or less, enter 0)**	10.	

Georgia Form 501
Fiduciary Income Tax Return
(Approved web2 version)

Page 2

2500804121

TAXPAYER'S FEIN

Schedule 1- Computation of Tax (continued)

11. 11a. **Georgia Estimated Tax Paid**	11a.	
11b. **Tax Withheld** (1099, G2-A, G2-LP and/or G2-RP)	11b.	
11c. **Schedule 5B Refundable Tax Credits** **(Cannot be claimed unless filed electronically)**	11c.	
11d. **Total** (Add Lines 11a, 11b and 11c)	11d.	
12. **Balance of tax due.** If Line 10 exceeds Line 11d, enter Line 10 less Line 11d	12.	
13. **Overpayment.** If Line 11d exceeds Line 10, enter Line 11d less Line 10	13.	
14. Amount from Line 13 to be credited to next year's estimated tax	14.	
15. **Interest**	15.	
16. **Late payment penalty**	16.	
17. **Late filing penalty**	17.	
18. Penalty for underpayment of estimated tax (UET)	18.	
19. **(If you owe)** Add Lines 12, 15 thru 18. **Make check payable to Georgia Department of Revenue.**	19.	
20. **(If you are due a refund)** Subtract the sum of Lines 14 thru 18 from Line 13. This is your refund.	20.	

Mail To: Georgia Department of Revenue Processing Center PO Box 740316 Atlanta, Georgia 30374-0316

Direct Deposit Options

20a. **Direct Deposit (For U.S. Accounts Only)** Type: Checking ☐ Routing Number

See Instructions in the IT-511 booklet for further details.
If you do not enter Direct Deposit information or if you are a first time filer you will be issued a paper check. Savings ☐ Account Number

DECLARATION: I/We declare under the penalties of perjury that I/we have examined this return (including accompanying schedules and statements) and to the best of my/our knowledge and belief, it is true, correct, and complete. If prepared by a person other than the taxpayer, this declaration is based on all information of which the preparer has knowledge.

SIGNATURE OF FIDUCIARY DATE PHONE NUMBER

By providing my e-mail address I am authorizing the Georgia Department of Revenue to electronically notify me at the below e-mail address regarding any updates to my account(s).

FIDUCIARY E-MAIL ADDRESS

☐ Check the box to authorize the Georgia Department of Revenue to discuss the contents of this return with the named preparer.

SIGNATURE OF PREPARER OTHER THAN FIDUCIARY DATE PREPARER'S IDENTIFICATION NUMBER

NAME OF PREPARER OTHER THAN FIDUCIARY PHONE NUMBER

THE FIDUCIARY MUST ATTACH TO THIS RETURN A COPY OF ITS FEDERAL RETURN AND SUPPORTING SCHEDULES

Georgia Form 501
Fiduciary Income Tax Return
(Approved web2 version)

Page 3

2500804131

TAXPAYER'S FEIN

Schedule 2 - Adjustments to Income

ADDITIONS		
1. Municipal bond interest - Other states	1.	
2. Income tax deduction other than Georgia	2.	
3. Expense allocable to exempt income (Other than U.S. obligations)	3.	
4. Net operating loss carryover deducted on the Federal return	4.	
5. Other	5.	
6. **TOTAL ADDITIONS**	6.	

SUBTRACTIONS		
7. Interest - U.S. Government Obligations (Must be reduced by direct and indirect interest expense)	7.	
8. Income Tax Refund other than Georgia	8.	
9. Reserved	9.	
10. Other	10.	
11. **TOTAL SUBTRACTIONS**	11.	
12. **NET ADJUSTMENT:** Total additions less total subtractions. (Enter here and on Line 2, Schedule 1 or Schedule 4, Line 7)	12.	

Schedule 3 - Beneficiaries' Share of Income (For each Beneficiary complete Name, Address, City, State, ZIP, Country, ID Number and Share of Income)

A	Name	ID Number		Share of Income
	Address			
	City	State	ZIP	Country
B	Name	ID Number		Share of Income
	Address			
	City	State	ZIP	Country
C	Name	ID Number		Share of Income
	Address			
	City	State	ZIP	Country
D	**Enter total** (Including additional Beneficiaries' Share of Income from attached schedule). Enter here and on Line 4, Schedule 1 or Line 12, Schedule 4			

Georgia Form 501
Fiduciary Income Tax Return
(Approved web2 version)

Page 4

2500804141

TAXPAYER'S FEIN ____________

Schedule 4 - Computation of Georgia Taxable Income For Part Year and Nonresident Fiduciary (ROUND TO NEAREST DOLLAR)

Enter your Residency Status with the appropriate number........................ ☐ Part Year Resident ____________ to ____________

	Total Income From All Sources Column A	Georgia Source Income Column B
1. Interest Income .... 1.		
2. Dividend Income .... 2.		
3. Business Income or (loss) .... 3.		
4. Other Income or (loss) .... 4.		
5. Total Income (Add Lines 1 through 4).................... 5.		
6. Total deductions used in arriving at Adjusted Total Income from Form 1041 .... 6.		
7. Net Adjustments from Schedule 2 .... 7.		
8. Total (Line 5 minus Line 6 plus or minus Line 7) .... 8.		

9. Ratio: Divide Line 8 Col. B by Line 8 Col. A (% cannot be negative and cannot exceed 100%) Enter percentage here .... 9.	
10. Exemptions: (Trusts $1350, Estates $2700) .... 10.	
11. Part Year/Nonresident exemption (Multiply Line 9 by Line 10) .... 11.	
12. Beneficiaries share of GA income from Schedule 3.................... 12.	
13. Total Deductions (Add Lines 11 and 12) .... 13.	
14. Georgia taxable income before GA NOL (Line 8 Col. B less Line 13). Enter here and on Form 501 Line 7a. .... 14.	

CREDITS MUST BE FILED ELECTRONICALLY

Georgia Form 501
Fiduciary Income Tax Return
(Approved web2 version)

Page 5

2500804151

TAXPAYER'S FEIN

Schedule 5 - Credit Usage and Carryover (ROUND TO NEAREST DOLLAR)

1. **Complete a separate schedule for each Credit Code.**
2. Total the amounts on Line 13 of each schedule and enter the total on the credit line of the return.
3. If there is a credit eligible for carryover to this tax year, please complete a schedule even if the credit is not used for this tax year.
4. See the instructions for a list of credit codes.
5. See the relevant forms, statutes, and regulations to determine how the credit is allocated to the owners and to determine when carryovers expire.
6. If the credit for a particular credit code originated with more than one person or company, enter separate information on Lines 3 through 9 below.
7. The credit certificate number is issued by the Department of Revenue for credits that are preapproved. If applicable, please enter the Department of Revenue credit certificate number where indicated.
8. Before the Line 14 carryover is applied to next tax year, the amount must be reduced by any amounts elected to be applied to withholding for this tax year and by any carryovers that have expired.

For the credit generated this tax year, list the Company Name, ID Number, and Credit Certificate number if applicable. Purchased credits should also be included. If the credit originated with this taxpayer, enter this taxpayer's name and ID# below.

1. Credit Code	
2. Credit remaining from previous years (do not include amounts elected to be applied to withholding)	
3. Company Name	ID Number
Credit Certificate #	Credit Generated this Tax Year
4. Company Name	ID Number
Credit Certificate #	Credit Generated this Tax Year
5. Company Name	ID Number
Credit Certificate #	Credit Generated this Tax Year
6. Company Name	ID Number
Credit Certificate #	Credit Generated this Tax Year
7. Company Name	ID Number
Credit Certificate #	Credit Generated this Tax Year
8. Company Name	ID Number
Credit Certificate #	Credit Generated this Tax Year
9. Company Name	ID Number
Credit Certificate #	Credit Generated this Tax Year
10. Total available credit for this tax year (sum of Lines 2 through 9)	10.
11. Enter the amount of the credit sold (only certain credits can be sold, see instructions)	11.
12. List the credit allocated to the beneficiaries (See Schedule 6)	12.
13. Credit used for this tax year, enter here and on 501 Line 9b	13.
14. Potential carryover to next tax year (Line 10 less Lines 11,12, and 13)	14.

CREDITS MUST BE FILED ELECTRONICALLY

Exhibit 13.8 IRS Form 706 United States Estate (and Generation-Skipping Transfer) Tax Return

Form **706**
(Rev. August 2019)
Department of the Treasury
Internal Revenue Service

United States Estate (and Generation-Skipping Transfer) Tax Return

▶ **Estate of a citizen or resident of the United States (see instructions). To be filed for decedents dying after December 31, 2018.**
▶ **Go to *www.irs.gov/Form706* for instructions and the latest information.**

OMB No. 1545-0015

Part 1—Decedent and Executor

1a Decedent's first name and middle initial (and maiden name, if any)	1b Decedent's last name			2 Decedent's social security no.
3a City, town, or post office; county; state or province; country; and ZIP or foreign postal code	3b Year domicile established	4 Date of birth		5 Date of death
6a Name of executor (see instructions)	6b Executor's address (number and street including apartment or suite no.; city, town, or post office; state or province; country; and ZIP or foreign postal code) and phone no.			
6c Executor's social security number (see instructions)	Phone no.			

6d If there are multiple executors, check here ☐ and attach a list showing the names, addresses, telephone numbers, and SSNs of the additional executors.

7a Name and location of court where will was probated or estate administered | 7b Case number

8 If decedent died testate, check here ▶ ☐ and attach a certified copy of the will. 9 If you extended the time to file this Form 706, check here ▶ ☐

10 If Schedule R-1 is attached, check here ▶ ☐ 11 If you are estimating the value of assets included in the gross estate on line 1 pursuant to the special rule of Reg. section 20.2010-2(a)(7)(ii), check here ▶ ☐

Part 2—Tax Computation

1	Total gross estate less exclusion (from Part 5—Recapitulation, item 13)		1
2	Tentative total allowable deductions (from Part 5—Recapitulation, item 24)		2
3a	Tentative taxable estate (subtract line 2 from line 1)		3a
b	State death tax deduction		3b
c	Taxable estate (subtract line 3b from line 3a)		3c
4	Adjusted taxable gifts (see instructions)		4
5	Add lines 3c and 4		5
6	Tentative tax on the amount on line 5 from Table A in the instructions		6
7	Total gift tax paid or payable (see instructions)		7
8	Gross estate tax (subtract line 7 from line 6)		8
9a	Basic exclusion amount	9a	
b	Deceased spousal unused exclusion (DSUE) amount from predeceased spouse(s), if any (from Section D, Part 6—Portability of Deceased Spousal Unused Exclusion)	9b	
c	Restored exclusion amount (see instructions)	9c	
d	Applicable exclusion amount (add lines 9a, 9b, and 9c)	9d	
e	Applicable credit amount (tentative tax on the amount in line 9d from Table A in the instructions)	9e	
10	Adjustment to applicable credit amount (May not exceed $6,000. See instructions.)	10	
11	Allowable applicable credit amount (subtract line 10 from line 9e)		11
12	Subtract line 11 from line 8 (but do not enter less than zero)		12
13	Credit for foreign death taxes (from Schedule P). (Attach Form(s) 706-CE.)	13	
14	Credit for tax on prior transfers (from Schedule Q)	14	
15	Total credits (add lines 13 and 14)		15
16	Net estate tax (subtract line 15 from line 12)		16
17	Generation-skipping transfer (GST) taxes payable (from Schedule R, Part 2, line 10)		17
18	Total transfer taxes (add lines 16 and 17)		18
19	Prior payments (explain in an attached statement)		19
20	Balance due (or overpayment) (subtract line 19 from line 18)		20

Under penalties of perjury, I declare that I have examined this return, including accompanying schedules and statements, and to the best of my knowledge and belief, it is true, correct, and complete. Declaration of preparer (other than the executor) is based on all information of which preparer has any knowledge.

Sign Here

▶ Signature of executor ▶ Date

▶ Signature of executor ▶ Date

Paid Preparer Use Only

Print/Type preparer's name	Preparer's signature	Date	Check ☐ if self-employed	PTIN
Firm's name ▶			Firm's EIN ▶	
Firm's address ▶			Phone no.	

For Privacy Act and Paperwork Reduction Act Notice, see instructions. Cat. No. 20548R Form **706** (Rev. 8-2019)

Form 706 (Rev. 8-2019)

Estate of: | **Decedent's social security number**

Part 3—Elections by the Executor

Note: For information on electing portability of the decedent's DSUE amount, including how to opt out of the election, see Part 6—Portability of Deceased Spousal Unused Exclusion.
Note: Some of the following elections may require the posting of bonds or liens.

Please check "Yes" or "No" for each question. See instructions.

			Yes	No
1	Do you elect alternate valuation?	1		
2	Do you elect special-use valuation? If "Yes," you must complete and attach Schedule A-1	2		
3	Do you elect to pay the taxes in installments as described in section 6166? If "Yes," you must attach the additional information described in the instructions. **Note: By electing section 6166 installment payments, you may be required to provide security for estate tax deferred under section 6166 and interest in the form of a surety bond or a section 6324A lien.**	3		
4	Do you elect to postpone the part of the taxes due to a reversionary or remainder interest as described in section 6163?	4		

Part 4—General Information

Note: Please attach the necessary supplemental documents. **You must attach the death certificate.** See instructions.

Authorization to receive confidential tax information under Reg. section 601.504(b)(2)(i); to act as the estate's representative before the IRS; and to make written or oral presentations on behalf of the estate:

Name of representative (print or type)	State	Address (number, street, and room or suite no., city, state, and ZIP code)

I declare that I am the ☐ attorney/ ☐ certified public accountant/ ☐ enrolled agent (check the applicable box) for the executor. I am not under suspension or disbarment from practice before the Internal Revenue Service and am qualified to practice in the state shown above.

Signature	CAF number	Date	Telephone number

1 Death certificate number and issuing authority (attach a copy of the death certificate to this return).

2 Decedent's business or occupation. If retired, check here ▶ ☐ and state decedent's former business or occupation.

3a Marital status of the decedent at time of death:
☐ Married ☐ Widow/widower ☐ Single ☐ Legally separated ☐ Divorced

3b For all prior marriages, list the name and SSN of the former spouse, the date the marriage ended, and whether the marriage ended by annulment, divorce, or death. Attach additional statements of the same size if necessary.

4a Surviving spouse's name	4b Social security number	4c Amount received (see instructions)

5 Individuals (other than the surviving spouse), trusts, or other estates who receive benefits from the estate (do not include charitable beneficiaries shown in Schedule O) (see instructions).

Name of individual, trust, or estate receiving $5,000 or more	Identifying number	Relationship to decedent	Amount (see instructions)
All unascertainable beneficiaries and those who receive less than $5,000 ▶			
Total			

If you answer "Yes" to any of the following questions, you must attach additional information as described.

		Yes	No
6	Is the estate filing a protective claim for refund? If "Yes," complete and attach two copies of Schedule PC for each claim.		
7	Does the gross estate contain any section 2044 property (qualified terminable interest property (QTIP) from a prior gift or estate)? See instructions		
8a	Have federal gift tax returns ever been filed? If "Yes," attach copies of the returns, if available, and furnish the following information.		
b	Period(s) covered — c Internal Revenue office(s) where filed		
9a	Was there any insurance on the decedent's life that is not included on the return as part of the gross estate?		
b	Did the decedent own any insurance on the life of another that is not included in the gross estate?		

Page 2

Form 706 (Rev. 8-2019)

Estate of: | **Decedent's social security number**

Part 4—General Information *(continued)*

If you answer "Yes" to any of the following questions, you must attach additional information as described.		Yes	No
10	Did the decedent at the time of death own any property as a joint tenant with right of survivorship in which **(a)** one or more of the other joint tenants was someone other than the decedent's spouse, and **(b)** less than the full value of the property is included on the return as part of the gross estate? If "Yes," you must complete and attach Schedule E		
11a	Did the decedent, at the time of death, own any interest in a partnership (for example, a family limited partnership), an unincorporated business, or a limited liability company; or own any stock in an inactive or closely held corporation?		
b	If "Yes," was the value of **any** interest owned (from above) discounted on this estate tax return? If "Yes," see the instructions on reporting the total accumulated or effective discounts taken on Schedule F or G		
12	Did the decedent make any transfer described in sections 2035, 2036, 2037, or 2038? See instructions. If "Yes," you must complete and attach Schedule G		
13a	Were there in existence at the time of the decedent's death any trusts created by the decedent during his or her lifetime?		
b	Were there in existence at the time of the decedent's death any trusts not created by the decedent under which the decedent possessed any power, beneficial interest, or trusteeship?		
c	Was the decedent receiving income from a trust created after October 22, 1986, by a parent or grandparent?		
	If "Yes," was there a GST taxable termination (under section 2612) on the death of the decedent?		
d	If there was a GST taxable termination (under section 2612), attach a statement to explain. Provide a copy of the trust or will creating the trust, and give the name, address, and phone number of the current trustee(s).		
e	Did the decedent at any time during his or her lifetime transfer or sell an interest in a partnership, limited liability company, or closely held corporation to a trust described in line 13a or 13b?		
	If "Yes," provide the EIN for this transferred/sold item. ▶		
14	Did the decedent ever possess, exercise, or release any general power of appointment? If "Yes," you must complete and attach Schedule H		
15	Did the decedent have an interest in or a signature or other authority over a financial account in a foreign country, such as a bank account, securities account, or other financial account?		
16	Was the decedent, immediately before death, receiving an annuity described in the "General" paragraph of the instructions for Schedule I or a private annuity? If "Yes," you must complete and attach Schedule I		
17	Was the decedent ever the beneficiary of a trust for which a deduction was claimed by the estate of a predeceased spouse under section 2056(b)(7) and which is not reported on this return? If "Yes," attach an explanation		

Part 5—Recapitulation.

Note: If estimating the value of one or more assets pursuant to the special rule of Reg. section 20.2010-2(a)(7)(ii), enter on both lines 10 and 23 the amount noted in the instructions for the corresponding range of values. See instructions for details.

Item no.	Gross estate		Alternate value	Value at date of death
1	Schedule A—Real Estate	1		
2	Schedule B—Stocks and Bonds	2		
3	Schedule C—Mortgages, Notes, and Cash	3		
4	Schedule D—Insurance on the Decedent's Life (attach Form(s) 712)	4		
5	Schedule E—Jointly Owned Property (attach Form(s) 712 for life insurance)	5		
6	Schedule F—Other Miscellaneous Property (attach Form(s) 712 for life insurance)	6		
7	Schedule G—Transfers During Decedent's Life (att. Form(s) 712 for life insurance)	7		
8	Schedule H—Powers of Appointment	8		
9	Schedule I—Annuities	9		
10	Estimated value of assets subject to the special rule of Reg. section 20.2010-2(a)(7)(ii)	10		
11	Total gross estate (add items 1 through 10)	11		
12	Schedule U—Qualified Conservation Easement Exclusion	12		
13	Total gross estate less exclusion (subtract item 12 from item 11). Enter here and on line 1 of Part 2—Tax Computation	13		

Item no.	Deductions		Amount
14	Schedule J—Funeral Expenses and Expenses Incurred in Administering Property Subject to Claims	14	
15	Schedule K—Debts of the Decedent	15	
16	Schedule K—Mortgages and Liens	16	
17	Total of items 14 through 16	17	
18	Allowable amount of deductions from item 17 (see the instructions for item 18 of the Recapitulation)	18	
19	Schedule L—Net Losses During Administration	19	
20	Schedule L—Expenses Incurred in Administering Property Not Subject to Claims	20	
21	Schedule M—Bequests, etc., to Surviving Spouse	21	
22	Schedule O—Charitable, Public, and Similar Gifts and Bequests	22	
23	Estimated value of deductible assets subject to the special rule of Reg. section 20.2010-2(a)(7)(ii)	23	
24	Tentative total allowable deductions (add items 18 through 23). Enter here and on line 2 of the Tax Computation	24	

Page 3

Form 706 (Rev. 8-2019)

Estate of: | **Decedent's social security number**

Part 6—Portability of Deceased Spousal Unused Exclusion (DSUE)

Portability Election

A decedent with a surviving spouse elects portability of the DSUE amount, if any, by completing and timely filing this return. No further action is required to elect portability of the DSUE amount to allow the surviving spouse to use the decedent's DSUE amount.

Section A. Opting Out of Portability

The estate of a decedent with a surviving spouse may opt out of electing portability of the DSUE amount. Check here and do not complete Sections B and C of Part 6 only if the estate opts **NOT** to elect portability of the DSUE amount. ☐

Section B. Qualified Domestic Trust (QDOT)

	Yes	No
Are any assets of the estate being transferred to a QDOT?		

If "Yes," the DSUE amount portable to a surviving spouse (calculated in Section C, below) is preliminary and shall be redetermined at the time of the final distribution or other taxable event imposing estate tax under section 2056A. See instructions for more details.

Section C. DSUE Amount Portable to the Surviving Spouse (To be completed by the estate of a decedent making a portability election.)

Complete the following calculation to determine the DSUE amount that can be transferred to the surviving spouse.

1	Enter the amount from line 9d, Part 2—Tax Computation	1	
2	Reserved	2	
3	Enter the value of the cumulative lifetime gifts on which tax was paid or payable. See instructions . . .	3	
4	Add lines 1 and 3	4	
5	Enter amount from line 10, Part 2—Tax Computation	5	
6	Divide amount on line 5 by 40% (0.40) (do not enter less than zero)	6	
7	Subtract line 6 from line 4	7	
8	Enter the amount from line 5, Part 2—Tax Computation	8	
9	Subtract line 8 from line 7 (do not enter less than zero)	9	
10	DSUE amount portable to surviving spouse (Enter lesser of line 9 or line 9a, Part 2—Tax Computation) . .	10	

Section D. DSUE Amount Received From Predeceased Spouse(s) (To be completed by the estate of a deceased surviving spouse with DSUE amount from predeceased spouse(s))

Provide the following information to determine the DSUE amount received from deceased spouses.

A Name of Deceased Spouse (dates of death after December 31, 2010, only)	B Date of Death (enter as mm/dd/yy)	C Portability Election Made?		D If "Yes," DSUE Amount Received From Spouse	E DSUE Amount Applied by Decedent to Lifetime Gifts	F Year of Form 709 Reporting Use of DSUE Amount Listed in col. E	G Remaining DSUE Amount, if any (subtract col. E from col. D)
		Yes	No				
Part 1 — DSUE RECEIVED FROM LAST DECEASED SPOUSE							
Part 2 — DSUE RECEIVED FROM OTHER PREDECEASED SPOUSE(S) AND USED BY DECEDENT							
Total (for all DSUE amounts from predeceased spouse(s) applied) . .							

Add the amount from Part 1, column D, and the total from Part 2, column E. Enter the result on line 9b, Part 2—Tax Computation . . . . ▶

Exhibit 13.9 IRS Form 709 United States Gift (and Generation-Skipping Transfer) Tax Return

Form **709**

Department of the Treasury
Internal Revenue Service

United States Gift (and Generation-Skipping Transfer) Tax Return

Go to *www.irs.gov/Form709* for instructions and the latest information.
(For gifts made during calendar year 2024)

OMB No. 1545-0020

2024

Part I General Information

1 Donor's first name and middle initial	2 Donor's last name	3 Donor's social security number
4 Address (number and street). If you have a P.O. box, see instructions.		5 Apt. no.
6 City, town, or post office. If you have a foreign address, also complete spaces below.	7 State	8 ZIP code
9 Foreign country name	10 Foreign province/state/county	11 Foreign postal code
12 Legal residence (domicile)	13 Citizenship (see instructions)	

		Yes	No
14	If the donor died during the year, check here ☐ and enter date of death ______ , ______ .		
15	If an amended return, check here ☐		
16	If you extended the time to file this Form 709, check here ☐		
17	Enter the total number of donees listed on Schedule A. Count each person only once ______		
18a	Have you (the donor) previously filed a Form 709 (or 709-A) for any other year? If "No," skip line 18b		
b	Has your address changed since you last filed Form 709 (or 709-A)?		
19	**Gifts by spouses to third parties.** Did you and your spouse make gifts to third parties? See instructions. (If the answer is "Yes," complete Part III on page 2.)		
20	Have you applied a deceased spousal unused exclusion (DSUE) amount received from a predeceased spouse to a gift or gifts reported on this or a previous Form 709? If "Yes," complete Schedule C		
21	Does any gift or other transfer reported on this Form 709 include a digital asset (or a financial interest in a digital asset)? See instructions		

Part II Tax Computation

1	Enter the amount from Schedule A, Part 4, line 11	1	
2	Enter the amount from Schedule B, line 3	2	
3	Total taxable gifts. Add lines 1 and 2	3	
4	Tax computed on amount on line 3 (see *Table for Computing Gift Tax* in instructions)	4	
5	Tax computed on amount on line 2 (see *Table for Computing Gift Tax* in instructions)	5	
6	Balance. Subtract line 5 from line 4	6	
7	Applicable credit amount. If donor has DSUE amount from predeceased spouse(s) or Restored Exclusion Amount, enter amount from Schedule C, line 5; otherwise, see instructions	7	
8	Enter the applicable credit against tax allowable for all prior periods from Schedule B, line 1, col. (c)	8	
9	Balance. Subtract line 8 from line 7. Do not enter less than zero	9	
10	Enter 20% (0.20) of the amount allowed as a specific exemption for gifts made after September 8, 1976, and before January 1, 1977. See instructions	10	
11	Balance. Subtract line 10 from line 9. Do not enter less than zero	11	
12	Applicable credit. Enter the smaller of line 6 or line 11	12	
13	Credit for foreign gift taxes. See instructions	13	
14	Total credits. Add lines 12 and 13	14	
15	Balance. Subtract line 14 from line 6. Do not enter less than zero	15	
16	Generation-skipping transfer taxes from Schedule D, Part 3, col. (g), total	16	
17	**Total tax.** Add lines 15 and 16	17	
18	Gift and generation-skipping transfer taxes prepaid with extension of time to file	18	
19	If line 18 is less than line 17, enter **balance due**. See instructions	19	
20	If line 18 is greater than line 17, enter **amount to be refunded**	20	

Sign Here

Under penalties of perjury, I declare that I have examined this return, including any accompanying schedules and statements, and to the best of my knowledge and belief, it is true, correct, and complete. Declaration of preparer (other than donor) is based on all information of which preparer has any knowledge.

May the IRS discuss this return with the preparer shown below? See instructions. ☐ Yes ☐ No

Signature of donor | Date

Paid Preparer Use Only

Preparer's name	Preparer's signature	Date	Check ☐ if self-employed	PTIN
Firm's name			Firm's EIN	
Firm's address			Phone no.	

For Disclosure, Privacy Act, and Paperwork Reduction Act Notice, see the instructions for this form. Cat. No. 16783M Form **709** (2024)

Form 709 (2024) Page 2

Part III Spouse's Consent on Gifts to Third Parties

		Yes	No
1	**Gifts by spouses to third parties.** Do you consent to have the gifts (including generation-skipping transfers) made by you and by your spouse to third parties during the calendar year considered as made one-half by each of you? See instructions. (If the answer is "Yes," the following information must be furnished. **If the answer is "No," skip lines 2–7.**)		
2	Name of consenting spouse		
3	SSN of consenting spouse		
4	Were you married to one another during the entire calendar year? See instructions		
5	If line 4 is "No," check whether ☐ married ☐ divorced or ☐ widowed/deceased, and give date. See instructions		
6	Will a gift tax return for this year be filed by your spouse? If "Yes," mail both returns in the same envelope		
7	**Consent of Spouse.** Have you obtained required spousal consent for gifts made to third parties to be considered as made one-half by each spouse? If "Yes," **you must attach a Notice of Consent.** See instructions		

Form **709** (2024)

Key Terms

charitable deduction
credit
death tax
deduction
generation-skipping transfer tax
gross estate
inheritance tax
taxable estate

Review Questions

1. What is the difference between death taxes and inheritance taxes?
2. Why must the Internal Revenue Service be notified of a taxpayer's death?
3. Does the duty to pay personal income taxes end upon a taxpayer's death?
4. Under what circumstances may an estate earn income? What is the process for reporting such income?
5. What is part of a decedent's gross estate?
6. When calculating estate taxes, what is the difference between a deduction and a credit?
7. In Georgia, can a credit be claimed for the payment of state estate taxes? Why or why not?
8. How do we arrive at the amount of a decedent's taxable estate?
9. What kinds of gifts are subject to the federal gift tax, and what tax return(s) should be filed to report the same?
10. What is a generation-skipping transfer tax?

Practical Assignment

Research the annual gift tax exclusion amount and the amount of the unified credit for the last five years. Prepare a chart detailing your findings and provide a citation for each source of your information.

Chapter 14

Ethical Considerations

Learning Objectives

Upon completion of this chapter, you should be able to:

- List and describe the ethical rules applicable to lawyers and paralegals.
- Discuss potential ethical issues that may arise in this practice area.
- Explain the consequences of unethical behavior.

Lawyers and paralegals, like many other professionals, have a **code of ethics**, a standard of conduct by which they must abide. These standards govern the legal team's interactions with their clients, the courts, and the general public as they perform their services. The **American Bar Association (ABA)**, founded in 1898, and one of the world's largest voluntary professional organizations, developed the **Model Rules of Professional Conduct** for attorneys in 1983. Similar rules preceded them, but the Model Rules represent the current iteration of the ethical guidelines for legal professionals. Most jurisdictions, including the State of Georgia, have adopted these rules, in part or in whole. To practice law in Georgia, one must receive a license from and thereby become a member of the **State Bar of Georgia**. This licensing agency for Georgia attorneys is sometimes referred to as the **Georgia Bar**. As a result of their membership, Georgia attorneys are bound by the **Georgia Rules of Professional Conduct**, which closely mirror the Model Rules.

In this chapter, we will explore some of these ethical rules and discuss their impact on the work that the legal team must do on behalf of estate planning clients in Georgia. While doing so, we will discuss how, in recent times, the use of artificial intelligence to complete legal work has caused unique ethical concerns. Finally, we will outline the consequences for lawyers and paralegals who conduct themselves unethically.

Competence

> A lawyer shall provide competent representation to a client. **Competent representation** as used in this Rule means that a lawyer shall not handle a matter which the lawyer knows or should know to be beyond the lawyer's level of competence without associating another lawyer who the original lawyer reasonably believes to be competent to handle the matter in question. Competence requires the legal knowledge, skill, thoroughness and preparation reasonably necessary for the representation [emphasis added].
>
> Source: Georgia Rules of Professional Conduct, Rule 1.1.

The first rule we will examine deals with an attorney's duty to provide competent representation to his or her client. As stated in Rule 1.1 above, the attorney must exercise the requisite knowledge, skill, thoroughness, and preparation called for by the client's circumstances. For the estate planning attorney, this involves being honest (with yourself and the client) about what you know and do not know. For example, if the attorney only has experience drafting basic wills for middle-class clients and a potential billionaire client comes in for a consultation seeking to have a complex trust created to avoid major tax consequences, competence may dictate that the attorney refers the client to another attorney for representation.

Another aspect of competence is doing what other reasonable, similarly situated attorneys would do under the client's circumstances. In Chapter 12, we discussed all the various steps of estate administration and the importance of proper timing in completing them. A competent attorney, oftentimes with assistance from his or her paralegal, will have conducted an independent investigation of the client's assets and ensured that the estate is administered and closed properly within the time prescribed by Georgia law.

Also related to competence, Formal Opinion 512, issued by the ABA's Standing Committee on Ethics and Professional Responsibility in July 2024, addresses the ethical obligations of attorneys related to the use of **generative artificial intelligence (GAI)** tools. As the opinion indicates, there are numerous definitions of **artificial intelligence (AI)**, but "[a]t its essence, AI involves computer technology, software, and systems that perform tasks traditionally requiring human intelligence." GAI tools are defined as programs used in the legal environment to create "new content, including text, images, audio, video, and software code in response to a user's prompts and questions." Additionally, according to the opinion, "GAI tools may assist lawyers in tasks such as legal research, contract review, due diligence, document review, regulatory compliance, and drafting letters, contracts, briefs, and other legal documents." According to the ABA, to use GAI competently, "lawyers must have a reasonable understanding of the capabilities and limitations of the specific GAI technology that the lawyer might use. This means that lawyers should either acquire a reasonable understanding of the benefits and risks of the GAI tools that they employ in their practices or draw on the expertise of others who can provide guidance about the relevant GAI tool's capabilities and limitations." Although it is a useful, relatively new technology, some of the dangers of AI are already evident. For example, in the summer of 2023, the misuse of ChatGPT by two New York attorneys who filed briefs citing fabricated cases made national headlines, and in the summer of 2024, a Florida foreclosure attorney claimed that his name and bar number were used in a court filing generated by artificial intelligence and he had nothing to do with the case. These examples are cautionary tales illustrating the importance of technological competence.

Confidentiality

> A lawyer shall maintain in confidence all information gained in the professional relationship with a client, including information which the client has requested to be held inviolate or the disclosure of which would be embarrassing or would likely be detrimental to the client, unless the client gives informed consent, except for disclosures that are impliedly authorized in order to carry out the representation, or are required by these Rules or other law, or by order of the Court.
>
> Source: Georgia Rules of Professional Conduct, Rule 1.6(a).

Maintaining a client's privacy, also known as **confidentiality**, is another important ethical obligation of the estate planning attorney and paralegal. As we discussed in Chapter 2, the client is sharing extremely personal and sensitive information regarding family, finances, and medical wishes. According to Rule 1.6(a), legal professionals may not disclose this information unless one of the listed exceptions to the rule applies. Therefore, the legal team must avoid discussing their clients and cases outside of the office. No information regarding the client, whether positive or negative, should be shared with a third party without the client's consent or unless one of the other exceptions referenced above applies.

Related to maintaining confidentiality when using artificial intelligence, the ABA's Formal Opinion 512 indicates that "[b]efore lawyers input information relating to the representation of a client into a GAI tool, they must evaluate the risks that the information will be disclosed to or accessed by others outside the firm. Lawyers must also evaluate the risk that the information will be disclosed to or accessed by others *inside* the firm who will not adequately protect the information from improper disclosure or use."

A big part of abiding by the terms of the confidentiality rule is figuring out who the client is, which can be unclear at times. Ultimately, it is crucial because it is the client to whom the lawyer owes a fiduciary duty, and this duty of confidentiality we are discussing here. For example, suppose Anne schedules an appointment with an attorney for the attorney to draft her elderly grandmother's will. In the initial interview with the attorney, both Anne and her grandmother are present, but Anne does most of the talking, completes her grandmother's estate planning questionnaire, and pays the attorney's fee to draft the will. Who is the client in this scenario? Is it Anne or her grandmother? One might be tempted to say that the client is Anne since she initiated the contact with the firm, is more vocal, and pays for the representation. However, we have learned previously that a will is an indication of the *testator's* intentions. Hence, the testator and the client in this scenario is Anne's grandmother. Therefore, the attorney owes a fiduciary duty only to the grandmother, and at some point, the attorney will need to have a conversation with the client outside of Anne's presence. In that conversation, the legal team will need to confirm that the questionnaire and the will are reflections of the grandmother's true intentions and that she is acting voluntarily, free from undue influence. Moreover, it would behoove the law firm to obtain the grandmother's consent (preferably in writing) to discuss the will and its contents in Anne's presence and to have Anne continue to act as an agent for her grandmother.

Conflicts of Interest

> A lawyer shall not represent or continue to represent a client if there is a significant risk that the lawyer's own interests or the lawyer's duties to another client, a former client, or a third person will materially and adversely affect the representation of the client …
>
> Source: Georgia Rules of Professional Conduct, Rule 1.7.

Rule 1.7 introduces us to yet another ethical consideration for lawyers and paralegals: the avoidance of **conflicts of interest**. This means that the legal team must refrain from engaging in situations that do not represent their client's best interest. As indicated in Rule 1.7, generally, the lawyer and his or her paralegal must give the client complete, undivided loyalty. If a member of the legal team is acting to further his or her own agenda or that of a third party, the duty has been breached. It is important to note that this duty extends to former clients as well as current clients. Rule 1.8 outlines several transactions that may give rise to a conflict of interest, including business transactions with a client, loans to a client, and accepting fees from someone other than the client.

Other specific examples of possible conflicts in an estate planning context, include, but are not limited to the following: (1) the attorney is representing multiple estate planning clients at the same time (e.g., a couple who would like wills drafted, but whose interests may diverge and the wills are not mutual); (2) a drafting attorney is named an executor or trustee under the will; or, (3) a drafting attorney or his or her close relative is a named as a beneficiary under the will.

It is important to note that while generally, it is best for the attorney to avoid representation where a potential conflict of interest exists, representation may still be possible. Many exceptions to the rules outlined above exist. In those cases, the rules provide that if the client is made aware of the potential conflict of interest and gives informed consent in the form of a written waiver, the representation may continue.

Clients with Diminished Capacity

> (a) When a client's capacity to make adequately considered decisions in connection with a representation is diminished, whether because of minority, mental impairment or for some other reason, the lawyer shall, as far as reasonably possible, maintain a normal client-lawyer relationship with the client.
>
> (b) When the lawyer reasonably believes that the client has diminished capacity, is at risk of substantial physical, financial or other harm unless action is taken and cannot adequately act in the client's own interest, the lawyer may take reasonably necessary protective action, including consulting with individuals or entities that have the ability to take action to protect the client and, in appropriate cases, seeking the appointment of a guardian ad litem, conservator or guardian.
>
> Source: Georgia Rules of Professional Conduct, Rule 1.14.

The next potential ethical dilemma in this area of the law that we will address is dealing with clients with diminished capacity. As we discussed previously, to create a valid will or trust, the client must have capacity. Incapacity or **diminished capacity** may occur because the client is underage or suffering from mental or physical health issues. Rule 1.14(a) indicates that despite this diminished capacity, a normal attorney-client relationship can ensue. However, according to 1.14(b), the attorney must assess the client's situation carefully and if the situation poses a risk of substantial physical, financial, or other harm to the client, a normal attorney-client relationship is no longer possible, and the attorney must engage and consult with those who can assist in serving the client's best interests.

Consider the example of Anne and her grandmother from earlier in this chapter. According to the fact pattern, Anne was taking a great deal of initiative in establishing the attorney-client relationship for her grandmother since Anne's grandmother was elderly. However, since Anne's grandmother was still capable of a normal attorney-client relationship, best practices dictated that the attorney should consult primarily with Anne's grandmother related to drafting her will. Now, suppose that in addition to being elderly, Anne's grandmother was diagnosed with advanced Alzheimer's and had only intermittent **moments of lucidity**. In other words, according to her treating medical professionals, she had only limited times when she had clear perception and rational thought. Given this situation, the rule requires the attorney to make a judgment call. As we discussed in Chapter 5, O.C.G.A. § 53-4-11(a) indicates that a testator must demonstrate only "a decided and rational desire as to the disposition of property." Before drafting any documents, it might make sense for the estate planning attorney to consult with the grandmother's medical team to confirm when such capacity exists. Then, in all likelihood, it will be necessary for the attorney to consult with Anne's grandmother during a moment of lucidity to understand her intentions for the documents and/or have her execute a power of attorney or other documents to allow Anne to act as her agent to make decisions concerning the legal representation when her grandmother cannot act for herself.

Legal Fees

> (a) A lawyer shall not make an agreement for, charge, or collect an unreasonable fee or an unreasonable amount for expenses . . .
>
> (b) The scope of the representation and the basis or rate of the fee and expenses for which the client will be responsible shall be communicated to the client, preferably in writing, before or within a reasonable time after commencing the representation, except when the lawyer will charge a regularly represented client on the same basis or rate. Any changes in the basis or rate of the fee or expenses shall also be communicated to the client.
>
> Source: Georgia Rules of Professional Conduct, Rule 1.5.

Oftentimes, to fulfill the ethical responsibilities related to fees, estate planning attorneys will use a writing at the start of the representation known as an **engagement letter** or **retainer letter**. This communication should clearly outline the scope of the legal representation and the fees related to the same. In addition, it is recommended that attorneys bill clients regularly (perhaps monthly) so clients are fully aware of the fees and costs related to their representation and are less likely to complain about them.

According to the Georgia Rules, estate planning fees may be high, but can be justified if they are reasonable. The factors to be considered in determining the reasonableness of an attorney's fees are outlined in Rule 1.5(a):

1. the time and labor required, the novelty and difficulty of the questions involved, and the skill requisite to perform the legal service properly;
2. the likelihood that the acceptance of the particular employment will preclude other employment by the lawyer;
3. the fee customarily charged in the locality for similar legal services;
4. the amount involved and the results obtained;
5. the time limitations imposed by the client or by the circumstances;
6. the nature and length of the professional relationship with the client;
7. the experience, reputation, and ability of the lawyer or lawyers performing the services; and
8. whether the fee is fixed or contingent.

Moreover, regarding the use of artificial intelligence to render estate planning services, the ABA's Formal Opinion 512 indicates that "[t]he factors set forth in Rule 1.5(a) also apply when evaluating the reasonableness of charges for GAI tools when the lawyer and client agree on a flat or contingent fee. For example, if using a GAI tool enables a lawyer to complete tasks much more quickly than without the tool, it may be unreasonable under Rule 1.5 for the lawyer to charge the same flat fee when using the GAI tool as when not using it." Suppose Attorney Alice has an hourly billable rate of $300, and it usually takes her five hours to draft estate planning documents, so she has established a flat fee of $1500 for her estate planning clients. However, recently, she has begun using a GAI tool that helps her produce the same documents in one hour. Under those circumstances, Attorney Alice's flat fee of $1500 would likely be deemed unreasonable and may need to be changed. Additionally, Formal Opinion 512 indicates that, based on Rule 1.5(b), "before charging the client for the use of the GAI tools or services, the lawyer must explain the basis for the charge, preferably in writing." The engagement letter described earlier could be a useful tool for communicating to the client if and how GAI will be used during the course of the representation.

Safekeeping Property

> (a) A lawyer shall hold funds or other property of clients or third persons that are in a lawyer's possession in connection with a representation separate from the lawyer's own funds or other property.... Other property shall be identified as such and appropriately safeguarded. Complete records of such account funds and other property shall be kept by the lawyer and shall be preserved for a period of six years after termination of the representation.

Source: Georgia Rules of Professional Conduct, Rule 1.15(I).

The final ethical rule that we will address in this chapter relates to the safekeeping of client property. During the representation of an estate planning client or administering an estate, the attorney may be asked to receive funds or property on behalf of the client. The concern with this rule is avoiding possible mismanagement or mishandling of client property by the attorney or his or her agents. As Rule 1.15(I)(a) indicates, these funds or property must not be commingled with property or funds of the attorney or his or her firm, under any circumstances. Instead, client property should be held separately, and client funds should be placed in a distinct account known as a client **escrow account** or **trust account**.

Moreover, when clients request that the attorney hold certain property for them, under Rule 1.15(I)(a), the attorney must keep track of the location of such property and exercise due diligence in safeguarding it. For example, after the client executes his or her will at the signing ceremony, the client may ask his or her attorney to keep the original will. As we indicated previously, only one original is typically executed by the testator. Therefore, the originally signed will must be safeguarded at all costs. In the case where the attorney is asked to retain the original will, it would be advisable for the attorney to maintain careful records of the will's exact location and to store it in a fireproof, waterproof safe or vault.

Consequences for Unethical Behavior

Now that you are aware of some of the ethical rules and dilemmas an estate planning attorney and his or her paralegal may face, we will move on to a discussion of the consequences of their unethical behavior. A dissatisfied client may file a grievance with the Georgia Bar if the client believes that the attorney has behaved unethically.

The Office of the General Counsel of the State Bar of Georgia which receives the complaint, will review it to determine if the claims are legitimate. If so, the General Counsel's Office will give the attorney notice of the complaint and a chance to respond, and then conduct an informal investigation. Thereafter, the General Counsel may either: (1) dismiss the grievance if it is found unwarranted or resolved; or (2) refer the matter to the State Disciplinary Board for a more formal investigation. Again, if the Board finds that no ethical rules were violated, it may dismiss the complaint. However, if the attorney is found to have violated one or more of the Georgia Rules of Professional Conduct, the attorney may be penalized.

Unethical attorneys are subject to various **sanctions**, which are forms of disciplinary action imposed by the State Bar of Georgia as their licensing agency. These sanctions vary in degree based on the nature of the ethical violation. Rule 4-102 describes the levels of attorney discipline in the State of Georgia. Exhibit 14.1, which follows, illustrates the same, starting with the least severe sanction known as a formal admonition, and then culminating in the most serious form, which is disbarment. To avoid this most serious sanction, some attorneys, who know that disbarment is likely, may choose to voluntarily surrender their law licenses. In effect, with a **voluntary surrender of license**, these attorneys choose to "quit" before they are "fired" by the State Bar of Georgia.

Exhibit 14.1 Levels of Attorney Discipline

	Disciplinary Action	Description
1	Formal Admonition	a confidential letter to the attorney that declares the conduct to have been improper but does not limit the right to practice
2	Investigative Panel Reprimand	a confidential meeting of the Investigative Panel after which the Panel declares the attorney's conduct to have been improper but does not limit the right to practice
3	Review Panel Reprimand	a public meeting of the Review Panel after which the Panel declares the attorney's conduct to have been improper but does not limit the right to practice
4	Public Reprimand	a judge of a superior court in open court publicly declares the attorney's conduct to have been improper but does not limit the right to practice
5	Suspension	public disciplinary action that removes the attorney from the practice of law in Georgia for a definite period of time or until satisfaction of certain conditions imposed as a part of the suspension
6	Disbarment	public disciplinary action that removes the attorney from the practice of law in the State of Georgia

In addition to bar sanctions, attorneys who behave unethically may face other consequences. A client may choose to sue the attorney in civil court for **malpractice**. Legal malpractice is an attorney's breach of the fiduciary duty owed to the client to provide the standard of care, skill, and diligence that the attorney owed to the client, which breach has caused the client damages. A court may award money damages or other forms of restitution to clients if it determines that the attorney is liable. If the attorney's wrongdoing is criminal, the government may also bring a criminal action against the attorney. If the court finds that the attorney has violated criminal laws, he or she may be fined or imprisoned.

Since paralegals are not members of the Georgia Bar, they are not subject to the sanctions outlined in Rule 4-102 and summarized in Exhibit 14.1; however, they too may face consequences for their unethical behavior. As agents of the attorneys who supervise them, paralegals must abide by the Georgia Rules of Professional Conduct. Although a license is not required to be a paralegal in Georgia, if a paralegal has successfully completed one of the national certification exams, he or she may lose that certification as a result of an ethical violation. Moreover, the employing attorney may demote or fire the paralegal. Finally, like the attorney, a paralegal who engages in unethical behavior may be subject to civil or criminal lawsuits, fines, and imprisonment.

Given these potentially serious outcomes, both attorneys and paralegals should avoid even the appearance of impropriety.

Key Terms

American Bar Association (ABA)
artificial intelligence (AI)
code of ethics
competent representation
confidentiality
conflict of interest
diminished capacity
disbarment
engagement letter
escrow account
formal admonition
generative artificial intelligence (GAI) tools
Georgia Bar/State Bar of Georgia
Georgia Rules of Professional Conduct
Investigative Panel reprimand
malpractice
Model Rules of Professional Conduct
moments of lucidity
public reprimand
retainer letter
Review Panel reprimand
sanctions
suspension
trust account
voluntary surrender of license

Review Questions

1. What code of ethics governs Georgia attorneys? Are paralegals also bound by these rules? If so, why?
2. What is competent representation?
3. Why is confidentiality important for estate planning lawyers and paralegals?
4. Give examples of transactions that may create a potential conflict of interest.

5. Under what circumstances may a client have diminished capacity? What is the implication for an attorney working with this client?
6. What is a client trust account, and why is it necessary?
7. What are the possible sanctions for an attorney who has engaged in unethical behavior?
8. What are the possible consequences for a paralegal who has engaged in unethical behavior?
9. Is it possible for a paralegal to be disbarred? Why or why not?
10. What are the elements of a malpractice claim?

Practical Assignment

Visit the website for the State Bar of Georgia, www.gabar.org. Under the "For the Public" dropdown tab, click on "Recent Attorney Discipline." As you scroll down, you will find a list of attorneys who have been disbarred, suspended, or reprimanded recently. To get the specific details related to each sanction imposed by the State Bar, click on the sanction type listed below the attorney's name. Write about one of the disciplinary actions you have reviewed, describing the attorney, the ethical rule(s) that he or she violated, and the punishment the attorney received. Then, describe your reaction to what you have read concerning this attorney. What did you find surprising? Be sure to provide the properly formatted citation for the ethical case.

Appendix A

Selected Sections of the Official Code of Georgia Annotated

Reprinted with the permission of LexisNexis

Chapter 1

O.C.G.A. § 53-1-2(17)

"Will" means the legal declaration of an individual's testamentary intention regarding that individual's property or other matters. Will includes the will and all codicils to the will.

Chapter 2

O.C.G.A. § 15-19-50

The practice of law in this state is defined as:

(1) Representing litigants in court and preparing pleadings and other papers incident to any action or special proceedings in any court or other judicial body;

(2) Conveyancing;

(3) The preparation of legal instruments of all kinds whereby a legal right is secured;

(4) The rendering of opinions as to the validity or invalidity of titles to real or personal property;

(5) The giving of any legal advice; and

(6) Any action taken for others in any matter connected with the law.

O.C.G.A. § 15-19-51(a)

It shall be unlawful for any person other than a duly licensed attorney at law:

(1) To practice or appear as an attorney at law for any person other than himself in any court of this state or before any judicial body;

(2) To make it a business to practice as an attorney at law for any person other than himself in any of such courts;

(3) To hold himself out to the public or otherwise to any person as being entitled to practice law;

(4) To render or furnish legal services or advice;

(5) To furnish attorneys or counsel;

(6) To render legal services of any kind in actions or proceedings of any nature;

(7) To assume or use or advertise the title of "lawyer," "attorney," "attorney at law," or equivalent terms in any language in such manner as to convey the impression that he is entitled to practice law or is entitled to furnish legal advice, services, or counsel; or

(8) To advertise that either alone or together with, by, or through any person, whether a duly and regularly admitted attorney at law or not, he has, owns, conducts, or maintains an office for the practice of law or for furnishing legal advice, services, or counsel.

O.C.G.A. § 15-19-56(a)

Any person, corporation, or voluntary association violating Code Section 15-19-51, 15-19-53, 15-19-54, or 15-19-55 shall be guilty of a misdemeanor.

Chapter 3

O.C.G.A. § 44-6-20

An absolute or fee simple estate is one in which the owner is entitled to the entire property with unconditional power of disposition during his life and which descends to his heirs and legal representatives upon his death intestate.

O.C.G.A. § 44-6-120

Unless otherwise specifically provided by statute and unless the document or instrument provides otherwise, a tenancy in common is created wherever from any cause two or more persons are entitled to the simultaneous possession of any property. Tenants in common may have unequal shares, but they will be held to be equal unless the contrary appears. The fact of inequality shall not give the person holding the greater interest any privileges as to possession which are superior to those of the person owning a lesser interest so long as the tenancy continues.

O.C.G.A. § 44-6-190(a)(2)

Any instrument of title in favor of two or more persons shall be construed to create interests in common without survivorship between or among the owners unless the instrument expressly refers to the takers as "joint tenants," "joint tenants and not as tenants in common," or "joint tenants with survivorship" or as taking "jointly with survivorship."

O.C.G.A. § 53-1-20(b)

Any person to whom an interest in property is transferred or who succeeds to property by contract or by operation of law may renounce the property in whole or in part as provided in this Code section. A person may renounce even if a spendthrift or similar restriction applies to the property renounced. Persons who may renounce include fiduciaries acting on behalf of an individual, such as personal representatives, trustees, conservators, or guardians, as well as duly authorized attorneys in fact, whether acting on behalf of an individual or fiduciary.

O.C.G.A. § 53-12-2(9)

"Property" means any type of property, whether real or personal, tangible or intangible, legal or equitable, and shall include digital assets and electronic communications, as such terms are defined in Code Section 53-13-2.

Chapter 4

O.C.G.A. § 53-1-5(a)

An individual who feloniously and intentionally kills or conspires to kill or procures the killing of another individual forfeits the right to take an interest from the decedent's estate and to serve as a personal representative or trustee of the decedent's estate or any trust created by the decedent. For purposes of this Code section, the killing or conspiring to kill or procuring another to kill is felonious and intentional if the killing would constitute murder or felony murder or voluntary manslaughter under the laws of this state.

O.C.G.A. § 53-2-1(b)(2)

The half-blood, whether on the maternal or paternal side, are considered equally with the whole-blood, so that the children of any common parent are treated as brothers and sisters to each other.

O.C.G.A. § 53-2-1(c)

Except as provided in subsection (d) of this Code section, when a decedent died without a will, the following rules shall determine such decedent's heirs:

(1) Upon the death of an individual who is survived by a spouse but not by any child or other descendant, the spouse is the sole heir. If the decedent is also survived by any child or other descendant, the spouse shall share equally with the children, with the descendants of any deceased child taking that child's share, per stirpes; provided, however, that the spouse's portion shall not be less than a one-third share;

(2) If the decedent is not survived by a spouse, the heirs shall be those relatives, as provided in this Code section, who are in the nearest degree to the decedent in which there is any survivor;

(3) Children of the decedent are in the first degree, and those who survive the decedent shall share the estate equally, with the descendants of any deceased child taking, per stirpes, the share that child would have taken if in life;

(4) Parents of the decedent are in the second degree, and those who survive the decedent shall share the estate equally;

(5) Siblings of the decedent are in the third degree, and those who survive the decedent shall share the estate equally, with the descendants of any deceased sibling taking, per stirpes, the share that sibling would have taken if in life; provided, however, that, subject to the provisions of paragraph (1) of subsection (f) of Code Section 53-1-20, if no sibling survives the decedent, the nieces and nephews who survive the decedent shall take the estate in equal shares,

with the descendants of any deceased niece or nephew taking, per stirpes, the share that niece or nephew would have taken if in life;

(6) Grandparents of the decedent are in the fourth degree, and those who survive the decedent shall share the estate equally;

(7) Uncles and aunts of the decedent are in the fifth degree, and those who survive the decedent shall share the estate equally, with the children of any deceased uncle or aunt taking, per stirpes, the share that uncle or aunt would have taken if in life; provided, however, that, subject to the provisions of paragraph (1) of subsection (f) of Code Section 53-1-20, if no uncle or aunt of the decedent survives the decedent, the first cousins who survive the decedent shall share the estate equally; and

(8) The more remote degrees of kinship shall be determined by counting the number of steps in the chain from the relative to the closest common ancestor of the relative and decedent and the number of steps in the chain from the common ancestor to the decedent. The sum of the steps in the two chains shall be the degree of kinship, and the surviving relatives with the lowest sum shall be in the nearest degree and shall share the estate equally.

O.C.G.A. § 53-2-3

The rights of inheritance of a child born out of wedlock shall be as follows:

(1) A child born out of wedlock may inherit in the same manner as though legitimate from or through the child's mother, the other children of the mother, and any other maternal kin;

(2) A child born out of wedlock may not inherit from or through the child's father, the other children of the father, or any paternal kin by reason of the paternal kinship, unless:

  (i) A court of competent jurisdiction has entered an order declaring the child to be legitimate, under the authority of Code Section 19-7-22 or such other authority as may be provided by law;

  (ii) A court of competent jurisdiction has otherwise entered a court order establishing paternity;

  (iii) The father has executed a sworn statement signed by him attesting to the parent-child relationship;

  (iv) The father has signed the birth certificate of the child; or

  (v) There is other clear and convincing evidence that the child is the child of the father.

O.C.G.A. § 53-2-5

An individual conceived by artificial insemination and presumed legitimate in accordance with Code Section 19-7-21 shall be considered a child of the parents and entitled to inherit under the laws of intestacy from the parents and from relatives of the parents, and the parents and relatives of the parents shall likewise be entitled to inherit as heirs from and through such individual.

O.C.G.A. § 53-2-50

As used in this article, the term "escheat" is the reversion of property to the state upon a failure of heirs of a decedent to appear and make claim for or against property owned by the decedent at death for which no other disposition was provided either by will or otherwise.

O.C.G.A. § 53-3-1(c)

The surviving spouse and minor children of a testate or intestate decedent are entitled to year's support in the form of property for their support and maintenance for the period of 12 months from the date of the decedent's death.

Chapter 5

O.C.G.A. § 53-4-2

A will shall take effect instantly upon the death of the testator however long probate may be postponed.

O.C.G.A. § 53-4-3

No particular form is necessary to constitute a will. To determine whether an instrument is a will, the test is the intention of the maker to be gathered from the whole instrument, read in light of the surrounding circumstances. If the intention is to convey a present interest, though the possession is postponed until after death, the instrument is not a will. If the intention is to convey an interest accruing and having effect only at death, the instrument is a will.

O.C.G.A. § 53-4-5(a)

A written statement or list meeting the requirements of subsection (b) of this Code section shall dispose of items of tangible personal property, other than money, not otherwise specifically disposed of by the testator's will. If more than one otherwise effective writing exists, then, to the extent of any conflict among the writings, the provisions of a more recent writing revoke the inconsistent provisions of each prior writing.

O.C.G.A. § 53-4-10(a)

Every individual 14 years of age or older may make a will, unless laboring under some legal disability arising either from a want of capacity or a want of perfect liberty of action.

O.C.G.A. § 53-4-11(a)

Testamentary capacity exists when the testator has a decided and rational desire as to the disposition of property.

O.C.G.A. § 53-4-12

A will must be freely and voluntarily executed. A will is not valid if anything destroys the testator's freedom of volition, such as fraudulent practices upon the testator's fears, affections, or sympathies; misrepresentation; duress; or undue influence whereby the will of another is substituted for the wishes of the testator.

O.C.G.A. § 53-4-20

(a) A will shall be in writing and shall be signed by the testator or by some other individual in the testator's presence and at the testator's express direction. A testator may sign by mark or by any name that is intended to authenticate the instrument as the testator's will.

(b) A will shall be attested and subscribed in the presence of the testator by two or more competent witnesses. A witness to a will may attest by mark. Another individual may not subscribe the name of a witness, even in that witness's presence and at that witness's direction.

(c) A codicil shall be executed by the testator and attested and subscribed by witnesses with the same formality as a will.

O.C.G.A. § 53-4-21

Knowledge of the contents of a will by the testator is necessary to the validity of a will. If the testator can read, the testator's signature or acknowledgment of that signature is presumed to show such knowledge.

O.C.G.A. § 53-4-22(a)

Any individual who is competent to be a witness and age 14 or over may witness a will.

O.C.G.A. § 53-4-24(c)

A self-proved will or codicil may be admitted to probate without the testimony of any subscribing witness, but otherwise it shall be treated no differently from a will or codicil that is not self-proved. In particular, without limiting the generality of the foregoing sentence, a self-proved will or codicil may be contested, revoked, or amended in exactly the same fashion as a will or codicil that is not self-proved.

O.C.G.A. § 53-4-31

(a) A joint will is one will signed by two or more testators that deals with the distribution of the property of each testator. A joint will may be probated as each testator's will.

(b) Mutual wills are separate wills of two or more testators that make reciprocal dispositions of each testator's property.

O.C.G.A. § 53-4-40

A will may be changed or revoked by the testator at any time prior to the testator's death.

O.C.G.A. § 53-4-42

(a) A revocation may be express or implied.

(b) An express revocation occurs when the testator by writing or action expressly annuls a will. An express revocation takes effect instantly.

(c) An implied revocation results from the execution of a subsequent inconsistent will that does not by its terms expressly revoke the previous will. An implied revocation takes effect only when the subsequent inconsistent will becomes effective. If the subsequent inconsistent will fails to become effective from any cause, the implied revocation is not completed.

Chapter 6

O.C.G.A. § 44-5-81

If a gift is of substantial benefit, the law will presume its acceptance unless the contrary is shown. A parent, guardian, or friend may accept a gift for a minor. The officers of a corporation may accept a gift for the corporation.

O.C.G.A. § 53-4-55

In the construction of all wills, the court shall seek diligently for the intention of the testator and shall give effect to such intention as far as it may be consistent with the rules of law. Provided the proof of intention is clear and convincing, the court may transpose sentences or clauses, change conjunctions, and supply or delete words in cases in which a sentence or clause as it stands is unintelligible or inoperative in context.

O.C.G.A. § 53-4-59

Testamentary gifts may be specific, demonstrative, general, or residuary. A specific testamentary gift directs the delivery of property particularly designated. A demonstrative testamentary gift designates the fund or property from which the gift is to be satisfied but nevertheless is an unconditional gift of the amount or value specified. A general testamentary gift does not direct the delivery of any particular property. A residuary testamentary gift includes all the property of the estate that is not effectively disposed of by other provisions of the will.

O.C.G.A. § 53-4-63

(a) Unless otherwise directed, the debts of the testator and expenses of administration of the estate shall be paid out of the residuum. Unless otherwise provided in the will, a residuary gift or any part thereof, including a residuary gift to a surviving spouse in lieu of year's support, shall be deemed a gift of the net residuum or part thereof remaining after all debts of the testator and expenses of administration of the estate, including taxes, have been paid.

(b) If the residuum proves to be insufficient for the payment of the debts of the testator and the expenses of administration of the estate, then general testamentary gifts shall abate pro rata to make up the deficiency. If general testamentary gifts are insufficient, then demonstrative testamentary gifts shall abate in the same manner. If both general and demonstrative gifts are insufficient, then specific gifts shall abate in the same manner.

(c) After the estate assets in the hands of the personal representative are exhausted, a creditor may proceed against each beneficiary for that beneficiary's pro rata share of the debts to the extent a testamentary gift has been distributed to that beneficiary.

(d) Realty and personalty shall be equally liable for the payment of debts.

(e) Unless otherwise expressly directed in the will, nothing in this Code section shall be deemed to limit any rights to reimbursement for federal estate taxes, generation-skipping transfer taxes, or any other taxes that may be available to personal representatives under federal law.

Chapter 7

O.C.G.A. § 10-6B-5

(a) A power of attorney shall be:

(1) Signed by the principal or by another individual in such principal's presence at the principal's express direction;

(2) Attested in the presence of the principal by a competent witness who is not also named as an agent in the power of attorney being attested; and

(3) Attested as set forth in Code Section 44-2-15, in the presence of the principal, by an individual who is not a witness for purposes of paragraph (2) of this subsection and who is not also named as an agent in the power of attorney being attested.

(b) The individuals provided for in paragraphs (2) and (3) of subsection (a) of this Code section shall not be required to attest to the signature of any person other than the principal or the individual signing at the principal's express direction.

O.C.G.A. § 31-32-5(a)

Any person of sound mind who is emancipated or 18 years of age or older may execute a document which:

(1) Appoints a health care agent;

(2) Directs the withholding or withdrawal of life-sustaining procedures or the withholding or withdrawal of the provision of nourishment or hydration when the declarant is in a terminal condition or state of permanent unconsciousness; or

(3) Covers matters contained in both paragraphs (1) and (2) of this subsection.

Such document shall be in writing, signed by the declarant or by some other person in the declarant's presence and at the declarant's express direction, and witnessed in accordance with the provisions of subsection (c) of this Code section.

O.C.G.A. § 31-32-5(c)

(1) An advance directive for health care shall be attested and subscribed in the presence of the declarant by two witnesses who are of sound mind and at least

18 years of age, but such witnesses do not have to be together or present when the declarant signs the advance directive for health care.

(2) Neither witness can be a person who:

(A) Was selected to serve as the declarant's health care agent;

(B) Will knowingly inherit anything from the declarant or otherwise knowingly gain a financial benefit from the declarant's death; or

(C) Is directly involved in the declarant's health care.

(3) Not more than one of the witnesses may be an employee, agent, or medical staff member of the health care facility in which the declarant is receiving health care.

O.C.G.A. § 31-32-7

(a) A health care agent shall not have the authority to make a particular health care decision different from or contrary to the declarant's decision, if any, if the declarant is able to understand the general nature of the health care procedure being consented to or refused, as determined by the declarant's attending physician based on such physician's good faith judgment.

(b) A health care agent shall be under no duty to exercise granted powers or to assume control of or responsibility for the declarant's health care; provided, however, that when granted powers are exercised, the health care agent shall use due care to act for the benefit of the declarant in accordance with the terms of the advance directive for health care. A health care agent shall exercise granted powers in such manner as the health care agent deems consistent with the intentions and desires of the declarant. If a declarant's intentions and desires are unclear, the health care agent shall act in the declarant's best interest considering the benefits, burdens, and risks of the declarant's circumstances and treatment options.

(c) A health care agent may act in person or through others reasonably employed by the health care agent for that purpose but may not delegate authority to make health care decisions.

(d) A health care agent may sign and deliver all instruments, negotiate and enter into all agreements, and do all other acts reasonably necessary to implement the exercise of the powers granted to the health care agent. A health care agent shall be authorized to accompany a declarant in an ambulance or air ambulance if in the opinion of the ambulance personnel protocol permits a passenger and to visit or consult in person with a declarant who is admitted to a health care facility if the health care facility's protocol permits such visitation.

(e) The form of advance directive for health care contained in Code Section 31-32-4 shall, and any different form of advance directive for health care may, include the following powers, subject to any limitations appearing on the face of the form:

(1) The health care agent is authorized to consent to and authorize or refuse, or to withhold or withdraw consent to, any and all types of medical care, treatment, or procedures relating to the physical or mental health of the declarant, including any medication program, surgical procedures, life-sustaining procedures, or provision of nourishment or hydration for the declarant, but not including sterilization or involuntary hospitalization or involuntary treatment covered by Title 37;

(2) The health care agent is authorized to admit the declarant to or discharge the declarant from any health care facility;

(3) The health care agent is authorized to contract for any health care facility or service in the name of and on behalf of the declarant and to bind the declarant to pay for all such services, and the health care agent shall not be personally liable for any services or care contracted for or on behalf of the declarant;

(4) At the declarant's expense and subject to reasonable rules of the health care provider to prevent disruption of the declarant's health care, the health care agent shall have the same right the declarant has to examine and copy and consent to disclosure of all the declarant's medical records that the health care agent deems relevant to the exercise of the agent's powers, whether the records relate to mental health or any other medical condition and whether they are in the possession of or maintained by any physician, psychiatrist, psychologist, therapist, health care facility, or other health care provider, notwithstanding the provisions of any statute or other rule of law to the contrary; and

(5) Unless otherwise provided, the health care agent is authorized to direct that an autopsy of the declarant's body be made; to make an anatomical gift of any part or all of the declarant's body pursuant to Article 6 of Chapter 5 of Title 44, the "Georgia Revised Uniform Anatomical Gift Act"; and to direct the final disposition of the declarant's body, including funeral arrangements, burial, or cremation.

(f) A court may remove a health care agent if it finds that the health care agent is not acting properly.

(g) With respect to mental health care, the duties and responsibilities of a health care agent under this chapter shall be subordinate to the duties and responsibilities of a mental health care agent under Chapter 11 of Title 37 and subject to the terms of a psychiatric advance directive executed by the declarant before, simultaneously with, or after the advance directive for health care under which the health care agent is acting.

O.C.G.A. § 44-5-141(3)

"Anatomical gift" means a donation of all or part of a human body to take effect after the donor's death for the purpose of transplantation, therapy, research, or education.

O.C.G.A. § 44-5-143

(a) A donor may make an anatomical gift:

(1) By authorizing a statement or symbol indicating that the donor has made an anatomical gift to be imprinted on the donor's driver's license or identification card;

(2) In a will;

(3) During a terminal illness or injury of the donor, by any form of communication addressed to at least two adults, at least one of whom is a disinterested witness;

(4) By granting power pursuant to a durable power of attorney for health care or advance directive for health care under Chapter 32 of Title 31; or

(5) As provided in subsection (b) of this Code section.

(b) A donor or other person authorized to make an anatomical gift under Code Section 44-5-142 may make a gift by a donor card or other record signed by the donor or other person making the gift or by authorizing that a statement or symbol indicating that the donor has made an anatomical gift be included on a donor registry. If the donor or other person is physically unable to sign a record, the record may be signed by another individual at the direction of the donor or other person and shall:

(1) Be witnessed by at least two adults, at least one of whom is a disinterested witness, who have signed at the request of the donor or the other person; and

(2) State that it has been signed and witnessed as provided in paragraph (1) of this subsection.

(c) Revocation, suspension, expiration, or cancellation of a driver's license or identification card upon which an anatomical gift is indicated does not invalidate the gift.

(d) An anatomical gift made by will takes effect upon the donor's death whether or not the will is probated. Invalidation of the will after the donor's death does not invalidate the gift.

Chapter 8

O.C.G.A. § 53-12-4

(a) As to real property, the validity of a trust shall be determined by the law of the situs of the real property.

(b) As to all other property, the validity of a trust shall be determined by:

(1) The law of the jurisdiction designated in the trust instrument unless the effect of the designation is contrary to the public policy of the jurisdiction having the most significant relationship to the matter at issue; or

(2) In the absence of an effective designation in the trust instrument, the law of the jurisdiction having the most significant relationship to the matter at issue.

O.C.G.A. § 53-12-20(b)

An express trust shall have, ascertainable with reasonable certainty:

(1) An intention by a settlor to create such trust;

(2) Trust property;

(3) Except for charitable trusts or a trust for care of an animal, a beneficiary who is reasonably ascertainable at the time of the creation of such trust or reasonably ascertainable within the period of the rule against perpetuities;

(4) A trustee; and

(5) Trustee duties specified in writing or provided by law.

O.C.G.A. § 53-12-21(a)

No formal words shall be necessary to create an express trust.

O.C.G.A. § 53-12-23

A person has capacity to create an inter vivos trust to the extent that such person has legal capacity to transfer title to property inter vivos. A person has capacity to create a testamentary trust to the extent that such person has legal capacity to devise or bequeath property by will.

O.C.G.A. § 53-12-40

(a) A settlor shall have no power to modify or revoke a trust in the absence of an express reservation of such power.

(b) A power to revoke shall be deemed to include a power to modify, and an unrestricted power to modify shall be deemed to include a power to revoke.

(c) Any revocation or modification of an express trust shall be in writing and signed by the settlor.

O.C.G.A. § 53-12-61

(a) The trust instrument may confer upon a trustee or other person a power to modify, consolidate, divide, or terminate the trust without court approval.

(b) During the settlor's lifetime, the court shall approve a petition to modify or terminate a noncharitable irrevocable trust, even if the modification or termination is inconsistent with a material purpose of the trust, if the settlor and all the beneficiaries consent to such modification or termination and the trustee has received notice of the proposed modification or termination. A settlor's power to consent to such trust's modification or termination may be exercised by:

(1) An agent under a power of attorney only to the extent expressly authorized by the power of attorney and the terms of the trust;

(2) The settlor's conservator with the approval of the court supervising the conservatorship if an agent is not so authorized; or

(3) The settlor's guardian with the approval of the court supervising the guardianship if an agent is not so authorized and a conservator has not been appointed.

(c) Following the settlor's death the court shall approve a petition to:

(1) Modify a noncharitable irrevocable trust if all the beneficiaries consent, the trustee has received notice of the proposed modification, and the court concludes that modification is not inconsistent with any material purpose of such trust; and

(2) Terminate a noncharitable irrevocable trust if all the beneficiaries consent, the trustee has received notice of the proposed termination, and the court concludes that continuance of such trust is not necessary to achieve any material purpose of such trust.

(d) The court may, upon petition:

(1) Modify the trust if, owing to circumstances not anticipated by the settlor, modification would further the purposes of such trust;

(2) Modify the administrative provisions of a trust if continuation of such trust under its existing provisions would impair such trust's administration;

(3) Modify the trust by the appointment of an additional trustee or special fiduciary if such appointment is necessary or helpful to the administration of such trust;

(4) Modify the trust to achieve the settlor's tax objectives, with such modification to have either prospective or retroactive effect;

(5) Order the division of a single trust into two or more trusts or the consolidation of two or more trusts, whether created by the same or different trust instruments or by the same or different persons, into a single trust if the division or consolidation would be helpful to the administration of such trust or trusts; or

(6) Terminate a trust and order distribution of the trust property if the:

(A) Costs of administration are such that the continuance of such trust, the establishment of such trust if it is to be established, or the distribution from a probate estate would defeat or substantially impair the purposes of such trust;

(B) Purpose of such trust has been fulfilled or become illegal or impossible to fulfill; or

(C) Continuance of such trust would impair the accomplishment of the purposes of such trust.

(e) A proceeding to approve a proposed modification or termination under this Code section may be commenced by a trustee or beneficiary. A proceeding to approve a proposed modification or termination under subsection (b) of this Code section may be commenced by a trustee, beneficiary, or settlor. In the case of an unfunded testamentary trust, a petition for modification or termination under this Code section may be filed by the personal representative of the settlor's estate.

(f) No later than 30 days after filing the petition for modification or termination, notice of a petition to modify or terminate a trust under subsection (d) of this Code section shall be given to the settlor, the trustee, all the beneficiaries, any holder of a power of appointment over the trust property, and such other persons as the court may direct.

(g) The court may modify or terminate a trust as provided in this Code section regardless of whether it contains spendthrift provisions or other similar protective provisions.

(h) An order under subsection (d) of this Code section shall conform as nearly as practicable to the intention of the settlor.

(i) Distribution of the trust property under an order for termination shall be made to or among the current beneficiaries and the vested remainder beneficiaries, or, if there are no vested remainder beneficiaries, among the current beneficiaries and the contingent remainder beneficiaries. The order shall specify the appropriate share, if any, of each current and remainder beneficiary who is to share in the proceeds of the trust so as to conform as nearly as practicable to the intention of the settlor. The order may direct that the interest of a minor beneficiary, or any portion thereof, be converted into qualifying property and distributed to a custodian pursuant to Article 5 of Chapter 5 of Title 44, "The Georgia Transfers to Minors Act."

O.C.G.A. § 53-12-62

(a) As used in this Code section, the term:

  (1) "Original trust" refers to the trust from which principal is being distributed.

  (2) "Second trust" refers to the trust to which assets are being distributed from the original trust, whether a separate trust or an amended version of the original trust.

(b)

  (1) As used in this subsection, the term "current beneficiary" means a person who, on the date of distribution to the second trust, is a distributee or permissible distributee of trust income or principal.

(2) Unless the original trust instrument expressly provides otherwise, a trustee, other than a person who contributed property to the trust, with authority to invade the principal of the original trust to make distributions to or for the benefit of one or more of the beneficiaries may also, independently or with court approval, exercise such authority by distributing all or part of the principal of the original trust to a trustee of a second trust; provided, however, that the second trust shall not include as a:

(A) Current beneficiary any person that is not a current beneficiary of income or principal of the original trust; or

(B) Beneficiary any person that is not a beneficiary of the original trust.

(c) Except as provided in this Code section, a trustee may exercise the power to invade the principal of the original trust under subsection (b) of this Code section without the consent of the settlor or the beneficiaries of the original trust if such trustee provides written notice of such trustee's decision to exercise the power to such settlor, if living, and those persons then entitled to annual reports from the trustee of the original trust. Such notice shall:

(1) Describe the manner in which such trustee intends to exercise such power;

(2) Specify the date such trustee proposes to distribute to the second trust; and

(3) Be delivered at least 60 days before the proposed distribution to the second trust.

(d) The exercise of the power to invade the principal of the original trust under subsection (b) of this Code section shall be by an instrument in writing, signed and acknowledged by the trustee, and filed with the records of the original trust.

(e) The exercise of the power to invade the principal of the original trust under subsection (b) of this Code section shall not extend the permissible period of the rule against perpetuities that applies to such original trust.

(f) This Code section shall not be construed to abridge the right of any trustee who has a power of invasion to distribute property in further trust that arises under any other law or under common law, and nothing in this Code section shall be construed to imply that the common law does not permit the exercise of a power to invade the principal of a trust in the manner authorized under subsection (b) of this Code section.

(g) A second trust may confer a power of appointment upon a beneficiary of the original trust to whom or for the benefit of whom the trustee has the power to distribute the principal of such original trust. For purposes of this subsection, the permissible appointees of the power of appointment conferred upon a beneficiary may include persons who are not beneficiaries of such original trust or second trust.

(h) If any contribution to the original trust qualified for the annual exclusion under Section 2503(b) of the federal Internal Revenue Code, as it existed on February 1, 2018, the marital deduction under Section 2056(a) or 2523(a) of the federal Internal Revenue Code, as it existed on February 1, 2018, or the charitable deduction under Section 170(a), 642(c), 2055(a), or 2522(a) of the federal Internal Revenue Code, as it existed on February 1, 2018, is a direct skip qualifying for treatment under Section 2642(c) of the federal Internal Revenue Code, as it existed on February 1, 2018, or qualified for any other specific tax benefit that would be lost by the existence of the authorized trustee's authority under subsection (b) of this Code section for income, gift, estate, or generation-skipping transfer tax purposes under the federal Internal Revenue Code, then the authorized trustee shall not have the power to distribute the principal of a trust pursuant to subsection (b) of this Code section in a manner that would prevent the contribution to the original trust from qualifying for such exclusion, deduction, or other tax benefit or would reduce such exclusion, deduction, or other tax benefit that was originally claimed with respect to such contribution.

(i) The exercise of the power to invade the principal of the original trust under subsection (b) of this Code section shall be subject to the following limitations:

(1) The second trust need not qualify as a grantor trust for federal income tax purposes, even if the original trust does qualify as a grantor trust, except that if such original trust qualifies as a grantor trust because of the application of Section 672(f)(2)(A) of the federal Internal Revenue Code, as it existed on February 1, 2018, such second trust may not include or omit a term that, if included in or omitted from the original trust instrument, would have prevented such original trust from qualifying under such section;

(2) The second trust may qualify as a grantor trust for federal income tax purposes, even if the original trust does not so qualify, except that if such original trust does not so qualify and such second trust will so qualify, in whole or in part, with respect to the settlor, such second trust shall grant such settlor or another person a power that would cause such second trust to cease to be a grantor trust for federal income tax purposes unless such settlor objects in a writing delivered to the trustee before the date the trustee proposes to distribute from such original trust to such second trust; and

(3) When both the original trust and the second trust qualify as grantor trusts for federal income tax purposes and such original trust grants the settlor or another person the power to cause such original trust to cease

to be a grantor trust, such second trust shall grant an equivalent power to the settlor or another person unless such settlor objects in a writing delivered to the trustee before the date the trustee proposes to distribute from such original trust to such second trust.

(j) During any period when the original trust owns stock in a Subchapter "S" corporation as defined in Section 1361(a)(1) of the federal Internal Revenue Code, as it existed on February 1, 2018, an authorized trustee shall not exercise a power authorized by subsection (b) of this Code section to distribute part or all of the stock of the Subchapter "S" corporation to a second trust that is not a permitted shareholder under Section 1361(c)(2) of the federal Internal Revenue Code, as it existed on February 1, 2018.

(k) A trustee or other person that reasonably relies on the validity of a distribution of property of the original trust to the second trust under subsection (b) of this Code section or any other law or common law shall not be liable for any action or failure to act as a result of such reliance.

(l) This Code section shall not create or imply a duty for a trustee to exercise a power conferred by this Code section.

(m) If exercise of the power to invade the principal of the original trust would be effective under subsection (b) of this Code section except that the second trust in part does not comply with this Code section, such exercise of the power shall be effective, a provision in such second trust that is not permitted under this Code section shall be void to the extent necessary to comply with this Code section, and a provision required by this Code section to be in such second trust that is not contained in such second trust shall be deemed to be included in such second trust to the extent necessary to comply with this Code section.

(n) The settlor of the original trust shall be deemed to be the settlor of the second trust with respect to the portion of the principal of the original trust subject to the exercise of the power to invade the principal of such original trust under subsection (b) of this Code section.

(o) A debt, liability, or other obligation enforceable against property of the original trust shall be enforceable to the same extent against the property when held by the second trust after exercise of the power to invade the principal of such original trust under subsection (b) of this Code section.

(p) This Code section shall not apply to a trust held solely for charitable purposes.

O.C.G.A. § 53-12-132(a)

A constructive trust is a trust implied whenever the circumstances are such that the person holding legal title to property, either from fraud or otherwise, cannot enjoy the beneficial interest in the property without violating some established principle of equity.

O.C.G.A. § 53-12-133

In all cases in which a trust is sought to be implied, the court may hear parol evidence of the nature of the transaction, the circumstances, and the conduct of the parties, either to imply or rebut the trust.

O.C.G.A. § 53-12-221

(a) A trustee may be removed:

(1) In accordance with the provisions of the trust instrument; or

(2) Upon petition to the court by any interested person showing good cause.

(b) In the discretion of the court, in order to protect the trust property or the interests of any beneficiary, on its own motion or on motion of a cotrustee or other interested person, the court may compel the trustee whose removal is being sought to surrender trust property to a cotrustee, a receiver, or temporary trustee pending a decision on a petition for removal of a trustee or pending appellate review of such decision. To the extent the court deems necessary, the powers of the trustee also may be suspended.

O.C.G.A. § 53-12-240

(a) The duties contained in this part are in addition to and not in limitation of the common law duties of the trustee, except to the extent inconsistent therewith.

(b) Upon acceptance of a trusteeship, the trustee shall administer the trust in good faith, in accordance with its provisions and purposes.

O.C.G.A. § 53-12-243

(a) On reasonable request by any qualified beneficiary, the trustee shall provide the qualified beneficiary with a report of information, to the extent relevant to that beneficiary's interest, about the assets, liabilities, receipts, and disbursements of the trust, the acts of the trustee, and the particulars relating to the administration of such trust, including the trust provisions that describe or affect such beneficiary's interest.

(b)

(1) A trustee shall account at least annually, at the termination of the trust, and upon a change of trustees to each qualified beneficiary of an irrevocable trust to whom income is required or authorized in the trustee's discretion to be distributed currently, and to any person who may revoke the trust. At the termination of the trust, the trustee shall also account to each remainder beneficiary. Upon a change of trustees, the trustee shall also account to the successor trustee. In full satisfaction of this obligation, the trustee may deliver the accounting to the guardian or conservator of any qualified beneficiary who is not sui juris.

(2) An accounting furnished to a qualified beneficiary pursuant to paragraph (1) of this subsection shall contain a statement of receipts and disbursements of principal and income that have occurred during the

last complete fiscal year of the trust or since the last accounting to that beneficiary and a statement of the assets and liabilities of the trust as of the end of the accounting period.

(c) A trustee shall not be required to report information or account to a qualified beneficiary who has waived in writing the right to a report or accounting and has not withdrawn that waiver.

(d) Subsections (a) and (b) of this Code section shall not apply to the extent that the terms of the trust provide otherwise or the settlor of the trust directs otherwise in a writing delivered to the trustee.

(e) Nothing in this Code section shall affect the power of a court to require or excuse an accounting.

O.C.G.A. § 53-12-261

(a) A trustee of an express trust, without court authorization, shall be authorized to exercise:

(1) Powers conferred by the trust instrument; and

(2) Except as limited by the trust instrument:

(A) All powers over the trust property that an unmarried competent owner has over individually owned property;

(B) Any other powers appropriate to achieve the proper investment, management, and distribution of the trust property; and

(C) Any other powers conferred by this chapter.

(b) Without limiting the authority conferred by subsection (a) of this Code section, a trustee of an express trust, without court authorization, shall be authorized:

(1) To sell, exchange, grant options upon, partition, or otherwise dispose of any property or interest therein which the fiduciary may hold from time to time, at public or private sale or otherwise, with or without warranties or representations, upon such terms and conditions, including credit, and for such consideration as the fiduciary deems advisable and to transfer and convey the property or interest therein which is at the disposal of the fiduciary, in fee simple absolute or otherwise, free of all trust. The party dealing with the fiduciary shall not be under a duty to follow the proceeds or other consideration received;

(2) To invest and reinvest in any property which the fiduciary deems advisable, including, but not limited to, common or preferred stocks, bonds, debentures, notes, mortgages, or other securities, in or outside the United States; insurance contracts on the life of any beneficiary or of any person in whom a beneficiary has an insurable interest or in annuity contracts for any beneficiary; any real or personal property; investment trusts, including the securities of or other interests in any open-end or

closed-end management investment company or investment trust registered under the federal Investment Company Act of 1940, 15 U.S.C. Section 80a-1, et seq.; and participations in common trust funds;

(3) To the extent and upon such terms and conditions and for such periods of time as the fiduciary shall deem necessary or advisable, to continue or participate in the operation of any business or other enterprise, whatever its form or organization, including, but not limited to, the power:

(A) To effect incorporation, dissolution, or other change in the form of the organization of the business or enterprise;

(B) To dispose of any interest therein or acquire the interest of others therein;

(C) To contribute or invest additional capital thereto or to lend money thereto in any such case upon such terms and conditions as the fiduciary shall approve from time to time; and

(D) To determine whether the liabilities incurred in the conduct of the business are to be chargeable solely to the part of the property held by the fiduciary set aside for use in the business or to the property held by the fiduciary as a whole.

In all cases in which the fiduciary is required to file accounts in any court or in any other public office, it shall not be necessary to itemize receipts, disbursements, and distributions of property; but it shall be sufficient for the fiduciary to show in the account a single figure or consolidation of figures, and the fiduciary shall be permitted to account for money and property received from the business and any payments made to the business in lump sum without itemization;

(4) To form a corporation or other entity and to transfer, assign, and convey to the corporation or entity all or any part of the property held by the fiduciary in exchange for the stock, securities, or obligations of or other interests in any such corporation or entity and to continue to hold the stock, securities, obligations, and interests;

(5) To continue any farming operation and to do any and all things deemed advisable by the fiduciary in the management and maintenance of the farm and the production and marketing of crops and dairy, poultry, livestock, orchard, and forest products, including, but not limited to, the power:

(A) To operate the farm with hired labor, tenants, or sharecroppers;

(B) To lease or rent the farm for cash or for a share of the crops;

(C) To purchase or otherwise acquire farm machinery, equipment, and livestock;

(D) To construct, repair, and improve farm buildings of all kinds needed, in the fiduciary's judgment, for the operation of the farm;

(E) To make or obtain loans or advances at the prevailing rate or rates of interest for farm purposes, such as for production, harvesting, or marketing; or for the construction, repair, or improvement of farm buildings; or for the purchase of farm machinery, equipment, or livestock;

(F) To employ approved soil conservation practices, in order to conserve, improve, and maintain the fertility and productivity of the soil;

(G) To protect, manage, and improve the timber and forest on the farm and to sell the timber and forest products when it is to the best interest of the persons to whom the fiduciary owes a duty of care;

(H) To ditch, dam, and drain damp or wet fields and areas of the farm when and where needed;

(I) To engage in the production of livestock, poultry, or dairy products and to construct such fences and buildings and to plant pastures and crops as may be necessary to carry on such operations;

(J) To market the products of the farm; and

(K) In general, to employ good husbandry in the farming operation;

(6) To manage real property:

(A) To improve, manage, protect, and subdivide any real property;

(B) To dedicate, or withdraw from dedication, parks, streets, highways, or alleys;

(C) To terminate any subdivision or part thereof;

(D) To borrow money for the purposes authorized by this paragraph for the periods of time and upon the terms and conditions as to rates, maturities, and renewals as the fiduciary shall deem advisable and to mortgage or otherwise encumber the property or part thereof, whether in possession or reversion;

(E) To lease the property or part thereof, the lease to commence at the present or in the future, upon the terms and conditions, including options to renew or purchase, and for the period or periods of time as the fiduciary deems advisable even though the period or periods may extend beyond the duration of the estate or trust;

(F) To make gravel, sand, oil, gas, and other mineral leases, contracts, licenses, conveyances, or grants of every nature and kind which are lawful in the jurisdiction in which the property lies;

(G) To manage and improve timber and forests on the property, to sell the timber and forest products, and to make grants, leases, and contracts with respect thereto;

(H) To modify, renew, or extend leases;

(I) To employ agents to rent and collect rents;

(J) To create easements and to release, convey, or assign any right, title, or interest with respect to any easement on the property or part thereof;

(K) To erect, repair, or renovate any building or other improvement on the property and to remove or demolish any building or other improvement in whole or in part; and

(L) To deal with the property and every part thereof in all other ways and for such other purposes or considerations as it would be lawful for any person owning the same to deal with such property either in the same or in different ways from those specified elsewhere in this paragraph;

(7) To lease personal property held by the fiduciary or part thereof, the lease to commence at the present or in the future, upon the terms and conditions, including options to renew or purchase, and for the period or periods of time as the fiduciary deems advisable even though the period or periods may extend beyond the duration of the estate or trust;

(8)

(A) To pay debts, taxes, assessments, compensation of the fiduciary, and other expenses incurred in the collection, care, administration, and protection of the property held by the fiduciary; and

(B) To pay from the estate or trust all charges that the fiduciary deems necessary or appropriate to comply with laws regulating environmental conditions and to remedy or ameliorate any such conditions which the fiduciary determines adversely affect the property held by the fiduciary or otherwise are liabilities of the estate or trust and to apportion all such charges among the several bequests and trusts and the interests of the beneficiaries in such manner as the fiduciary deems fair, prudent, and equitable under the circumstances;

(9) To receive additional property from any source and to administer the additional property as a portion of the appropriate estate or trust under the management of the fiduciary, provided that the fiduciary shall not be required to receive the property without the fiduciary's consent;

(10) In dealing with one or more fiduciaries of the estate or any trust created by the decedent or the settlor or any spouse or child of the decedent or settlor and irrespective of whether the fiduciary is a personal representative or trustee of such other estate or trust:

(A) To sell real or personal property of the estate or trust to such fiduciary or to exchange such property with such fiduciary upon such terms and conditions as to sale price, terms of payment, and security as shall seem advisable to the fiduciary; and the fiduciary shall be under no duty to follow the proceeds of any such sale; and

(B) To borrow money from the estate or trust for such periods of time and upon such terms and conditions as to rates, maturities, renewals, and securities as the fiduciary shall deem advisable for the purpose of paying debts of the decedent or settlor, taxes, the costs of the administration of the estate or trust, and like charges against the estate or trust or any part thereof or of discharging any other liabilities of the estate or trust and to mortgage, pledge, or otherwise encumber such portion of the estate or trust as may be required to secure the loan and to renew existing loans;

(11) To borrow money for such periods of time and upon such terms and conditions as to rates, maturities, renewals, and security as the fiduciary shall deem advisable for the purpose of paying debts, taxes, or other charges against the estate or trust or any part thereof and to mortgage, pledge, or otherwise encumber such portion of the property held by the fiduciary as may be required to secure the loan and to renew existing loans either as maker or endorser;

(12) To make loans out of the property held by the fiduciary, including loans to a beneficiary on terms and conditions the fiduciary considers to be fair and reasonable under the circumstances, and the fiduciary has a lien on future distributions for repayment of those loans;

(13) To vote shares of stock or other ownership interests held by the fiduciary, in person or by proxy, with or without power of substitution;

(14) To hold a security in the name of a nominee or in other form without disclosure of the fiduciary relationship, so that title to the security may pass by delivery; but the fiduciary shall be liable for any act of the nominee in connection with the security so held;

(15) To exercise all options, rights, and privileges to convert stocks, bonds, debentures, notes, mortgages, or other property into other stocks, bonds, debentures, notes, mortgages, or other property; to subscribe for other or additional stocks, bonds, debentures, notes, mortgages, or other property; and to hold the stocks, bonds, debentures, notes, mortgages, or other property so acquired as investments of the estate or trust so long as the fiduciary shall deem advisable;

(16) To unite with other owners of property similar to any which may be held at any time by the fiduciary, in carrying out any plan for the consolidation or merger, dissolution or liquidation, foreclosure, lease, or sale of the property or the incorporation or reincorporation, reorganization, or readjustment of the capital or financial structure of any corporation, company, or association the securities of which may form any portion of

an estate or trust; to become and serve as a member of a shareholders' or bondholders' protective committee; to deposit securities in accordance with any plan agreed upon; to pay any assessments, expenses, or sums of money that may be required for the protection or furtherance of the interest of the beneficiaries to whom the fiduciary owes a duty of care with reference to any such plan; and to receive as investments of the estate or trust any securities issued as a result of the execution of such plan;

(17) To adjust the interest rate from time to time on any obligation, whether secured or unsecured, constituting a part of the estate or trust;

(18) To continue any obligation, whether secured or unsecured, upon and after maturity, with or without renewal or extension, upon such terms as the fiduciary shall deem advisable, without regard to the value of the security, if any, at the time of the continuance;

(19) To foreclose, as an incident to the collection of any bond, note, or other obligation, any deed to secure debt or any mortgage, deed of trust, or other lien securing the bond, note, or other obligation and to bid in the property at the foreclosure sale or to acquire the property by deed from the mortgagor or obligor without foreclosure; and to retain the property so bid in or taken over without foreclosure;

(20) To carry such insurance coverage as the fiduciary shall deem advisable;

(21) To collect, receive, and issue receipts for rents, issues, profits, and income of the estate or trust;

(22)

(A) To compromise, adjust, mediate, arbitrate, or otherwise deal with and settle claims involving the fiduciary or the property held by the fiduciary;

(B) To compromise, adjust, mediate, arbitrate, bring or defend actions on, abandon, or otherwise deal with and settle claims in favor of or against the estate or trust as the fiduciary shall deem advisable; the fiduciary's decision shall be conclusive between the fiduciary and the beneficiaries to whom the fiduciary owes a duty of care and the person against or for whom the claim is asserted, in the absence of fraud by such persons and, in the absence of fraud, bad faith, or gross negligence of the fiduciary, shall be conclusive between the fiduciary and the beneficiaries to whom the fiduciary owes a duty of care; and

(C) To compromise all debts, the collection of which are doubtful, belonging to the estate or trust when such settlements will advance the interests of those represented;

(23) To employ and compensate, out of income or principal or both and in such proportion as the fiduciary shall deem advisable, persons deemed by the fiduciary needful to advise or assist in the administration of the estate or trust, including, but not limited to, agents, accountants, brokers, attorneys at law, attorneys in fact, investment brokers, rental agents, realtors, appraisers, and tax specialists; and to do so without liability for any neglect, omission, misconduct, or default of the agent or representative, provided such person was selected and retained with due care on the part of the fiduciary;

(24) To acquire, receive, hold, and retain undivided the principal of several trusts created by a single trust instrument until division shall become necessary in order to make distributions; to hold, manage, invest, reinvest, and account for the several shares or parts of shares by appropriate entries in the fiduciary's books of account and to allocate to each share or part of share its proportionate part of all receipts and expenses; provided, however, that this paragraph shall not defer the vesting in possession of any share or part of share of the trust;

(25) To set up proper and reasonable reserves for taxes, assessments, insurance premiums, depreciation, obsolescence, amortization, depletion of mineral or timber properties, repairs, improvements, and general maintenance of buildings or other property out of rents, profits, or other income received;

(26) To value property held by the fiduciary and to distribute such property in cash or in kind, or partly in cash and partly in kind, in divided or undivided interests, as the fiduciary finds to be most practical and in the best interest of the distributees, the fiduciary being able to distribute types of assets differently among the distributees;

(27) To transfer money or other property distributable to a beneficiary who is under age 21, an adult for whom a guardian or conservator has been appointed, or an adult who the fiduciary reasonably believes is incapacitated by distributing such money or property directly to the beneficiary or applying it for the beneficiary's benefit, or by:

(A) Distributing it to the beneficiary's conservator or, if the beneficiary does not have a conservator, the beneficiary's guardian;

(B) Distributing it to the beneficiary's custodian under "The Georgia Transfers to Minors Act" or similar state law and, for that purpose, creating a custodianship and designating a custodian;

(C) Distributing it to the beneficiary's custodial trustee under the Uniform Custodial Trust Act as enacted in another state and, for that purpose, creating a custodial trust; or

(D) Distributing it to any other person, whether or not appointed guardian or conservator by any court, who shall, in fact, have the care and custody of the person of the beneficiary.

The fiduciary shall not be under any duty to see to the application of the distributions so made if the fiduciary exercised due care in the selection of the person, including the beneficiary, to whom the payments were made; and the receipt of the person shall be full acquittance to the fiduciary;

(28) To determine:

(A) What is principal and what is income of any estate or trust and to allocate or apportion receipts and expenses, as between principal and income, in the exercise of the fiduciary's discretion and, by way of illustration and not limitation of the fiduciary's discretion, to charge premiums on securities purchased at a premium against principal or income or partly against each;

(B) Whether to apply stock dividends and other noncash dividends to income or principal or to apportion them as the fiduciary shall deem advisable; and

(C) What expenses, costs, and taxes, other than estate, inheritance, and succession taxes and other governmental charges, shall be charged against principal or income or apportioned between principal and income and in what proportions;

(29) To make, modify, and execute contracts and other instruments, under seal or otherwise, as the fiduciary deems advisable; and

(30) To serve without making and filing inventory and appraisement, without filing any annual or other returns or reports to any court, and without giving bond; but a personal representative shall furnish to the income beneficiaries, at least annually, a statement of receipts and disbursements.

(c) The exercise of a power shall be subject to the fiduciary duties prescribed by this chapter.

(d) If a probate court grants to a personal representative any of the powers contained in this Code section, then as used in this Code section the term:

(1) "Beneficiary" includes a distributee of the estate;

(2) "Trust" includes the estate held by the personal representative; and

(3) "Trustee" or "fiduciary" includes the personal representative.

O.C.G.A. § 53-12-301(a)

If a trustee commits a breach of trust, or threatens to commit a breach of trust, a beneficiary shall have a cause of action to seek:

(1) To recover damages;

(2) To compel the trustee to perform the trustee's duties;

(3) To require an accounting;

(4) To enjoin the trustee from committing a breach of trust;

(5) To compel the trustee to redress a breach of trust by payment of money or otherwise;

(6) To appoint a temporary trustee to take possession of the trust property and administer the trust or to suspend a trustee with or without the appointment of a temporary trustee;

(7) To remove the trustee; and

(8) To reduce or deny compensation of the trustee.

Chapter 9

O.C.G.A. § 44-6-201(a)

A nonvested property interest is invalid unless:

(1) When the interest is created, it is certain either to vest or to terminate within the lifetime of an individual then alive or within 21 years after the death of that individual; or

(2) The interest either vests or terminates within 360 years after its creation.

O.C.G.A. § 53-12-80(d)

A spendthrift provision shall not be valid as to the following claims against a beneficiary's right to a current distribution to the extent the distribution would be subject to garnishment under Article 1 of Chapter 4 of Title 18 if the distribution were disposable earnings:

(1) Alimony or child support;

(2) Taxes or other governmental claims;

(3) Tort judgments;

(4) Judgments or orders for restitution as a result of a criminal conviction of the beneficiary; or

(5) Judgments for necessaries.

The ability of a creditor or assignee to reach a beneficiary's interest under this subsection shall not apply to the extent that it would disqualify the trust as a special needs trust established pursuant to 42 U.S.C. Sections 1396p(d)(4)(A) or 1396p(d)(4)(C).

O.C.G.A. § 53-12-170(b)

Charitable purposes shall include:

(1) The relief of poverty;

(2) The advancement of education;

(3) The advancement of ethics and religion;

(4) The advancement of health;

(5) The advancement of science and the arts and humanities;

(6) The protection and preservation of the environment;

(7) The improvement, maintenance, or repair of cemeteries, other places of disposition of human remains, and memorials;

(8) The prevention of cruelty to animals;

(9) Governmental purposes; and

(10) Other similar subjects having for their object the relief of human suffering or the promotion of human civilization.

Chapter 10

O.C.G.A. § 29-4-1

(a) The court may appoint a guardian for an adult only if the court finds the adult lacks sufficient capacity to make or communicate significant responsible decisions concerning his or her health or safety.

(b) No guardian, other than a guardian ad litem, shall be appointed for an adult except pursuant to the procedures of this chapter.

(c) No guardian shall be appointed for an adult unless the appointment is in the best interest of the adult.

(d) No guardian shall be appointed for an adult within two years after the denial or dismissal on the merits of a petition for the appointment of a guardian for that adult unless the petitioner shows a significant change in the condition or circumstances of the adult.

(e)

(1) No adult shall be presumed to be in need of a guardian unless adjudicated to be in need of a guardian pursuant to this chapter.

(2) An adult shall not be presumed to be in need of a guardian solely because of a finding of criminal insanity or incompetence to stand trial or a finding of a need for treatment or services pursuant to:

(A) Code Section 37-1-1;

(B) Code Sections 37-3-1 through 37-3-6;

(C) Articles 2 through 6 of Chapter 3 of Title 37;

(D) Code Sections 37-4-1 through 37-4-3 and 37-4-5 through 37-4-8;

(E) Articles 2 through 5 of Chapter 4 of Title 37;

(F) Code Section 37-5-3;

(G) Code Sections 37-7-1, 37-7-2, and 37-7-4 through 37-7-7; and

(H) Articles 2 through 6 of Chapter 7 of Title 37.

(f) All guardianships ordered pursuant to this chapter shall be designed to encourage the development of maximum self-reliance and independence in the adult and shall be ordered only to the extent necessitated by the adult's actual and adaptive limitations after a determination that less restrictive alternatives to the guardianship are not available or appropriate.

O.C.G.A. § 29-4-2

(a) Only an individual may serve as guardian of an adult, except in the event a public guardian or the Department of Human Services is appointed pursuant to subsection (b.1) of Code Section 29-4-3.

(b) No individual may be appointed as guardian of an adult who:

(1) Is a minor, a ward, or a protected person;

(2) Has a conflict of interest with the adult unless the court determines that the conflict of interest is insubstantial or that the appointment would be in the adult's best interest; or

(3) Is an owner, operator, or employee of a long-term care or other caregiving institution or facility at which the adult is receiving care, unless related to the adult by blood, marriage, or adoption.

(c) No entity may be appointed as guardian of an adult which:

(1) Has a conflict of interest with the adult unless the court determines that the conflict of interest is insubstantial or that the appointment would be in the adult's best interest; or

(2) Is a long-term care or other caregiving institution or facility at which the adult is receiving care.

O.C.G.A. § 29-4-3(b)

Individuals who are eligible have preference in the following order:

(1) The individual last nominated by the adult in accordance with the provisions of subsection (c) of this Code section;

(2) The spouse of the adult or an individual nominated by the adult's spouse in accordance with the provisions of subsection (d) of this Code section;

(3) An adult child of the adult or an individual nominated by an adult child of the adult in accordance with the provisions of subsection (d) of this Code section;

(4) A parent of the adult or an individual nominated by a parent of the adult in accordance with the provisions of subsection (d) of this Code section;

(5) A guardian appointed during the minority of the adult;

(6) A guardian previously appointed in Georgia or another state;

(7) A friend, relative, or any other individual;

(8) Any other person, including a volunteer to the court, found suitable and appropriate who is willing to accept the appointment; and

(9) The county guardian.

O.C.G.A. § 29-5-1

(a) The court may appoint a conservator for an adult only if the court finds the adult lacks sufficient capacity to make or communicate significant responsible decisions concerning the management of his or her property.

(b) No conservator, except a conservator for the estate of an individual who is missing or who is believed to be dead, shall be appointed for any adult except pursuant to the procedures of this chapter.

(c) No conservator shall be appointed for an adult unless the appointment is in the best interest of the adult.

(d) No conservator shall be appointed for an adult within two years after the denial or dismissal on the merits of a petition for the appointment of a conservator for that adult unless the petitioner shows a significant change in the condition or circumstances of the adult.

(e)

(1) No adult shall be presumed to be in need of a conservator unless adjudicated to be in need of a conservator pursuant to this chapter.

(2) An adult shall not be presumed to be in need of a conservator solely because of a finding of criminal insanity or incompetence to stand trial or a finding of a need for treatment or services pursuant to:

(A) Code Section 37-1-1;

(B) Code Sections 37-3-1 through 37-3-6;

(C) Articles 2 through 6 of Chapter 3 of Title 37;

(D) Code Sections 37-4-1 through 37-4-3 and 37-4-5 through 37-4-8;

(E) Articles 2 through 5 of Chapter 4 of Title 37;

(F) Code Section 37-5-3;

(G) Code Sections 37-7-1, 37-7-2, and 37-7-4 through 37-7-7; and

(H) Articles 2 through 6 of Chapter 7 of Title 37.

(f) All conservatorships ordered pursuant to this chapter shall be designed to encourage the development of maximum self-reliance and independence in the adult and shall be ordered only to the extent necessitated by the adult's actual and adaptive limitations after a determination that less restrictive alternatives to the conservatorship are not available or appropriate.

O.C.G.A. § 29-5-2

No person may be appointed or continue to serve as conservator of the estate of an adult who:

(1) Is a minor, a ward, or a protected person;

(2) Who has a conflict of interest with the adult unless the court determines that the conflict of interest is insubstantial or that the appointment clearly would be in the adult's best interest; or

(3) Is an owner, operator, or employee of a long-term care or other caregiving institution or facility at which the adult is receiving care, unless related to the adult by blood, marriage, or adoption.

O.C.G.A. § 29-5-3(b)

Persons who are eligible and not disqualified have preference in the following order:

(1) The person last nominated by the adult in accordance with the provisions of subsection (c) of this Code section;

(2) The spouse of the adult or a person nominated by the adult's spouse in accordance with the provisions of subsection (d) of this Code section;

(3) An adult child of the adult or a person nominated by an adult child of the adult in accordance with the provisions of subsection (d) of this Code section;

(4) A parent of the adult or a person nominated by a parent of the adult in accordance with the provisions of subsection (c) of this Code section;

(5) A conservator appointed during the minority of the adult;

(6) A conservator previously appointed in Georgia or another state;

(7) A friend, relative, or any other person; or

(8) The county guardian.

Chapter 11

O.C.G.A. § 53-1-2(2)

"Administrator with the will annexed" means any person, other than an executor, appointed and qualified to administer a testate estate, including a testate estate already partially administered and from any cause unrepresented.

O.C.G.A. § 53-1-2(12)

"Personal representative" means any administrator, administrator with the will annexed, county administrator, or executor.

O.C.G.A. § 53-6-2

Any person who, without authority of law, wrongfully intermeddles with or converts the personalty of a decedent whose estate is unrepresented shall be deemed an executor de son tort and as such shall be liable to the creditors and heirs or beneficiaries of the estate for double the value of the property so possessed and converted. Such executor shall not be allowed to set off any debt due the executor by the decedent or voluntarily paid by the executor out of the assets. If the executor dies, the executor's personal representative shall be liable in the same manner and to the same extent as would the executor were the executor still living.

O.C.G.A. § 53-6-10

(a) No formal words are necessary for the nomination of an executor. An expression by the testator of a desire that the person carry into effect the testator's wishes shall amount to a nomination as executor.

(b) Unless adjudged unfit, nominated executors shall have the right to qualify in the order set out in the will.

(c) An individual who has not reached the age of majority may be nominated as an executor but may not qualify until reaching the age of majority.

(d) If the will names a person to fill a vacancy in the office of executor or provides a method of selecting a personal representative to fill the vacancy, any vacancy shall be filled or selection made as provided in the will.

O.C.G.A. § 53-6-13

Unless another nominated executor qualifies within the time provided in Code Section 53-6-11, the probate court shall appoint an administrator with the will annexed of a testate estate when:

(1) No executor is nominated in the will;

(2) The nominated executor has not reached the age of majority, to serve until the disability ceases;

(3) The executor dies, resigns, or otherwise becomes disqualified to serve; or

(4) A testate estate is unrepresented for any other reason.

O.C.G.A. § 53-6-14(b)

An administrator with the will annexed may be unanimously selected by the beneficiaries of the will who are capable of expressing a choice unless the sole beneficiary is the decedent's surviving spouse and an action for divorce or separate maintenance was pending between the decedent and the surviving spouse at the time of death. When no such unanimous selection is made, the probate court shall make the appointment that will best serve the interests of the estate, considering the following preferences:

(1) Any beneficiary or the trustee of any trust that is a beneficiary under the will; or

(2) Those persons listed in paragraphs (3) through (5) of Code Section 53-6-20.

O.C.G.A. § 53-6-20

An administrator may be unanimously selected by all the heirs of a deceased intestate unless the sole heir is the decedent's surviving spouse and an action for divorce or separate maintenance was pending between the deceased intestate and the surviving spouse at the time of death. With respect to any heir who is not sui juris, consent may be given by the guardian of the individual. When no such unanimous selection is made, the probate court shall make the appointment that will best serve the interests of the estate, considering the following order of preferences:

(1) The surviving spouse, unless an action for divorce or separate maintenance was pending between the deceased intestate and the surviving spouse at the time of death;

(2) One or more other heirs of the intestate or the person selected by the majority in interest of them;

(3) Any other eligible person;

(4) Any creditor of the estate; or

(5) The county administrator.

O.C.G.A. § 53-6-30

(a) The probate court may at any time and without service or notice to anyone grant temporary letters of administration on an unrepresented estate to continue in full force and effect until the temporary administrator is discharged or a personal representative is appointed.

(b) The probate court may appoint such person as temporary administrator as the court determines to be in the best interests of the estate. Pending an issue of devisavit vel non upon any paper propounded as a will that has not been admitted to probate in common form, the executor nominated in the purported will shall have preference in the appointment of a temporary administrator.

(c) There shall be no appeal from an order granting temporary letters of administration, either to the superior court under subsection (a) of Code Section 5-3-2 or to the Supreme Court or the Court of Appeals under subsection (a) of Code Section 15-9-123.

O.C.G.A. § 53-6-60(a)

Personal representatives shall be compensated as specified in either the will or any written agreement entered into prior to the decedent's death or a written agreement signed by all the beneficiaries of a testate estate or all the heirs of an intestate estate. A written agreement between a testator and a personal representative shall be valid and binding upon the estate of the testator as fully and completely as if set forth in and made a part of the will.

O.C.G.A. § 53-6-60(b)

If the personal representative's compensation is not specified in the will or any separate written agreement, the personal representative for services rendered shall be entitled to compensation equal to:

(1) Two and one-half percent commission on all sums of money received by the personal representative on account of the estate, except on money loaned by and repaid to the personal representative, and 2 1/2 percent commission on all sums paid out by the personal representative, either for debts, legacies, or distributive shares;

(2) Ten percent commission on the amount of interest made if, during the course of administration, the personal representative shall receive interest on money loaned by the personal representative in that capacity and shall include the same on the return to the probate court so as to become chargeable therewith as a part of the corpus of the estate;

(3) Reasonable compensation, as determined in the discretion of the probate court and after such notice, if any, as the court shall direct, for the delivery

over of property in kind, not exceeding 3 percent of the appraised value and, in cases where there has been no appraisal, not over 3 percent of the fair value as found by the judge, irrespective of whether delivery over in kind is made pursuant to proceedings for that purpose in the probate court and irrespective of whether the property, except money, is tangible or intangible, personal or real; and

(4) In the discretion of the probate court, compensation for working land for the benefit of the parties in interest in no case exceeding 10 percent of the annual income of the property so managed.

O.C.G.A. § 53-6-61

Personal representatives shall be allowed reasonable expenses incurred in the administration of the estate, including without limitation expenses for travel, the expenses and premiums incurred in securing a bond, and the expenses of counsel and other agents. Such reasonable expenses shall be determined after such notice, if any, as the court shall direct.

O.C.G.A. § 53-7-54(a)

If a personal representative or temporary administrator commits a breach of fiduciary duty or threatens to commit a breach of fiduciary duty, a beneficiary of a testate estate or heir of an intestate estate shall have a cause of action:

(1) To recover damages;

(2) To compel the performance of the personal representative's or temporary administrator's duties;

(3) To enjoin the commission of a breach of fiduciary duty;

(4) To compel the redress of a breach of fiduciary duty by payment of money or otherwise;

(5) To appoint another personal representative or temporary administrator to take possession of the estate property and administer the estate;

(6) To remove the personal representative or temporary administrator; and

(7) To reduce or deny compensation to the personal representative or temporary administrator.

O.C.G.A. § 53-7-56

(a) A personal representative may resign:

  (1) In the manner and under the circumstances described in the will;

  (2) Upon petition to the probate court, showing that the resignation has been requested in writing by all heirs of an intestate estate or all beneficiaries of a testate estate; or

  (3) Upon petition to the probate court, showing to the satisfaction of the court that:

(A) The personal representative is unable to continue serving due to age, illness, infirmity, or other good cause;

(B) Greater burdens have developed upon the office of personal representative than those that originally were contemplated or should have been contemplated when the personal representative was qualified and the additional burdens would work a hardship upon the personal representative;

(C) Disagreement exists between one or more of the beneficiaries or heirs and the personal representative in respect to the personal representative's management of the estate, which disagreement and conflict appear deleterious to the estate;

(D) The resignation of the personal representative will result in or permit substantial financial benefit to the estate;

(E) The resigning personal representative is one of two or more acting personal representatives and the other personal representatives will continue in office with no adversity to the estate contemplated; or

(F) The resignation would not be disadvantageous to the estate.

(b) A personal representative's petition to resign shall be made to the probate court and the court shall cause citation to issue and service of notice to be made upon all the heirs of an intestate estate or the beneficiaries of a testate estate in the manner provided by Chapter 11 of this title.

Chapter 12

O.C.G.A. § 53-7-30

Unless otherwise provided by will or relieved under Code Section 53-7-32 or 53-7-33, the personal representative shall prepare an inventory of all the property of the decedent. The personal representative shall file the inventory with the probate court and shall deliver a copy of the inventory to the beneficiaries of a testate estate or the heirs of an intestate estate by first-class mail within six months after the qualification of the personal representative. It shall not be necessary to mail a copy of the inventory to any beneficiary or heir who is not sui juris or for the court to appoint a guardian for such person. The time for filing the inventory may be extended by the probate court for good cause shown. The inventory shall state that it contains a true statement of all the property of the decedent within the knowledge of the personal representative and shall be verified in the same manner as a petition filed in the probate court. The inventory shall state that the inventory has been mailed to all beneficiaries or heirs who are entitled to receive the inventory and shall provide the name of any beneficiary or heir who has waived the right to receive the inventory, as provided in Code Section 53-7-32.

O.C.G.A. § 53-7-40

Unless otherwise provided by law, all property of the estate, both real and personal, shall be liable for the payment of claims against the estate in the following order:

(1) Year's support for the family;

(2) Funeral expenses, whether or not the decedent leaves a surviving spouse, in an amount which corresponds with the circumstances of the decedent in life. If the estate is solvent, the personal representative is authorized to provide a suitable protection for the grave;

(3) Other necessary expenses of administration;

(4) Reasonable expenses of the decedent's last illness;

(5) Unpaid taxes or other debts due the state or the United States;

(6) Judgments, secured interests, and other liens created during the lifetime of the decedent, to be paid according to their priority of lien. Secured interests and other liens on specific property shall be preferred only to the extent of such property; and

(7) All other claims.

Chapter 13

O.C.G.A. § 48-12-1(a)

On and after July 1, 2014, there shall be no estate taxes levied by the state and no estate tax returns shall be required by the state.

Appendix B

Selected Sections of the Internal Revenue Code

Chapter 9

I.R.C. § 2010. Unified credit against estate tax

(a) General rule

A credit of the applicable credit amount shall be allowed to the estate of every decedent against the tax imposed by section 2001.

(b) Adjustment to credit for certain gifts made before 1977

The amount of the credit allowable under subsection (a) shall be reduced by an amount equal to 20 percent of the aggregate amount allowed as a specific exemption under section 2521 (as in effect before its repeal by the Tax Reform Act of 1976) with respect to gifts made by the decedent after September 8, 1976.

(c) Applicable credit amount

(1) In general

For purposes of this section, the applicable credit amount is the amount of the tentative tax which would be determined under section 2001(c) if the amount with respect to which such tentative tax is to be computed were equal to the applicable exclusion amount.

(2) Applicable exclusion amount

For purposes of this subsection, the applicable exclusion amount is the sum of:

(A) the basic exclusion amount, and

(B) in the case of a surviving spouse, the deceased spousal unused exclusion amount.

(3) Basic exclusion amount

(A) In general

For purposes of this subsection, the basic exclusion amount is $5,000,000.

(B) Inflation adjustment

In the case of any decedent dying in a calendar year after 2011, the dollar amount in subparagraph (A) shall be increased by an amount equal to—

(i) such dollar amount, multiplied by

(ii) the cost-of-living adjustment determined under section 1(f)(3) for such calendar year by substituting "calendar year 2010" for "calendar year 2016" in subparagraph (A)(ii) thereof.

If any amount as adjusted under the preceding sentence is not a multiple of $10,000, such amount shall be rounded to the nearest multiple of $10,000.

(C) Increase in basic exclusion amount

In the case of estates of decedents dying or gifts made after December 31, 2017, and before January 1, 2026, subparagraph (A) shall be applied by substituting "$10,000,000" for "$5,000,000".

(4) Deceased spousal unused exclusion amount

For purposes of this subsection, with respect to a surviving spouse of a deceased spouse dying after December 31, 2010, the term "deceased spousal unused exclusion amount" means the lesser of—

(A) the basic exclusion amount, or

(B) the excess of—

(i) the applicable exclusion amount of the last such deceased spouse of such surviving spouse, over

(ii) the amount with respect to which the tentative tax is determined under section 2001(b)(1) on the estate of such deceased spouse

(5) Special rules

(A) Election required

A deceased spousal unused exclusion amount may not be taken into account by a surviving spouse under paragraph (2) unless the executor of the estate of the deceased spouse files an estate tax return on which such amount is computed and makes an election on such return that such amount may be so taken into account. Such election, once made, shall be irrevocable. No election may be made under this subparagraph if such return is filed after the time prescribed by law (including extensions) for filing such return.

(B) Examination of prior returns after expiration of period of limitations with respect to deceased spousal unused exclusion amount

Notwithstanding any period of limitation in section 6501, after the time has expired under section 6501 within which a tax may be assessed under chapter 11 or 12 with respect to a deceased spousal unused exclusion amount, the Secretary may examine a return of the deceased spouse to make determinations with respect to such amount for purposes of carrying out this subsection.

(6) Regulations

The Secretary shall prescribe such regulations as may be necessary or appropriate to carry out this subsection.

(d) Limitation based on amount of tax

The amount of the credit allowed by subsection (a) shall not exceed the amount of the tax imposed by section 2001.

I.R.C. § 2523. Gift to spouse

(a) Allowance of deduction

Where a donor transfers during the calendar year by gift an interest in property to a donee who at the time of the gift is the donor's spouse, there shall be allowed as a deduction in computing taxable gifts for the calendar year an amount with respect to such interest equal to its value.

(b) Life estate or other terminable interest

Where, on the lapse of time, on the occurrence of an event or contingency, or on the failure of an event or contingency to occur, such interest transferred to the spouse will terminate or fail, no deduction shall be allowed with respect to such interest—

(1) if the donor retains in himself, or transfers or has transferred (for less than an adequate and full consideration in money or money's worth) to any person other than such donee spouse (or the estate of such spouse), an interest in such property, and if by reason of such retention or transfer the donor (or his heirs or assigns) or such person (or his heirs or assigns) may possess or enjoy any part of such property after such termination or failure of the interest transferred to the donee spouse; or

(2) if the donor immediately after the transfer to the donee spouse has a power to appoint an interest in such property which he can exercise (either alone or in conjunction with any person) in such manner that the appointee may possess or enjoy any part of such property after such termination or failure of the interest transferred to the donee spouse. For purposes of this paragraph, the donor shall be considered as having immediately after the transfer to the donee spouse such power to appoint even though such power cannot be exercised until after the lapse of time, upon the occurrence of an event or contingency, or on the failure of an event or contingency to occur.

An exercise or release at any time by the donor, either alone or in conjunction with any person, of a power to appoint an interest in property, even though not otherwise a transfer, shall, for purposes of paragraph (1), be considered as a transfer by him. Except as provided in subsection (e), where at the time of the transfer it is impossible to ascertain the particular person or persons who may receive from the donor an interest in property so transferred by him, such interest shall, for purposes of paragraph (1), be considered as transferred to a person other than the donee spouse.

(c) Interest in unidentified assets

Where the assets out of which, or the proceeds of which, the interest transferred to the donee spouse may be satisfied include a particular asset or assets with respect to which no deduction would be allowed if such asset or assets were transferred from the donor to such spouse, then the value of the interest transferred to such spouse shall, for purposes of subsection (a), be reduced by the aggregate value of such particular assets.

(d) Joint interests

If the interest is transferred to the donee spouse as sole joint tenant with the donor or as tenant by the entirety, the interest of the donor in the property which exists solely by reason of the possibility that the donor may survive the donee spouse, or that there may occur a severance of the tenancy, shall not be considered for purposes of subsection (b) as an interest retained by the donor in himself.

(e) Life estate with power of appointment in donee spouse

Where the donor transfers an interest in property, if by such transfer his spouse is entitled for life to all of the income from the entire interest, or all the income from a specific portion thereof, payable annually or at more frequent intervals, with power in the donee spouse to appoint the entire interest, or such specific portion (exercisable in favor of such donee spouse, or of the estate of such donee spouse, or in favor of either, whether or not in each case the power is exercisable in favor of others), and with no power in any other person to appoint any part of such interest, or such portion, to any person other than the donee spouse—

(1) the interest, or such portion, so transferred shall, for purposes of subsection (a) be considered as transferred to the donee spouse, and

(2) no part of the interest, or such portion, so transferred shall, for purposes of subsection (b)(1), be considered as retained in the donor or transferred to any person other than the donee spouse.

This subsection shall apply only if, by such transfer, such power in the donee spouse to appoint the interest, or such portion, whether exercisable by will or during life, is exercisable by such spouse alone and in all events. For purposes of this subsection, the term "specific portion" only includes a portion determined on a fractional or percentage basis.

(f) Election with respect to life estate for donee spouse

(1) In general

In the case of qualified terminable interest property—

(A) for purposes of subsection (a), such property shall be treated as transferred to the donee spouse, and

(B) for purposes of subsection (b)(1), no part of such property shall be considered as retained in the donor or transferred to any person other than the donee spouse.

(2) Qualified terminable interest property

For purposes of this subsection, the term "qualified terminable interest property" means any property—

(A) which is transferred by the donor spouse,

(B) in which the donee spouse has a qualifying income interest for life, and

(C) to which an election under this subsection applies.

(3) Certain rules made applicable

For purposes of this subsection, rules similar to the rules of clauses (ii), (iii), and (iv) of section 2056(b)(7)(B) shall apply and the rules of section 2056(b)(10) shall apply.

(4) Election

(A) Time and manner

An election under this subsection with respect to any property shall be made on or before the date prescribed by section 6075(b) for filing a gift tax return with respect to the transfer (determined without regard to section 6019(2)) and shall be made in such manner as the Secretary shall by regulations prescribe.

(B) Election irrevocable

An election under this subsection, once made, shall be irrevocable.

(5) Treatment of interest retained by donor spouse

(A) In general

In the case of any qualified terminable interest property—

(i) such property shall not be includible in the gross estate of the donor spouse, and

(ii) any subsequent transfer by the donor spouse of an interest in such property shall not be treated as a transfer for purposes of this chapter.

(B) Subparagraph (A) not to apply after transfer by donee spouse

Subparagraph (A) shall not apply with respect to any property after the donee spouse is treated as having transferred such property under section 2519, or such property is includible in the donee spouse's gross estate under section 2044.

(6) Treatment of joint and survivor annuities

In the case of a joint and survivor annuity where only the donor spouse and donee spouse have the right to receive payments before the death of the last spouse to die—

(A) the donee spouse's interest shall be treated as a qualifying income interest for life,

(B) the donor spouse shall be treated as having made an election under this subsection with respect to such annuity unless the donor spouse otherwise elects on or before the date specified in paragraph (4)(A),

(C) paragraph (5) and section 2519 shall not apply to the donor spouse's interest in the annuity, and

(D) if the donee spouse dies before the donor spouse, no amount shall be includible in the gross estate of the donee spouse under section 2044 with respect to such annuity.

An election under subparagraph (B), once made, shall be irrevocable.

(g) Special rule for charitable remainder trusts

(1) In general

If, after the transfer, the donee spouse is the only beneficiary who is not a charitable beneficiary (other than the donor) of a qualified charitable remainder trust, subsection (b) shall not apply to the interest in such trust which is transferred to the donee spouse.

(2) Definitions

For purposes of paragraph (1), the term "charitable beneficiary" and "qualified charitable remainder trust" have the meanings given to such terms by section 2056(b)(8)(B).

(h) Denial of double deduction

Nothing in this section or any other provision of this chapter shall allow the value of any interest in property to be deducted under this chapter more than once with respect to the same donor.

(i) Disallowance of marital deduction where spouse not citizen

If the spouse of the donor is not a citizen of the United States—

(1) no deduction shall be allowed under this section,

(2) section 2503(b) shall be applied with respect to gifts which are made by the donor to such spouse and with respect to which a deduction would be allowable under this section but for paragraph (1) by substituting "$100,000" for "$10,000", and

(3) the principles of sections 2515 and 2515A (as such sections were in effect before their repeal by the Economic Recovery Tax Act of 1981) shall apply, except that the provisions of such section 2515 providing for an election shall not apply.

This subsection shall not apply to any transfer resulting from the acquisition of rights under a joint and survivor annuity described in subsection (f)(6).

I.R.C. § 2601. Tax imposed

A tax is hereby imposed on every generation-skipping transfer (within the meaning of subchapter B).

Chapter 13

I.R.C. § 2001(c). Rate Schedules

If the amount with respect to which the tentative tax to be computed is:	The tentative tax is:
Not over $10,000	18 percent of such amount.
Over $10,000 but not over $20,000	$1,800, plus 20 percent of the excess of such amount over $10,000.
Over $20,000 but not over $40,000	$3,800, plus 22 percent of the excess of such amount over $20,000.
Over $40,000 but not over $60,000	$8,200 plus 24 percent of the excess of such amount over $40,000.
Over $60,000 but not over $80,000	$13,000, plus 26 percent of the excess of such amount over $60,000.
Over $80,000 but not over $100,000	$18,200, plus 28 percent of the excess of such amount over $80,000.
Over $100,000 but not over $150,000	$23,800, plus 30 percent of the excess of such amount over $100,000.
Over $150,000 but not over $250,000	$38,800, plus 32 percent of the excess of such amount over $150,000.
Over $250,000 but not over $500,000	$70,800, plus 34 percent of the excess of such amount over $250,000.
Over $500,000 but not over $750,000	$155,800, plus 37 percent of the excess of such amount over $500,000.
Over $750,000 but not over $1,000,000	$248,300, plus 39 percent of the excess of such amount over $750,000.
Over $1,000,000	$345,800, plus 40 percent of the excess of such amount over $1,000,000.

Source: http://uscode.house.gov/view.xhtml?req=granuleid:USC-prelim-title26-section2001&num=0&edition=prelim

I.R.C. § 2502(c). Tax to be paid by donor

The tax imposed by section 2501 shall be paid by the donor.

Appendix C

Estate Planning Hypothetical

William Noel is a resident of the State of Georgia and has come to your firm for estate planning advice. William (80 years old) is happily married to Eugenia Noel (78 years old) and they have three (3) children: their sons, George Noel (35 years old) and Steven Noel (30 years old), and their daughter, Betsy Noel (28 years old). In addition, William had a son, Henry Noel (40 years old), and a daughter, Bella Noel (39 years old), from his previous marriage to Virginia Noel. William has not seen or heard from Henry or Bella since Henry was about three (3) and Bella was two (2) years old.

George has no children but is married to Barry Johnson Noel. George wants no children. George is an attorney who practices estate planning and has been a responsible and respected member of the Georgia Bar for many years. Despite this, William does not regard George as one from whom he should take legal advice.

Steven is married to Lola Roberts and has two children: twins, Jaden and Braden Noel, who are seven (7) years old. Steven is independently wealthy due to his many savvy financial investments. Steven is not particularly close to William, but they share an amicable existence. However, William is very close to his grandsons, Jaden and Braden. William coordinates with Lola and makes a point to pick the boys up from school at least once a week. Steven is having an affair and Lola knows about it. She is considering getting a divorce from Steven. Steven, also contemplating divorce, has secretly asked his girlfriend, Minnie (21 years old), to marry him.

Betsy is ill with blood cancer and lives with William and Eugenia. She has been ill for many years and requires nursing care. Though very ill and not able to live independently, with proper care, she should live to attain the age of 60 years or older.

Regarding William's children from his prior marriage, you happen to know that Henry was a very successful poker player who lived out in Nevada with a net worth of millions of dollars. Henry has recently died. Henry never married and has no children. Henry's mother, Virginia, died years ago. Neither you nor William has any information concerning Bella.

William was the only child of Charles and Martha Noel. Charles was a landowner with over 100 acres of land in South Georgia. He died 30 years ago, leaving no will. After Charles' death, Martha took over his assets and cared for the land. Twenty years ago, when Martha died, she also left no will. Charles was able to gain possession of his parents' assets but never officially opened an estate administration. As a consequence of having pursued his own life and career, William has largely disregarded the land, and it has fallen into disrepair.

William is a healthy gentleman and he enjoys daily walks and his part-time job as a Walmart greeter. He earns about $12,000 per year at Walmart. He also gets Medicare and receives his retirement benefits from Ford where he was in middle management for more than forty years. He has a group term life insurance policy worth $200,000. He has a joint checking account with his wife which has a $9,000 balance. He owns a 2010 Ford in his own name, and he owns the home he lives in with his wife. The house is worth $100,000 and has equity of about $70,000. In addition, William has recently hit the lottery for $500,000. He wants to make sure that money is set aside for the education of Jaden and Braden and any other possible grandchildren that he may have.

William is a skin cancer survivor and has always supported the cause of the National Cancer Society. He participates in their 5k runs every year and regularly donates to organizations dedicated to finding a cure for cancer. He has mentioned that when he dies, he does not want his organs donated or his body donated to science. In addition, he is a lifelong member of the Main Street Baptist Church, and he purchased a funeral plot there where he would like to be buried when he dies. He never misses a Sunday service and generously gives to the church. He and his wife have begun to have a close relationship with a fellow church member, Benjamin Simmons, and his wife, Darlene Simmons. Darlene will regularly come and check on William. William has begun to trust them very much.

Finally, it is important to note that William is an avid fan of the Panthers, the football team at his beloved alma mater, Georgia Central University. Exhibit C.1, the Noel Family Tree, is located below.

Exhibit C.1 Noel Family Tree

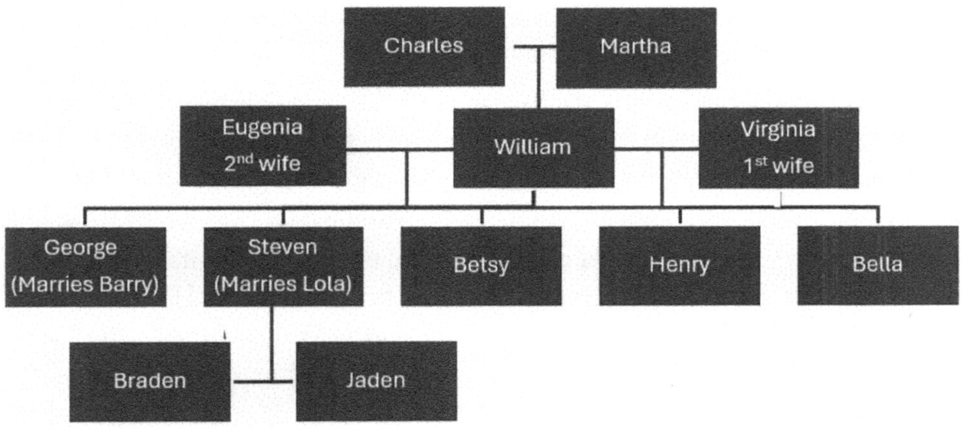

Questions for Consideration

1. Does William need a will? Why or why not?
2. What professionals does he need to help him create an estate plan?
3. What property should be disposed of in his will?
4. What family members need to be provided for in the will?
5. What are the steps you recommend that William take in drafting an estate plan?
6. Who could possibly witness his will? Who should probably be precluded from witnessing the will?
7. If the firm decides a trust is the better estate planning tool, what kind of trust would you recommend and why?
8. Is there a need for guardianship and/or conservatorship? For whom or what?
9. Does William need to administer the estate of his parents? Why or why not?
10. Could the attorney drafting the will also be a beneficiary of a gift under its terms?
11. Who would you recommend to serve as William's personal representative? Why?
12. What tax planning advice would you give William?
13. What other questions do you need answered?

Appendix D

Social Media/Website Suggestions

Forms

Free Legal Forms
https://www.ilrg.com/forms

Probate Forms
http://gaprobate.gov

Tax Forms-federal
www.irs.gov

Tax Forms-state
https://dor.georgia.gov/

Blawgs

American Academy of Estate Planning Attorneys
https://www.aaepa.com/blog/

Huffington Post
https://www.huffingtonpost.com/topic/estate-planning

Reddit
https://www.reddit.com/r/EstatePlanning

The New York Times
https://www.nytimes.com/topic/subject/estate-planning

Trial and Heirs
https://www.blog.trialandheirs.com/

Podcasts

Estate Planning Academy
https://podbay.fm/p/estate-planning-academy

Estate Planning Law Group of Georgia
https://letstalkestateplanning.com/estate-planning-podcast/

SR Law Group
https://www.srlawgrp.com/black-parents-aging-podcast

Your Life Simplified
https://www.marinerwealthadvisors.com/podcast/

Movies with Scenes about Estate Planning

https://thefarrelllawfirm.com/7-movies-with-unbelievable-scenes-about-estate-planning

http://gailrubin.com/public-speaking/estate-planning-film-clips/

https://willsandwellness.com/2014/06/10-best-estate-planning-movies/

https://www.youtube.com/playlist?list=PL583_3ThdbO2dobO5a5zmjpfeEyW4j4D-

Appendix E

Michael Jackson's Pour Over Will

LAST WILL

OF

MICHAEL JOSEPH JACKSON

I, MICHAEL JOSEPH JACKSON, a resident of the State of California, declare this to be my last Will, and do hereby revoke all former wills and codicils made by me.

I

I declare that I am not married. My marriage to DEBORAH JEAN ROWE JACKSON has been dissolved. I have three children now living, PRINCE MICHAEL JACKSON, JR., PARIS MICHAEL KATHERINE JACKSON and PRINCE MICHAEL JOSEPH JACKSON, II. I have no other children, living or deceased.

II

It is my intention by this Will to dispose of all property which I am entitled to dispose of by will. I specifically refrain from exercising all powers of appointment that I may possess at the time of my death.

III

I give my entire estate to the Trustee or Trustees then acting under that certain Amended and Restated Declaration of Trust executed on March 22, 2002 by me as Trustee and Trustor which is called the MICHAEL JACKSON FAMILY TRUST, giving effect to any amendments thereto made prior to my death. All such assets shall be held, managed and distributed as a part of said Trust according to its terms and not as a separate testamentary trust.

If for any reason this gift is not operative or is invalid, or if the aforesaid Trust fails or has been revoked, I give my residuary estate to the Trustee or Trustees named to act in the MICHAEL JACKSON FAMILY TRUST, as Amended and Restated on March 22, 2002, and I direct said Trustee or Trustees to divide, administer, hold and distribute the trust estate pursuant to the provisions of said Trust, as hereinabove referred to as such provisions now exist to the same extent and in the same manner as though that certain Amended and Restated Declaration of Trust, were herein set forth in full, but without giving effect to any subsequent amendments after the date of this Will. The Trustee, Trustees, or any successor Trustee named in such Trust Agreement shall serve without bond.

IV

I direct that all federal estate taxes and state inheritance or succession taxes payable upon or resulting from or by reason of my death (herein "Death Taxes") attributable to property which is part of the trust estate of the MICHAEL JACKSON FAMILY TRUST, including property which passes to said trust from my probate estate shall be paid by the Trustee of said trust in accordance with its terms. Death Taxes attributable to property passing outside this Will, other than property constituting the trust estate of the trust mentioned in the preceding sentence, shall be charged against the taker of said property.

V

I appoint JOHN BRANCA, JOHN McCLAIN and BARRY SIEGEL as co-Executors of this Will. In the event of any of their deaths, resignations, inability, failure or refusal to serve or continue to serve as a co-Executor, the other shall serve and no replacement need be named. The co-Executors serving at any time after my death may name one or more replacements to serve in the event that none of the three named individuals is willing or able to serve at any time.

The term "my executors" as used in this Will shall include any duly acting personal representative or representatives of my estate. No individual acting as such need post a bond.

I hereby give to my Executors, full power and authority at any time or times to sell, lease, mortgage, pledge, exchange or otherwise dispose of the property, whether real or personal comprising my estate, upon such terms as my Executors shall deem best, to continue any business enterprises, to purchase assets from my estate, to continue in force and pay insurance premiums on any insurance policy, including life insurance, owned by my estate, and for any of the foregoing purposes to make, execute and deliver any and all deeds, contracts, mortgages, bills of sale or other instruments necessary or desirable therefor. In addition, I give to my Executors full power to invest and reinvest the estate funds and assets in any kind of property, real, personal or mixed, and every kind of investment, specifically including, but not by way of limitation, corporate obligations of every kind and stocks, preferred or common, and interests in investment trusts and shares in investment companies, and any common trust fund administered by any corporate executor hereunder, which men of prudent discretion and intelligence acquire for their own account.

VI

Except as otherwise provided in this Will or in the Trust referred to in Article III hereof, I have intentionally omitted to provide for my heirs. I have intentionally omitted to provide for my former wife, DEBORAH JEAN ROWE JACKSON.

VII

If at the time of my death I own or have an interest in property located outside of the State of California requiring ancillary administration, I appoint my domiciliary Executors as ancillary Executors for such property. I give to said domiciliary Executors the following additional powers, rights and privileges to be exercised in their sole and absolute discretion, with reference to such property: to cause such ancillary administration to be commenced, carried on and completed; to determine what assets, if any, are to be sold by the ancillary Executors; to pay directly or to advance funds from the California estate to the ancillary Executors for the payment of all claims, taxes, costs and administration expenses, including compensation of the ancillary Executors and attorneys' fees incurred by reason of the ownership of such property and by such ancillary administration; and upon completion of such ancillary administration, I authorize and direct the ancillary Executors to distribute, transfer and deliver the residue of such property to the domiciliary Executors herein, to be distributed by them under the terms of this Will, it being my intention that my entire estate shall be administered as a unit and that my domiciliary Executors shall supervise and control, so far as permissible by local law, any ancillary administration proceedings deemed necessary in the settlement of my estate.

VIII

If any of my children are minors at the time of my death, I nominate my mother, KATHERINE JACKSON as guardian of the persons and estates of such minor children. If KATHERINE JACKSON fails to survive me, or is unable or unwilling to act as guardian, I nominate DIANA ROSS as guardian of the persons and estates of such minor children.

I subscribe my name to this Will this ____ day of ____, 2002.

MICHAEL JOSEPH JACKSON

On the date written below, MICHAEL JOSEPH JACKSON, declared to us, the undersigned, that the foregoing instrument consisting of five (5) pages, including the page signed by us as witnesses, was his Will and requested us to act as witnesses to it. He thereupon signed this Will in our presence, all of us being present at the same time. We now, at his request, in his presence and in the presence of each other, subscribe our names as witnesses.

Each of us is now more than eighteen (18) years of age and a competent witness and resides at the address set forth after his name.

Each of us is acquainted with MICHAEL JOSEPH JACKSON. At this time, he is over the age of eighteen (18) years and, to the best of our knowledge, he is of sound mind and is not acting under duress, menace, fraud, misrepresentation or undue influence.

We declare under penalty of perjury that the foregoing is true and correct.

Executed on July 7th, 2002 at 5:00 pm, Los Angeles, CA

______ Residing At ______

______ Residing At

______ Residing At

Glossary

A

A/B trust: A trust for married couples that divides in two upon the death of the first spouse.

administrator: A person appointed by the probate court to administer a decedent's estate.

administrator with the will annexed: A person appointed by the court to administer the estate of a testate person who has not named an executor or whose named executor(s) fail to qualify.

administratrix: A female appointed by the probate court to administer a decedent's estate.

advance directive for health care: A document in which a declarant names a health care agent to act on his or her behalf and outlines choices re: burial or cremation, treatment preferences, and decisions related to anatomical gifts.

agent: Someone who acts on behalf of a principal or declarant at his or her request.

ambulatory: Capable of being modified or revoked.

American Bar Association (ABA): One of the world's largest voluntary professional organizations founded in 1898 for attorneys.

anatomical gift: A gift of all or part of one's body.

ancillary administration: A legal procedure that runs parallel to a primary probate administration when the decedent owns property in multiple jurisdictions.

ancillary probate: See *ancillary administration*.

annual gift tax exclusion amount: The amount of gifts that may be transferred each year without incurring tax liability.

annual return: A status report regarding the estate that the personal representative submits to the probate court each year.

applicable exclusion amount: See *exclusion amount*.

artificial intelligence (AI): Computer technology, software, and systems that perform tasks traditionally requiring human intelligence.

assets: Any property a decedent may own that has value.

attestation clause: A closing section of the will appearing before the witnesses' signatures and addresses that acknowledges that the will formalities have been observed.

B

beneficial property: Property that one may be entitled to use or enjoy, but it is actually owned by someone else with legal title.

beneficiary: A person who is designated in a will or trust to take an interest in real or personal property.

bequest: A gift of personal property by will.

bundle of rights: The group of privileges belonging to owners of real property, including the rights to: (1) possess it, (2) use and control it, (3) enjoy it and exclude others from it, and (4) dispose of and encumber it.

bypass trust: See *credit shelter trust.*

C

caveat: A written document that states the reason(s) why a will contester objects to the will.

charitable deduction: The amount that can be donated to a qualifying charity without incurring liability for estate or gift taxes.

charitable trust: A trust that benefits a particular charity or the public in general and lowers or avoids the imposition of estate and gift taxes.

clause: An article or section of a document.

code of ethics: A standard of conduct that governs the interactions of a professional with the people and institutions with whom the professional interacts.

codicil: A written supplement or addition to an existing will that changes it.

competent representation: Using the requisite legal knowledge, skill, thoroughness and preparation necessary to serve a client well.

confidentiality: Maintaining a client's privacy.

conflict of interest: A situation that compromises the legal professional's ability to give the client complete and undivided loyalty.

conservator: A person appointed by the court to manage the property of another.

conservatorship: The appointment of someone to manage the property of another.

constructive trust: An implied trust established by operation of law for equitable purposes.

county administrator: A public official who is appointed to act as an administrator of an unrepresented estate if no one of a higher priority qualifies.

creator: See *settlor.*

credit: An amount of money that can be used to offset tax liability.

credit shelter trust: A trust that is designed to hold as much of the grantor's property as is sheltered from the federal estate tax by virtue of the unified credit.

Crummey powers: The right of a beneficiary under a life insurance trust to withdraw money which amounts to a present interest.

Crummey trust: A life insurance trust named after D. Clifford Crummey, its founder with certain provisions that allow gifts to the trust to qualify for the annual gift tax exclusion.

cy pres doctrine: The ability to modify a trust when the settlor's original intent is frustrated.

D

death tax: Another term for an estate tax, it is a tax paid by the estate as opposed to the beneficiary.

decedent: A person who has died.

declarant: A person who makes an advance directive for health care.

declaration of trust: A written document that is executed by the settlor as the sole trustee to create a trust.

deduction: An amount that may be subtracted from the gross estate.

demonstrative gift: A testator's gift of property (usually money) that must be taken from a specific source.

devise: A gift of real property by will.

devisee: A person who receives a gift of real property by will.

diminished capacity: A situation when a client's ability to make adequately considered decisions in connection to a representation is reduced.

disability insurance: Insurance that can be used to replace a portion of a worker's income when he or she is unable to work.

disbarment: A public disciplinary action that removes the attorney from the practice of law.

disclaimer: The refusal, rejection or renunciation of a gift of property.

disinherit: To preclude from receiving a gift.

disinheritance clause: See *no-contest clause.*

disinterested witnesses: Those who are not beneficiaries under a will, but are present to observe the testator's execution of the will.

dispose: To transfer property ownership or possession.

dispositive provisions: Clauses in a will by which the testator designates beneficiaries of his or her property.

domicile: The place of one's principal and permanent residence.

donor: See *settlor.*

durable: To be effective even if the principal becomes incapacitated and unable to handle matters on his or her own.

dynasty trust: See *generation-skipping trust.*

E

emancipated minor: Someone under the age of 18 who is no longer under the care, custody or control of parents.

employer identification number (EIN): An identification number that the IRS issues to a taxpayer.

engagement letter: A communication from an attorney to a client that should clearly outline the scope of representation and the fees related to the same.

equitable property: See *beneficial property.*

escheat: When the state gets an intestate decedent's property because no living beneficiary can be found.

escrow account: A separate bank account in which client funds that have been entrusted to his or her attorney is deposited.

estate: The property and assets owned by a person at death.

estate planning: Preparing for the transfer of property and assets upon one's death.

estate planning attorney: An individual authorized to practice law who specializes in wills, trusts, and estate administration.

estate planning questionnaire: A document used by the legal team to gather important facts and information from estate planning clients.

estate tax: Tax liability based on the value of the decedent's estate that exceeds the limits set by the taxing authority.

exclusion amount: The amount of property that can be placed in a trust and sheltered from federal gift and estate taxation by virtue of the unified credit.

execute: To sign.

executor: A person who the testator nominates in a will to ensure decedent's final wishes are honored and to settle the estate.

executor de son tort: Someone acting as a personal representative without having the property authority to do so who will be liable for this intermeddling.

executrix: A female who the testator nominates in a will to ensure decedent's final wishes are honored and to settle the estate.

exordium clause: An introductory will section that: (1) identifies the testator; (2) indicates the testator's domicile; (3) declares the document to be testator's will; and, (4) revokes any prior wills and codicils.

express revocation: The cancellation of a will by clearly stating in writing or acting in a manner that annuls the will.

express trust: A trust intentionally created by the settlor, usually under a written trust instrument that is signed by the settlor or his or her agent.

F

fee simple: The most complete or absolute form of ownership of real property.

fiduciaries: Those persons or organizations entrusted to act on behalf of an individual regarding his will, trust and/or estate.

final accounting: A comprehensive report of probate activities filed with the court before assets are distributed to beneficiaries or heirs and the estate is closed.

financial advisors: Accountants, bankers, financial planners, and investment managers who can assist someone in estate planning.

financial power of attorney: A document in which a principal nominates an agent to make certain business decisions on his or her behalf.

fixtures: Items so attached to the land that they become part of it.

formal admonition: A confidential disciplinary letter sent to an attorney that declares his or her conduct improper but does not limit the attorney's right to practice law.

formalities: Statutory requirements for a valid will.

four unities: Characteristics of a joint tenancy: (1) unity of possession, (2) unity of interest, (3) unity of time; and, (4) unity of title; commonly referred to by mnemonic "PITT."

G

general bequest: A gift from the testator that does not specify the precise property that the beneficiary will receive.

generation-skipping transfer tax: A tax imposed on outright gifts or transfers in trust that are above the exemption amount.

generation-skipping trust: A trust designed to last beyond the time permitted by the rule against perpetuities.

generative artificial intelligence (GAI) tools: Programs used to create new content, including text, images, audio, video, and software code in response to a user's prompts and questions that assist lawyers in tasks such as legal research, contract review, due diligence, document review, regulatory compliance, and drafting letters, contracts, briefs, and other legal documents.

Georgia Bar: See *State Bar of Georgia.*

Georgia Rules of Professional Conduct: The code of ethics applicable to attorneys who are members of the Georgia Bar.

gift tax: Tax liability based on a gift that has value that exceeds the annual or lifetime limits set forth by the taxing authority.

grantor: See *settlor.*

gross estate: The total value of all of the non-exempt estate assets.

guardian: Someone who looks after the affairs of another who is unable to manage his or her own affairs.

guardian ad litem: A person appointed to serve as an investigator and advocate for the best interests of a proposed ward.

guardianship: The appointment of someone to look after the personal affairs of another who is unable to manage his or her own affairs.

H

Health Insurance Portability and Accountability Act: A federal law that protects patients' health information

heir: A person entitled by laws of intestate succession to inherit the decedent's property.

heir determination worksheet: A tool that the personal representative may use in cases of intestacy to find the decedent's proper heirs-at-law.

HIPAA: See *Health Insurance Portability and Accountability Act.*

HIPAA Authorization and Waiver: A document that provides written authorization for certain uses and disclosures of protected health information.

holographic will: One that is completely handwritten and does not observe execution formalities, which is no longer valid in Georgia.

I

implied revocation: The cancellation of a will by executing a new, inconsistent and valid will.

implied trust: A trust that arises based on the nature of a transaction, facts and circumstances, and the conduct of the parties.

in terrorem clause: See *no-contest clause.*

incapacitated adult: An adult who, through illness or incidences, ceases to possess the ability to make responsible decisions for himself or a disabled person who reaches the age of majority.

incidents of ownership: The right to sell property, give it away, change the beneficiaries upon death, and to determine how it is managed and invested while the property is in a revocable trust.

inheritance tax: Another term for an estate tax; it is a tax paid by the beneficiary as opposed to the estate.

insurance agent: A person who sells insurance policies that may assist someone in estate planning.

intangible property: Real or personal property that represents an ownership interest in something and that has no physical substance.

inter vivos trust: See *living trust.*

Internal Revenue Code (I.R.C.): Federal tax laws, including those related to gift, income and estate taxes.

intestate: Dying without leaving a valid will.

intestate succession laws: State rules that outline how property should be distributed in the event the decedent has left no will or trust.

inventory: A comprehensive list of estate assets which must be submitted to the probate court.

Investigative Panel reprimand: A disciplinary action involving a confidential meeting of the Georgia Bar's Investigative Panel that declares an attorney's conduct improper but does not limit the attorney's right to practice law.

irrevocable life insurance trust (ILIT): A trust designed to hold life insurance on the life of the grantor or another person in order to exclude the life insurance proceeds payable on the death of the grantor from federal estate taxation.

irrevocable trust: A trust that generally cannot be altered, changed, modified or revoked after its creation, with some recent exceptions.

J

joint ownership: Two or more persons own the property concurrently.

joint tenancy: See *joint tenancy with the right of survivorship.*

joint tenancy with the right of survivorship: Ownership interests characterized by the four unities (PITT) and when one owner dies the remaining owner(s) get(s) the decedent's share.

joint tenant: A person who holds a joint tenancy.

joint will: One will signed by two or more testators that deals with the distribution of each testator's property.

L

last will and testament: The legal declaration of an individual's testamentary intention regarding that individual's property or other matters. The will includes the will and all codicils to the will.

legacy: See *bequest.*

legal advice: A statement or conclusion that applies the law or legal principles to the facts of a specific person's legal problem.

legal assistant: See *paralegal.*

legal property: Title to the property/ownership, including the right to manage and control the property, without an equitable or beneficial interest.

legitimation: The legal process by which children born out-of-wedlock obtain the same rights as those born within wedlock, including the right to inherit.

letter of instruction: A document written by the testator, which accompanies the will and contains more detailed information for his or her loved ones or executor.

letters of administration: A document which evidences the appointment and authority to administer an intestate estate.

letters of administration with the will annexed: A document which evidences the appointment and authority to administer a testate estate that is unrepresented.

letters of conservatorship: A court order appointing and authorizing a conservator to manage the ward's property.

letters of guardianship: A court order appointing and authorizing a guardian to manage the ward's personal affairs.

letters testamentary: A document which evidences the executor's appointment and authority to administer a testate estate.

liabilities: Financial obligations.

life estate: A right to property limited to a specific time period, usually the life tenant's lifetime or a third party's lifetime.

life insurance: Policies of insurance that are payable on the death of the insured that may be used as an estate planning tool.

life insurance trust: See *irrevocable life insurance trust.*

life tenant: A person who has right to a life estate.

living trust: A trust that becomes effective during the settlor's lifetime.

living will: See *advance directive for health care.*

long-term care insurance: An insurance policy designed to provide money to pay for nursing home and custodial care when an insured becomes chronically ill.

M

malpractice: An attorney's breach of the fiduciary duty owed to a client to provide the standard of skill, care, and diligence the attorney owed to the client, which breach causes the client damages.

marital property: Property acquired during marriage by either partner or gifted to the couple, which is considered property of both spouses for estate planning purposes.

marital trust: A trust designed to hold the remainder of the decedent's property and is sheltered from the federal estate tax by virtue of the unlimited marital deduction.

measuring life: The specific time period (either the life estate owner's lifetime or a third party's lifetime) that marks the duration of a life estate.

Model Rules of Professional Conduct: The current code of ethics for attorneys that was developed by the American Bar Association in 1983; these rules have been adopted in whole or in part by most states.

modification: Amendment of the will.

moments of lucidity: Those times when someone who is suffering from diminished capacity may have clear perception and rational thoughts.

mutual wills: Separate wills of two or more testators that make reciprocal dispositions of each testator's property.

N

no-contest clause: A provision that states that a will challenger will forfeit his or her right to inherit under the will due to the contest.

nonprobate property: Property that cannot be transferred by will or through laws of intestate succession. Examples include jointly owned property; trust property; life estates; and, retirement, pension and life insurance plans with named beneficiaries.

nuncupative will: Oral wills, which are no longer valid in Georgia.

O

O.C.G.A.: *See* Official Code of Georgia Annotated.

Official Code of Georgia Annotated: Georgia statutes, Title 53 of which contains laws related wills, trusts, probate and administration.

order for discharge: A probate court order granting the personal representative's request to close the estate of the decedent.

P

paralegal: A person with specialized legal knowledge that works under the supervision of the estate planning attorney to address client needs.

pay-on-death account: A bank account listing a beneficiary in the event the owner dies.

per stirpes: Latin for "by roots"; property is distributed in equal shares by representation, meaning by family groups.

personal property: All property which is movable in nature, has inherent value or is representative of value, and is not otherwise defined as realty.

personal representative: A person who will oversee the proper distribution of decedent's estate; the general term for the executor or administrator of a decedent's estate.

pet insurance: An insurance policy available for pet owners to protect against unexpected veterinary expenses.

pet trust: A trust that permits pet owners to provide instructions and set aside funds and other resources to care for their pets in the event of the owner's death or incapacitation.

petition for discharge: The document a personal representative files with the probate court to close the estate.

posthumously: After death.

postmortem estate planning: Estate planning taking place after a person dies.

pour over will: A basic will to go along with a trust, meant to capture any property not put in the name of the trust.

predecease: To die before someone else.

principal: A person who nominates an agent to act on his or her behalf.

probate: The court-supervised process of administering a decedent's estate, which includes determining the validity of the will, settling estate debts, and distributing property and assets.

probate property: Property that the decedent owns solely or as a tenant in common at death, which will be distributed as the decedent indicated in his or her will or through laws of intestate succession.

proposed ward: An alleged incapacitated adult for whom a guardian and/or conservator may be appointed.

prove: To have a court validate and accept a document as the authentic last will and testament of a decedent.

public reprimand: A disciplinary action involving a judge of a superior court in open court publicly declaring that an attorney's conduct was improper, but does not limit the attorney's right to practice law.

publication clause: See *exordium clause.*

Q

qualified terminable interest property (QTIP) trust: A trust that allows the grantor to transfer property in trust for his or her surviving spouse estate-tax free by virtue of the unlimited marital deduction, even though the surviving spouse is not given the right to determine the beneficiaries of the property upon his or her subsequent death.

R

real property: Land, buildings erected on the land, items affixed to the land and interests in the land, such as water and mineral rights.

reciprocal will: See *mutual will.*

remainderman: A person who has an interest to property at the time of death of the life tenant or the measuring life.

renunciation: A method of disclaiming property.

residuary clause: A will section that represents a catch-all provision, by which the testator disposes of all other property that has not been gifted in previous will provisions.

retainer letter: See *engagement letter.*

Review Panel reprimand: A disciplinary action involving a public meeting of the Georgia Bar's Review Panel that declares an attorney's conduct improper but does not limit the attorney's right to practice law.

revocable trust: A trust that can be modified or revoked entirely and becomes effective on the settlor's death.

revocation: Cancellation of a will.

rule against perpetuities: A law that provides that a property interest is invalid unless: (1) when created, it is certain to vest or terminate within the lifetime of an individual then alive or within 21 years after the death of that individual; or, (2) the interest vests or terminates within 360 years after its creation.

S

sanctions: Forms of disciplinary action imposed by the Georgia Bar on unethical attorneys who are members of the Bar.

self-proving affidavit: The sworn statements of testator and witnesses that allow a will to be proved without their testimony in court.

separate property: Real or personal property that was owned prior to marriage or acquired solely during marriage by gift or inheritance.

settlor: The person who creates a trust.

severalty: Ownership of property as the sole title holder.

slayer statute: A law stating that those who are responsible for a decedent's death are barred from inheritance of his or her estate.

special needs trust: A trust that enables the grantor to provide for the continuing care of a disabled spouse, child, relative or friend for those supplemental needs in excess of those provided for by public benefits programs.

specific bequest: The gift of a particular object from a testator to a beneficiary.

specific devise: The gift of a particular parcel of real property in a will.

specific legacy: The gift of a particular item of personal property in a will.

spendthrift: A person who spends money unwisely.

spendthrift trust: A trust that includes certain language giving the trustee wide latitude to avoid making distributions to a beneficiary when the distribution would go to a creditor, or when the trustee fears that the distribution would be wasted by the beneficiary.

standing: Having a beneficial interest in a legal matter.

State Bar of Georgia: The licensing authority for Georgia attorneys.

statutory form: A document created by the legislature to serve as a model form for public use.

successor executor: The person nominated to serve as executor under the will if the testator's primary choice is unwilling or unable to act.

successor trustee: The person nominated to serve as trustee under the will if the testator's primary choice is unwilling or unable to act.

sui juris: Having full legal rights and not being under the power or guardianship of another person.

supplemental needs trust: See *special needs trust.*

surviving parent: The parent remaining alive after the other has died.

survivorship clause: A will section that indicates that a beneficiary cannot inherit under the will unless he or she outlives the testator for a specified amount of time.

suspension: A public disciplinary action that removes an attorney from the practice of law in Georgia for a definite period of time or until satisfaction of certain conditions imposed as part of the disciplinary action.

T

tangible property: Real or personal property that can be physically touched.

taxable estate: The decedent's gross estate minus expenses, deductions, and exclusions.

taxpayer identification number (TIN): See *employer identification number (EIN).*

temporary administrator: A person the court appoints to preserve an unrepresented estate until a permanent administrator can be named.

tenancy in common: Joint ownership of property in which owners can pass their respective shares on to heirs or otherwise dispose of it individually.

tenant in common: A person who holds tenancy in common.

testamentary: Related to or arising out of a will.

testamentary trust: A trust that is created by a will.

testate: Dying having left a valid will.

testate succession: The transfer of property and assets pursuant to a decedent's will.

testator: A person who creates a will.

testatrix: A female who creates a will.

testimonium clause: A closing section of the will that marks its end and includes the date of execution before the testator's signature.

totten trust: See *transfer-on-death account.*

transfer-on-death account: An account which passes securities, such as stocks and bonds, directly to the named beneficiary upon the owner's death.

trust: An arrangement by which one person, the trustee, holds legal title to property for the benefit of another, the beneficiary.

trust account: See *escrow account.*

trust agreement: A written contract between the settlor and the trustee to create a trust.

trust corpus: See *trust property.*

trust fund: See *trust property.*

trust principal: See *trust property.*

trust property: Property or assets set aside in a trust or for special purposes.

trust res: See *trust property.*

trustee: A person who holds legal title to property for the trust beneficiary.

trustor: See *settlor.*

U

unauthorized practice of law (UPL): Engaging in the practice of law by persons or entities not authorized to practice law in the state.

unfit: Incapable of carrying out the duties associated with being a personal representative.

unified credit: A certain amount of assets that a person is allowed to give to another without paying gift, estate, or generation-skipping taxes.

unity of interest: Joint owners each owns an equal percentage of property.

unity of possession: Joint owners each has an undivided interest in the whole property.

unity of time: Joint owners take ownership of property at the same time.

unity of title: Joint owners take ownership in the same instrument (deed or will).

unlimited marital deduction: A deduction that allows one spouse to transfer property and assets without restriction to the other spouse at any time, without incurring liability for estate or gift taxes.

V

valid: Legally enforceable.

volition: Freedom of choice.

voluntary surrender of license: When attorneys potentially facing disbarment give up their license to practice law.

W

ward: A person for whom a guardian and/or a conservator has been appointed.

waste: The abuse or destruction of property, causing it to depreciate in value.

will: See *last will and testament.*

will contest: A lawsuit challenging the validity of a will.

Y

year's support: Entitlement for a decedent's spouse (who has not remarried) and unmarried minor children (not stepchildren).

Index